Ancient Monuments of Kashmir

Ancient Monuments of Kashmir

Akhtar Malik

ANMOL PUBLICATIONS PVT. LTD.
NEW DELHI - 110 002 (INDIA)

ANMOL PUBLICATIONS PVT. LTD.
H.O.: 4374/4B, Ansari Road, Darya Ganj,
New Delhi-110 002 (India)
Ph.: 23278000, 23261597
B.O.: No. 1015, Ist Main Road, BSK IIIrd Stage
IIIrd Phase, IIIrd Block,
Bangalore - 560 085 (India)
Visit us at: www.anmolpublications.com

Ancient Monuments of Kashmir

First Published, 2008

ISBN 978-81-261-3414-4

PRINTED IN INDIA

Printed at Mehra Offset Press, Delhi.

Contents

Preface

Architecture is one of the sources for tracing the various aspect of the culture of any region and any period. In India there in no dearth of ancient architectural monuments and literature dealing with the ancient Indian architecture is also available in plenty. The scope of the subject is vast but the present work, in order to get ourselves introduced to the subject, aims at tracing peculiar characteristic features of different types of architecture that flourished in Kashmir in ancient times. As the detail study of the subject is not aimed at we have selected here only the best examples representing the different styles of architecture for our purpose and focussed our attention on the survey of distinctive elements such as the technique, material, origin, plan, elevation, roof, tower, exterior, ceiling, interior etc. of each of the examples.

The archaeological heritage of Kashmir in the form of sites and monuments distributed almost all over the valley and contiguous areas reflects the glorious achievements of the past history of Kashmir. These monuments are of cardinal importance in the history of Indian art and architecture while, remains of proto-historic and historic periods as found in different sites in the Kashmir Valley are unique in ways more than one.

The present book contains an excellent account of the remains in the Valley besides the necessary background relating to the state and the people, sources, tradition and legends, political history and a discussion on architectural styles.

Akhtar Malik

1

Ancient Temples of Kashmir

Kashmir is bestowed with nature's bounties and the mystical environment has fascinated people irrespective of caste, creed and language. Scholars coming from far and wide have carried away with them its, immense spiritual wealth shedding the shackles of this materialistic work and merging with the ultimate.

The Kashmir valley blessed with the natural bounties is rightly celebrated as the valley of Gods. Apart from its natural beauty an added attraction are the ancient stone temples of Kashmir, noteworthy for unique architectural elements and fine stone carvings.

The Hindu temple represents the cosmological symbolism in an aesthetic grab. The Hindu temple is a symbol or rather an aggregate of various symbols. It is ritually invested with human personality (Vastupursha) and conceived in terms of human organism, which is the most evolved form. The scriptures say that the temple should be worshipped as Pursa. The names of the various limbs of the human body from the foot to the crown of the head are applied in Indian architectural texts to different parts of the temple structure.

The door of the temple is its mouth, the platform terminating the trunk to the superstructure, represents the shoulder of the Pursa; the projection, the arms and down to the wall, the leg and to the very bottom, to the lower most molding—the feet.

The temple is Pursa and conceived by means of Prakrti the feminine form.

We talked about the perfect body—the Vastupursha, but it is lifeless without the resident soul. The image in the temple, the Pratima is the very life of the temple. The sanctum called Garbhagriha is the house of the womb, it is here the regeneration is effected and the higher self of the devotee is reborn

Documentation officer, Indira Gandhi National Center for the Arts, Janpath, New Delhi.

A similar purpose is served by the superstructure, which is frequently designed as the mystical, Meru, Mandara or Kailasa—the function of which is to lead from a broad base to a point where all lines converge—the ultimate one.

The conceptualization and development of Hindu temple architecture was the result of the churning of cosmic ideas in the microcosm of natural setting. The temple was not a four-walled enclosure but an embodiment of the cosmos and the energy, which propels it. The main sanctum sanatorium, which houses the Garbagriha, the womb, is the personification of Pursha so as to define the relationship of cosmos and man. The image placed in the Garba Griha is the atman—the soul. The temples were laid according a well-defined plan. The temple building was a ritual and every stone laid was consecrated to God by the holy chant of the Brahmins.

Buddhism was introduced in Kashmir soon after the Buddha's demise and king Ashoka is said to have built stupas in the 3rd C.B.C. The Buddhist remains at Harwan, Hoina and Hutamer have revealed unique tiles depicting the fine workmanship.

With the background of Buddhist artistic tradition, Kashmiri artisans evolved a style of Hindu temple architecture with a distinct characteristic of its own. Kashmir temple exhibits a unique bland of foreign style and indigenous creativity that resulted in a distinctive architecture which was more suited to their geographic and climate conditions.

The temple builders of Kashmir were way ahead of their contemporaries of the plains and peninsular India. The 8th cent. Temples of Kashmir were constructed of evenly dressed ashlars masonry. Built of mammoth boulders, the joints were put together with lime mortar, which is seen at Wangat and also using steel dowels, used in the Martand temple. These engineering developments were in vague in the neighbouring Western region of Kashmir.

These refined techniques could not stand up the rigorous climate of the region and Human vandalism and only a few of the vast number of temples described eloquently by Pandit Kalhana in Rajatarangni have survived.

Kashmir lies in the heart of Asian continent, its geographic location has been of decisive importance for trade and cultural exchange. All the main trade routes connecting eastern and central Asia with Eastern Europe countries of near—east lay across the territory. There was exchange on the cultural and religious fronts as it was meeting place of the cultural waves. The craven routes from China, central Asia and Tibet met and this led to the great impact on their political, social and cultural structure.

The temple at Lodhu situated 20 kms from Srinagar is in midst of a spring. The springs are considered to be sacred sites. The temple is said to be earliest remaining stone structure.

The next stage in the temple architecture development may be studied in the Sankaracharya temple. In the Temple at Narasthan in district Pulwama, the pediment and arch motif if in process of development. Triangular canopies, sunken Trefoil niches and the enclosure wall around with prominent gateway is an approach to the final form of Hindu temple architecture of Kashmir.

7th & 8th century marked the culmination of art during the reign of Karakota rulers. Laltaditya Miktapida (724-761 AD) Ushered in an era of glory and prosperity in the kingdom. After gaining victories over Punjab and Kananuj and Bihar, he turned his attention to the bordering territories of Kashmir. He led the victorious army to Dardistan, Ladakh and Tibet. During the Karakota rule there was a crisis cross which brought an improvised style into being. We see a profound influence of

Chinese, apparent from faces and dresses, which are typically Mangoloid. Building art was a product of influences from different classical schools viz-Greko-Roman, Gandharan, while as the sculpture iconography reflects the tremendous central Asian impact.

Laltaditya built the famous and elegant Sun temple at Martand and Parihaskesva at his capital Parihasspara.

The Sun temple of Martand stands in the middle of a large courtyard having 86 fluted columns. The temple proper contains grabhagraha, antarala and lost mandapa, approached by a grand flight of steps. The pliant supporting the central shrine has two tiers; both with niches having 37 divine figures.

The second golden age of temple building was brought into being by the patronage of king Avantivarman the founder of Utpala dynasty. The king built two temples one dedicated to Shiva and other dedicated to Vishnu.

The final refinement of form and a more polished look may be seen in a group of temples erected by Sankaravarman who succeeded Avantivarman. During subsequent years due to constant wars between the weak kings and kingdoms temple activity gradually started receding. By the beginning of the 10th century the growth of style had come to an end but small shrines to be raised without any notable architectural development.

The offshoot of the Kashmir style of architecture is found in Northern Punjab and Northwest frontier. The temples at Amb, Malot, Bilot, Kafirkot (sites presently in Pakistan) exhibit some of the architectural elements like enclosed courtyard, pyramidal roof, and trefoil arches, fluted columns showing strong affinity with that of Kashmir. The influences are also found in the Western Himalayan architecture from Ladakh to Nepal.

The traditions never die. The elements of ancient Hindu architecture of Kashmir, which were buried a millennium ago, resurfaced in the form of Muslim shrines and residential houses in succeeding periods. The traditions together with the geographical conditions play a vital role in shaping the Kashmiri character.

Malana

A Lost Utopia in the Himalayas

Below the Chanderkhani pass of the Kulu Valley lies a small cluster of around two hundred stone roof houses constituting a village called Malana. Its inimitable culture and the temple of Jamlu distinguish the village. The village consists of around 1500 inhabitants and has an impeccable system of administration with a higher and lower court guided by the spirit of village God Jamlu. Malana stands out as an autonomous self-sufficient unit whose inhabitants claim Greek ancestry.

Some fanciful stories about the village called "a little Greece," as also its drug mafia with its do's and don'ts, are often published in newspapers and magaines. However, what distinguishes this village in the interior of the Himalayas is its architecture, language, worship rituals and autonomous administrative system. The unique geographical location of Malana has enabled it to preserve its biodiversity and it is an ecological haven.

Malana is connected to Kulu by three mountain passes— it can be reached from Parbati valley crossing over the 3180 metres Rashol Pass and via Nagar over the 3600 metres beautiful Chanderkhani pass. The easiest way to reach Malana is from Jari, which is a 23 km picturesque trek to Malana. Jari is two hours drive from Kulu and is situated at the confluence of the Malana and Manikaran *nallah*, which join to form the Parbati River.

Jari is an entry point to Malana. About 1.5 km from Jari is the Malana powerhouse and visitors have to register their names before entering the valley From the powerhouse to the dam is a 10 km trek and thereafter it is an uneven trek of 7 km to Malana.

The last 4 km stretch to Malana is treacherously uphill. But the greenery all around with interceptions of waterfalls and streams make the climb bearable. About 2 km from Malana powerhouse is Chowki, a small hamlet, and the only towering structure in the village is the Shiva temple. This is the nearest village to Malana. However, the people of Chowki have nothing in common with the Malanese.

According to a story from mythology, Jamdagni Rishi is the father of Parashuram, one of the 10 incarnations of Lord Vishnu. After his intense prayers, Shiva appeared before him. Jamdagni Rishi asked for a secluded place, full of nature's bounty. Shiva told him to go to Malana. The Rishi's two brothers followed him. In order to avoid them, he created a mist in the valley and told them that the place was not good. His brothers left his company and one went to Lahoul and the other to the Banjar Valley. Malana was already in the control of a *Rakshasa* when the Rishi reached there The *Rakshasa* Banasura resisted him.

The conflict between Jamdagni Rishi and Banasura ended with a peace treaty, according to which, administration and justice were to be handled separately. While administration was with Banasura, justice was kept under the preview of Jamdagni Rishi. In case of a dispute in the administration, it was to be sorted out by the judiciary. The Kanashi language was made mandatory for those living in Malana, as also the customs and traditions prevalent there. During the festivals, the first sacrifice was to be made to Banasura. With the passage of time, Jamdagni Rishi gained superiority over Banasura, but the village retained its traditions, which are still followed there.

Malana is divided into two—upper Malana (Dhara Beda) and lower Malana (Sor Beda). Except for two families of *Lohars* and *Julahas* who came to the village as drummers and were allowed to settle there, Malana is inhabited by only Rajputs. A stone-lined path goes through the centre of the village where people can be seen lazing around, or playing dice, locally called *panji*. For the outsiders, there is a long list of do's and don'ts to be followed in the village.

The people are friendly but outsiders are told to keep distance and not to touch anything in the village. Photography is allowed in the village, but not videography. The *Dharamshalas* (rest houses) in the centre court of the village are richly decorated with wooden carvings depicting flora and fauna, which include peacocks, horses, elephants, birds, dancers and various flowers. The *Dharamshalas* are meant for pilgrims visiting the shrine of Jamdagni Rishi on festive occasions.Houses in Malana are of two or three storeys and each storey has a specific name and purpose. The ground floor is called *khudang* which acts as a cattle shed and where the firewood and fodder for the sheep and goats are stored. The first floor called *Gaying* is used to store eatables, wood and for weaving woollen fabric. The top floor with an over hanging balcony is called *pati*. It is the living quarter. The houses are built of alternate bands of stone and timber. The inner walls are plastered with mud. The outer side is entirely made up of wood.

Kanashi, the language of Malana, does not resemble any of the dialects spoken in its neighbourhood but seems to be a mixture of Sanskrit and several Tibetan dialects. This sort of amalgamation makes it difficult for an alien to understand it. Language is also considered to be one of the secrets of the village and outsiders are not allowed to use it for communication. The *Julaha* and *Lohar* families who have been staying in the village since the last five decades are not allowed to speak Kanashi. There is a single teacher government primary school with 100 children on the rolls. The school building also houses an Ayurvedic dispensary and the *panchayat ghar*. There is a middle school with a science teacher, Sanskrit teacher and history teacher. The middle school was established in 1966. Although there are four teachers, the number of students is only 13. Up to the primary level midday meals are provided. Girl students are provided free books. So far only two students in the village have managed to reach class 12.

The people of Malana are very conscious about preserving their ecological heritage. According to the village rules, fixing nails on a tree and burning of fire in the forest of Malana are prohibited. Only dry twigs and branches are allowed to be carried away from the forest. Hunting is not allowed without the permission of the village council. The livelihood of Malana is farming and cattle rearing. They also collect herbs in the upper reaches, which find a good market. Two important festivals are celebrated in Malana. One called *Badoh mela* is celebrated in August and the other called *Fagdi mela* in February. On these festive occasions people from nearby villages come to this place. Holy relics of Jamdagni Rishi in the form of instruments, jewellery, garments are kept on display. Men and women dance in their traditional attire consisting of *Chola*, *kalgi* (round cap) and tight *pajams*, to the beats of the *Nagara*, *Shanani*, *Karnali* and *Narsingha*. Marriage is a simple affair without any priest or ritual.

The locals call it the *Rakshasi* marriage. The bride goes after the groom to his house. In case of divorce, the boy has to arrange a separate house, food etc. for the girl. Divorced women and widows can remarry. Polygamy is allowed for men. Similarly, there are not elaborate last rites. The dead are cremated and the rituals last three days.

The shrine of Renuka Devi is situated in lower Malana. The Shrine with its intricate woodwork is noteworthy for its architectural excellence. Horns of animals sacrificed in the temple complex are usually fixed on the facade of the temple. The original abode of Jamdagni Rishi is said be at Baginda, 15 km from Buntar. Another shrine of Jamdagni Rishi is at Tosh village, 6 km from Pulga. The village priest is the only person in the village to wear a white turban. The position passes from father to son.

The village has a democratic set up and the village council is called *Hakima* and consists of *Goor*, *Pujari* and *Kardar* representing higher court and *Jestha* the lower court. *Pujari* and *Kardar* are hereditary posts and are representatives of the *Jamlu devta*. *Kardar* is second in hierarchy. There are four elected members from the village called *Jestha*. Each *Jestha* can select one more member called *Pogudar* and the total elected members come to eight. Out of these eight, one person is elected as *Pradhan* (chief) and the other is *upapradhan*. *Goor* is a person said to be possessed by the spirit of Jamlu *devta*. Any person from the village can be a *goor*. Once a *goor* is identified and accepted, he has to wear a cap and keep long hair. When possessed, *goor* listens to the woes of the villagers and directs them to do remedies.

The village judicial system though outdated is novel in its own way. The unanimous decision of the lower court is sent to the higher court for final verdict. On the basis of this participatory court procedure some scholars trace the origin of

Malana Hakima to the ancient Greece. If a villager wants to take the help of police, he has to pay a fine of Rs. 1000 to the village council. In most cases, the guilty are fined. Anyone defying the decision of the village council is thrown out of the valley. In extreme cases of theft or misuse of the God's treasures, a stone is tied to the culprit and he is pushed down the mountain slopes.

Malana is an interesting study of how isolated villages retain their socio-cultural characteristics.

Malana—Shangrila in the Himalayas

A civilized society in a country like India originates in the village where people of different identities interact for mutual benefit, self-sufficiency and autonomy. All villages outwardly appear to be similar but each has its core, a soul, which is a distinct as one fingerprint from the other. There are what are called artist villages, epic villages, shrine villages, fringe villages and forsaken villages distinguished by their inhabitants and their traditions.

Of these, in Himachal Pradesh, the most distinctive are the shrine villages. In every such village there is a presiding deity recognized by people of all religions on the basis of faith only. Malana is one such village in the district Kulu that has preserved its age-old traditions and customs.

Below the Chanderkhani pass of the Kulu valley lies a small cluster of around two hundred stone roof houses constituting a village called Malana. Its inimitable culture and the temple of Jamlu distinguish the village. The village consists of around 1500 inhabitants and has an impeccable system of administration with even a higher and lower court guided by the spirit of village God Jamlu. Malana stands out as an autonomous self-created unit whose inhabitants claim Greek ancestry.

The Republic of Malana; a little Greece in Malana; the Drug Mafia in Malana; do's and don'ts in Malana—all sort of fanciful stories are being regularly published in newspapers and magazines. A Malanese is subject to all sorts of probes and investigations.

However, what distinguishes this village in the interior of the Himalayas are the striking characteristics such as:

- Persistent & adamant effort by the inhabitants to retain their unique age-old heritage.
- Inaccessibility of the village so far makes it a greater attraction for adventure tourists and scholars alike.
- Unique geographical location, which has preserved its biodiversity and is an ecological heaven.
- The village God is considered by the inhabitants as superior in power as compared to those of the other Gods in the Kulu valley.
- Their manner of worship in strikingly different from the usual Himachal traditional rituals.
- Some words of the language and the architectural motifs are arguably of Greek provenance.
- A strange legend exists related to Emperor Akbar legitimizing pre-eminence of the Jamlu devta.
- Language locally called Kanashi does not belong to the Indo-Aryan group and serves and acts as a medium of communication among the Malanese only. Architecture is also unique and each architectural structure has a specific purpose and bears a vernacular name.
- The motifs on the residential houses have no resemblance to those in the adjoining regions. The motifs have connotations, which could be of interest to scholars.
- An elected village judiciary enforces rules and regulations adopted over the centuries for the benefit of the Malanese.

Malana—Geographical Location

Malana valley is connected to Kulu by three mountain passes—it can be reached from Parbati valley crossing over the 3180 metres Rashol Pass and via Nagar over the 3600 metres beautiful Chanderkhani pass. They easiest way to reach Malana is from jari which is a 23 kms picturesque trek to Malana. Jari is two hours drive from Kulu and is situated at the confluence of the Malana and Manikaran nallah, which join to form the Parbati River.

Jari is an entry point to Malana. About one and half kilometres from Jari is the Malana powerhouse and one has to register his or her name here before entering the valley. From the power house to the dam is a 10 kms trek and thereafter it is an uneven trek of 7 kms to Malana. The last 4 kms stretch to Malana is a treacherous uphill trek. But the greenery all around with interceptions of waterfalls and streams keeps one's spirit high. About 2 kms from Malana powerhouse is Chowki, a small hamlet and the only towering structure in the village is the Shiva temple. This is the only village in the region, which is near to Malana separated by 15 kms. However, the people of Chowki have nothing in common with the Malanese.

A Peep into its History: Jamdangni Rishi in the days of yore worshipped Brahma, Vishnu and Mahesha. After his intense prayers, Shiva appeared before him and told him to ask for a boon. Jamdagani Rishi asked for a place, secluded and full of nature's bounty. Shiva told him to go to Malana. The Rishi's two brothers followed him. In order to avoid them he created mist in the valley and told his brothers that the place was not good and further said that if they want to stay they could. His brothers lift his company and one of them went to Lahoul and the other to the Banjar valley. Malana was already in the control of a big Rakshasa when Rishi reached there the Rakshasa retaliated, which resulted in a fight between the two.

The conflict between Jamdagni Rishi and Banasura ended with the understanding on the following terms :-

1. Administration and justice were to be handled separately
2. The members of the executive were to be selected in consultation with Banasura.
3. Justice was kept under the preview of Jamdagni Rishi.
4. In case of a dispute in the administration it was to be sorted out by the judiciary.
5. The Kanashi language was made mandatory for those living in Malana, and also the customs and traditions prevalent there.

During festivals, the first sacrifice was to be made to Banasura the Rakshasha. With the passage of time, Jamdagini Rishi gained superiority over Banasura, but the village retained its traditions which are still followed there.

Social Structure: An exotic atmosphere catches hold of the visitor once he enters the village—houses with their antique look and the people in their traditional attire—it seems to be a different world altogether.

Malana is divided into two divisions—upper Malana (Dhara Beda) and lower Mala (sor Beda). It is inhabited by Rajputs only besides two families of Lohars and Julahas who came to the village as drummers and were allowed to settle there. Malana Rajputs have four sub-divisions.

1. Dhamyani Rajputs
2. Dhurani Rajputs
3. Nagvani Rajputs
4. Pachani Rajputs

Dhamyani and Dhurani Rajputs stay in upper Malana and Nagvani and Pachani Rajputs reside in lower Malana. In terms of hierarchy the Dhamyani is on the top and Panchani is at number four. This division in terms of classes is for name sake as the people intermarry and share each other's burden.

A stone lined path goes through the centre of the village where people can be seen lazing on the ground or playing dice, locally called panji. For the outsiders, there is a long list of do's and don'ts to be followed in the village. Don't touch anything signboards forbidding one to touch anything are conspicuously placed in the village.

The people are friendly but outsiders are told to keep distance and not to touch anything in the village. Photography is allowed in the village, but not videography.

Most of the names of the villages are based on the name of the day they are born. For example:

A Sunday born person is Ahuta

A Monday born person is Suanru

A Tuesday born person is Mangal

A Wednesday born person is Budh or Bui

A Thursday born person is Bestru or Bei

A Friday born person is Shukru

A Saturday born person is Shani Charu or Sheyi

There is also the custom of a new born male baby being given the sane name as that of his grand father. Ladies call their husbands by name contrary to the tradition prevalent in the rest of India.

Architecture: The Dharamshalas (rest houses) in the Center Court of the village are richly decorated with wooden carvings depicting flora and fauna which include peacocks, horses, elephants, birds, dancers and various flowers. The Dharamshalas are meant for pilgrims visiting the shrine of Jamdagni Rishi on festive occasions.

Houses in Malana are two or three storied and each storey has a specific name and purpose. The ground floor is called khudang, which acts as a cattle shed and where the firewood and fodder for the sheep and goats are stored. The first floor called Gaying is used to store eatables, wool and fer weaving woollen fabric. The top floor with an over hanging balcony is called pati. It is the actual living quarter. The houses are built of alternate bands of stove and limber. The inner walls are plastered with mud. The outer side is entirely made up of wood and acts as a verandah.

Language: From the linguistic point of view Malana appears to be an island. The language of the village, called Kanashi, is unintelligible for outsiders from the Kullu or Parvati Valley, who speak dialects belonging to Indo-European family of languages. It has been classified as a Sino-Tibetan tongue, related to Milchang which is a sub-branch of Kinnauri (a group of dialects spoken in Kinnaur).

According to the 1961 census, language speakers were 563. Today the population of Malana is at least three times as large as 40 years ago.

Although villagers claim to be descendants of Alexander the Great soldiers there is no proved lexical link with Greek or Macedonian languages. The core of the Kanashi vocabulary consists of Tibetan and Hindi layers.

Language is also considered to be one of the secrets of the village and outsiders are not allowed to use it for communication. The two lower caste Julahas and Lohar families who have been staying in the village since the last five decades are not allowed to speak Kanashi. Selected thematic list of words with Tibetan (Milchang) and Hindi correspondences

Education: There is one Government primary school manned by one teacher Sh. Roshan Lal a resident of Kulu. There are 100 children on roll in this school. The school building also houses an Ayurvedic dispensary, panchayat ghar and also a middle school. There is another middle school headed by Sh. Naresh Patiyal, a science teacher with Sh. Jagpal Shastri sanskrit teacher and Sh. Jog Raj Rana history teacher. The middle school was established in 1996. Although there are four teachers the number of students is only 13. Up to the primary school midday meals are provided. Girl students are provided free books. So far only two students in the village have managed to reach class 12.

Ecological Heritage: The people of Malana are very conscious about preserving their ecological heritage. According to village rules, fixing nails on a tree is prohibited as that could damage the tree. Burning of fire is also prohibited in the forests of Malana. Only dry twigs and branches are permitted to be carried away from the forest. Similarly, hunting of wild animals is not allowed without the permission of the village council and is allowed only during specific periods of the year.

In case wild animals attack the herds of shep and goats of the villagers the hunters are sent from the village to the pastures to kill them. And if a bear is killed, the hunter is rewarded but has to deposit the fur in the Bhandara of the Devta.

Livelihood: The life of Malanese is not an easy one. Living in class proximity to nature, they have to face the extreme conditions of weather. Long winter months, snow avalanches, and some times the epidemics also encounter them. Their livelihood is based on farming and cattle rearing. Besides, they also collect herbs in the upper reaches which find good market.

There are a few shops in the village, but these meet the requirements of the villagers. During winter villagers spend most of their time weaving the yarn on a loom. Generally a coarse cloth is woven from which outfits like coats and pajamas are made. Ladies make shawls with decorated geometrical patterns. The ladies wrap shawls in typical kulu fashion.

The villagers rear cattle, sheep and goat. During summer they take them to their summer house for grazing, as fodder is easily available. A number of such houses are located throughout the length and breadth of Malana valley. These houses are abandoned on the onset of winter and the villagers start collecting fodder in their permanent houses for their cattle. The sheep and goats are given to the village shepherd who takes them down to Kulu, Bilaspur etc. for grazing. Kokia, villager from Malana has the largest number of sheep and goats. Villagers usually hand over the flock to him for grazing as he is the most trusted man.

Rajmah, honey, and potatoes of this region are also very famous. Maize and wheat are grown on rotation basis to have good yield.

Fairs and Festivals: There are two important festivals celebrated in Malana. One called Badoh mela celebrated in August and the other called Fagdi mela in February. On these festive occasion people from nearby villages come to this place. Holy relics of Jamdagani Rishi in the form of instruments, jewellery, garments are kept on display. Men and women dance in their traditional attire consisting of chola, kalgi (round cap) and tight pajams on the beats of the Nagara, Shahanai, Karnali and Narsingha.

Marriages: Except the two major functions in the village there is not any custom or ritual to be followed. Marriage is a simple affair for Malanese and is performed around the Mela in the village. Marriages are performed at an early age mostly below fifteen. The function lasts for only one night. They day marriage is fixed, the bridegroom wearing a turban and the traditional attire along with his friends and relatives visits the bride's house where a feast is arranged for the guests. Not more than 30-40 people accompany him. Rice, chapatti, dal and meat are served. Meanwhile, the bride also gets dressed up in the traditional attire and is bedecked with jewellery. The girl's parents and relatives present gifts to the girl and bless her. Thereafter the bride alongwith the bridegroom prepares for the onward journey. According to the custom, the bridegroom is the first to leave alongwith baratis. He holds a mashal (torch) in his hand.

Seeing this, the bride runs after him and ultimately lands in her in-laws, house. This is all about the marriage and the locals call it Rakshasi marriage. No ceremonies, no priest and no elaborate rituals.

The only place in the outside world that malanese keep relations with is the village Rasol. Rasol worships the goddess Reneuka, the wife of Jamlu, and that is why girls from Malana can marry here. Malanese are allowed to marry inside the village. If they marry an outsider they may never be allowed to re-enter the village.

Divorce too is not uncommon is as simple as the marriage. In case of divorce, according to the law of the land, the boy has to arrange a separate house, the food etc. for the girl. Divorced women can remarry. The Malanese can keep one or more wives.

Similarly, there are not elaborate last rituals to be performed at the time of death. The dead body is wrapped in a coffin and taken to the cremation ground and consumed to flames on a pyre. One member of the village, the Hakim attends it besides the family members and the ashes are kept at the cremation ground only. The rituals of the deceased last for three days. A goat is sacrificed for the purification of the house. On the death of the husband, the widow can remarry but after a gap of one year.

Religious Beliefs: The shrine of Renuka Devi is situated in lower Malana. The shrine with its intricate wood work is noteworthy for its architectural excellence. Horns of animals sacrificed in the temple complex are usually fixed on the facade of the temple. The original abode of Jamdagani Rishi is said be at Baginda, 15 kms from Buntar. Another shrine of Jamdagani Rishi is at Tosh village, 6 kms from Pulga.

The village priest Bua Ram, who is the only person in the village to wear a white turban, can be recognized form a distance. His forefathers have been there since ages to take care of the village-shrine and pass on the injunctions of the Jamlu Rishi to the villagers.

Bua Ram, the priest has a two-storied house, well decorated from outside and embellished with intricate wood carvings. His family members are to stay separately but they do visit him while providing food and other things to him. In the close vicnity of the priest's house is the abode of Jamdagni Rishi called Jamlu Rishi in the local dialect.

The post of the village priest is a hereditary one. Bua Ram has one son Bayi Ram and a daughter Suvari Devi. Bayi Ram has two sons Morsingh and Amarchand. The village is inhabited by Thakurs only except for two families belonging to the Julaha and Lohar castes.

They don't belong to this place and came here as drummers. While untouchability prevails, there are separate dharmsalas in the village for the lower caste people coming to the place to attend the festivals and other occasions.

Jamlu is the most revered and is considered to be the king. His courtiers are elected and they collect funds for the following services for the upkeep and maintenance of the civic amenities:

1. Land revenue from the villagers of Malana.
2. From outsiders who graze their cattle in Malana.
3. Offering of devotees in cash and gold and silver horses.
4. From the offering of visitors.

The administration of Malana is based on religious faith and to maintain the faith the elected members select Bhandaris among the villagers who are assigned the following tasks :

1. To collect tax on land from the area, which falls under the jurisdiction of the village shrine.
2. To deposit land and other revenues in the shrine treasury.
3. To maintain the income and expenditure account.
4. To collect and deposit the offerings.

5. To arrange funds for functions and festivals and to organize them.
6. To hold symbols of Jamlu devata during the religious processions.

The three-storied building near the courtyard is meant for keeping food and other necessities for the pilgrims. According to the rule of the land, nobody must remain hungry in the village. The visitors or pilgrims can get food from this place. To maintain this store house four persons from the village are selected every year.

There is a separate bhandar for the God, which is adjacent to his abode. In this huge bhandar are kept the food grains besides the offerings made in cash and gold and silver horses.

Village Administration: The village has a democratic set up and the village council is called Hakima and consists of Goor, Pujari and Kardar representing higher court and Jestha the lower court. Pujari and Kardar are hereditary posts and the representatives of the Jamlu devta. Kardar is second in hierarchy there are four elected members from the village called Jestha. Each Jestha can select one more member called Pogudar and total elected members come to eight. Out of these eight, one person is elected as Pradhan (sarpanch) and the other is a upapradhan.

Goor regarded as the voice of village—god, can be any person from the village. Any person can become Goor, who is regarded the voice of the village god. He is said to be possessed by the spirit of the Jamlu devta. There can be one or more Goor in the village. Magdu, the Goor of the Malana died in 1985 and nobody has taken his place so far. The people of Malana attribute it to domination of evil forces in the village. Once the Goor is identified, he is directed to wear a cap and keep long hair. On certain occasions the Goor dances is ecstasy and is possessed by the holy spirit of Jamlu Devta. On such occasions the Goor directs the villagers and also listens to their woes. Goor has an important positions in the village Hakima and is always consulted before making any judgement.

Dispute Redressal: The village judiciary system through primitive is novel in its own way and the decisions are unanimously taken by the lower court. The council of the lower court hears the case and accordingly delivers the judgment. The council members reach a consensus and the case then is referred to the higher court for the final verdict. This type of participatory courtship is rarely found in villages of India and in most of the cases taken up by the traditional panchayat the decision is the monopoly of the sarpanch who is hand in glove with the panchs.

Some scholars on the basis of this participatory court procedure have traced the origin of Malana Hakima to the ancient Greece. The Hakima are not rigid in their decisions and sometime they do revise them in the interest of village after studying the pros and cons. There are a number of cases which are taken up by the village council, like theft, grabbing of land, eloping with another person's wife etc. etc. Police intervention is not allowed to take place, but if the accused wants to seek the help of police he has to pay a fine of Rs.1,000/-to the village council.

The Malanese Judiciary has its own way of administering justice. In most cases the guilty is fined. In case of theft the offender has to return the whole amount and pay a certain amount to the treasury. In case some one revolts against the administration and judiciary his property is attached and the person is not allowed to stay in the valley. In case of theft or misuse of the God's treasures, the stones are tied to culprit and he is pushed down the mountain slopes.

Epilogue: The civilized modern world has a lot to learn from the Malanese. The way they settle their issues is a lesson to the urban elite. No law books, no clauses, no constitution, no lawyers, no policemen or police stations and yet the villagers live in mutual harmony, sharing their burden with each other. With basic minimum requirements, the Malanese over the centuries have learn to live in tune with nature. They may not have access to the luxuries of the modern world still once can see the glow of contentment on their innocent faces.

In fact an outsiders in Malana or any other village is an intruder. The village of Malana is like a well-knit family and it is but natural that nobody should interfere in their private affairs. If we really want to protect and preserve this heritage we should leave the affairs of the village in the hands of the Malanese. Only minimum interference to which they have unitedly shown restraint will help. They are happy to be part of benevolent nature. Malana with its unique life style, language and traditions has remained curiosity for the outsiders for the last four decades. Much has been written about it, but not in a proper perspective.

But how long can the unique identity of this land be maintained when the Malanese themselves are more or less succumbing to the evil of modernisation? There may be no roads in the village but the video parlours have made in roads in its sanctity. The dwellings too are changing and in fact, the village is going through a slow process of socio-cultural degradation and if this continues the day may not be far off when it will lose its unique identity.

A Historical Preview of Basholi

From the times immemorial Jammu province was divided into small petty states, Lakhanpur, Jasrota, Billawar, Ramnagar, Chinani, Baderwah, Kashtwar, Kirmachi, Akhnoor, Poonch and Basohili were the independent states of Jammu province. These independent states had to give the part of their revenue to the rulers of Delhi and Punjab. The rulers of these petty states constructed forts, palaces and temples in their domains.

From the historical point of view, Basholi ever held an important place among these autonomous petty states. Town of Basholi is situated on the northeast and is about 130 kms from Jammu proper. Basholi is famous for its distinctive Basholi School of paintings, which is known world wide owing to their peculiar style of paintings. Basholi paintings have carved a separate place in the field of art. Masterpieces of Basholi paintings are not only found in India but also in the museums abroad. Dogra Art Museum, Jammu is having a good collection of Basholi paintings.

Pal rulers of Basholi were patrons of art. During their regime Basholi paintings added new dimensions to the pahari art by blending so many novel elements and out of this add mixture evolved a peculiar and distinctive style of painting.

So many famous artists and painters hailing from different quarters of the country adorned the royal durbar of Basholi rulers. These artists received lot of patronage and encouragement by the Basholi rulers, which is indicative of their fine taste for art. Consequently these artists embellished the palace walls with their art. Basholi palace paintings were worth seeing once. Rang Mahal of Basholi Palace has been popular theme of discussion in the artistic circles of the country as well as abroad.

Much has been written on the buildings and palaces of Basholi. Many visitors from the country and abroad visited this place. Their travel accounts facilitated our imagination in building conjectural picture of the past glory and grandeur of Basholi. Now only ruins are left to tell the story of the glorious past of Basholi.

In 1835, G.T. Vinage, visited this place. He saw there the beautiful palace and buildings. He was fascinated to see the palace buildings. From his travel report it is clear that up to 1835, the palace building was intact and in good condition.

Few years' back Govt. started a painting school at Basholi, now the school is closed. While this was a welcome step, towards, keeping the traditions of art alive in this region. But the local people didn't cooperated regarding this matter.

Basholi paintings have a peculiar style. The colours used are also different. Some people have tried to relate it with the Kangra School of paintings. In my view Basholi region evolved a new and individual style of its own. In this style there may be some similarities with other schools as far as theme and content are concerned but the overall style is peculiar and distinctive.

Old forts and ruined palaces are still standing the ravages of time at Basholi. These ruins bear witness to the Basholi past and speak a lot about the culture and traditions of the past. In the past Basholi was sometimes independent and sometimes under the rule of Jammu. During the Mughal regime Basholi had to pay a part of its revenue to the Delhi Durbar and afterwards, the reins were taken over by the rising power of Sikhs.

In the building activity at Basholi, Mughal architecture is clearly evident. Among the ruins at Basholi are the palace and the fort. On the southern side of the palace is a fort and on the northern side is a temple. Ruins of the fort are on top of a hillock and the Devi temple is situated on the top of hill.

The palace has three sections-Durbar Hall, Sheesh Mahal and Rang Mahal. Raja Amrit Pal started construction of this palace and the construction work was completed in the reign of Raja Mahendra Pal. Now the palace is in ruins having a deserted look. Not only weathering and time factor played its role in deterioration but the vandalism of local people also contributed a lot in razing to the ground this marvellous palace building.

Plinth and the ground floor of this palace building are in stone. The first floor is made up of burnt bricks. Presently it is very difficult to locate the Rang Mahal and Shesh Mahal. Now what are left are the heaps of bricks and stones. There is a basement also which is still in good condition. On some standing walls, paintings are still seen. On the brick wall a layer of line plaster was applied and after a coat of fresh lime, painting was done. Paintings on these ruined palace walls still look fresh as if painted yesterday.

The palace building didn't collapse due to weathering and time factor but was raised to the ground by local people and the Government also didn't take any interest in these falling ruins. Now the Archaeological survey of India is looking after it. The palace of Basholi was a fabulous construction in the whole hilly area but Alas! destructive hands of man couldn't find any other target.

On the western side of the palace is a tank, which remains filled with water throughout the year. Temple, which is on the hill, is a modern construction. This Devi temple was constructed by repairing the earlier temple. This temple was repaired during the Dogra regime.

While proceeding towards River Ravi there is an ancient Shiva temple. The precise date of its construction is yet to be established. Besides Shiva linga there are a cluster of many other deities represented around the linga viz. Nandi, Bhairava, Hanuman and Ganesh. The roof of this temple is in terrace form. Adjacent to this very temple there is also a small temple of Shiva's consort Parvati.

In Basholi, on the bank of River Ravi are two caves. These caves are carved out from a huge rock the big cave is having two rooms. The outer room is square and the height of the ceiling is seven and a half feet. From the ceiling is hanging a bell. Room is having three niches; niche on the western side of the cave room is bigger than the other two Southern sides of the cave room leads to another room. On the left side of the entrance is a life size image. This image is of the founder of Basholi, Raja Vishva Rana. The image is in higher relief but the sculptor is not able to give it a realistic look. King is wearing a turban and round his waist is attached a sword. Second cave room is a as small one; the ceiling of this room is also very low and is of dome shaped. In the center of the room is a Shiva lingam. Presently the whole area is submerged under water.

In my opinion the history of this cave dates back to countries. Work of carving out this cave, appears to be that of skilled chisellers and to complete it must have taken years. Blue waters of River Ravi, the, lavishly green nearby hills and the snow clapped mountains in the backdrop make the environs suitable for meditation and spiritual study.

Outside the cave is a big boulder. On the eastern side of the boulder is a niche having the height of one meter. Inside the niche is the Shiva linga. On the backside of the niche are the relief images of Shiva and Parvati. On one side of the niche is a three-headed image of Shiva. Outside, on the top of the niche, is a carved image of Ganesh, on the left side of the niche is Nandi and on the right side is Hanuman. Some of the images are defaced beyond recognition. From the iconography point of view the work is not up to the mark and it also does not shows the excellence in chiseling work, but still the work is appreciable. About one and a half kilometres from Basholi is a small hamlet of Mahadera. There also is an ancient Shiva temple.

Old monuments are integral part of our cultural heritage, which has survived down the ages. These should be maintained and conserved at all costs for the posterity. These ruins are not merely heaps of stone boulders but they are the only witness of our past. We have to protect them and keep them alive. This is not an easy job but not even impossible all together.

Bala Devi of Balahama, Srinagar

Ancient Hindu Shrines in Kashmir are under constant threat of oblivion either due to neglect or destruction.

The village Balhama named after the Goddess Bala Devi is thirteen kilometres from Srinagar and is surrounded by the village Wuyan in the east, Khanmoh and Zewan in the north and Pampore in the west. The shrine of Bala Devi is connected with link roads from the National Highway IA via Sempore and Pampore town. From Sempore the Shrine is at a distance of 4 kms and from Pampore at a distance of two kilometres.

Bala Devi Shrine: The shrine of Bala Devi has Jagir has thirty kanals of land attached to it. Around the shrine proper are twelve brick pillars covered with the galvanised iron sheets. The space in between the pillars is fenced with grills. This sort of renovation was undertaken in 1975. Earlier the shrine was open on all sides. Around the five sacred devdar trees in the shrine are twenty stone idols of gods and goddesses. Painted with Vermillion these are of ancient date. There is also a Shiv Linga in the Shrine.

Mythology : Bata Devi is mentioned in Mahakala-Samhita, Mantra Mahodadhi, Sri Lalitopakhyan and Haritayan Samhita or Tripura-Rahasya.

The three eyed Bala Devi has the moon crescent above her forehead and she has in her hands the book and beads, and the other two hands are in Abhay and Dhyan Mudra. She is of red complexion and wears red clothes. Sometimes she is depicted holding Ankusa and Pasa in addition to beads and the book. She is bedecked with the necklace of gems and pearls.

The account of Sri Bala Devi is given in the 22nd chapter of Sri Lalitopakhyan which forms part of Brahmand Purana.

According to this text Sri Bala Devi is said to be the daughter of Sri Lalitmaha Tripura Sundari. At the age of nine years she become terribly angry after seeing the Bandasura and his thirty sons who were marching ahead for a war. Bala Devi requested her mother Maha Bhatarika Sri Lalita Tripura Sundari to allow her to fight with the Bandasura. Permission for which was not allowed by her mother because of her tender age. On her daughter's insistence she not only gave her the permission but also one of her shields and number of her attributes. With this preparation she proceeded on a chariot towards the battle field. After an intense fight she was able to kill the thirty sons of Bandasura.

In Haritayan Samhita or Tripura-Rahasya, (Chapter 63), Bala Devi at the age of eight years is said to have fought directly with Bandasura. Knowing that her mother won't give her the permission she quietly proceeded towards the battle field on a chariot followed by Mantrani and Dandani.

Bala Devi was able to pierce the mighty forces of Bandasura with her rain of arrows and then confronted the Kutilaksh, riding on a mighty elephant, the commander of the forces of Bandasura. Bala Devi showered the arrows on the elephant and thereafter killed Kutilaksh. Bala Devi alone destroyed the army of Bandasura and then directly confronted the Asura. Instead of attacking Bala Devi, Bandasura showered flowery arrows on the Devi. Seeing this the charioteer of Devi was astonished and asked the Devi the reason for the same. Bala Devi said, "In the last incarnation Bandasura was Mahadoot of Srilakshmi and his name was Manik Shekhar. He was an ardent devotee of Bagvati Lalita Maha Tripura Sundari. Because of the curse on him he became Asura and he was told to earn salvation only by being killed by me. Knowing that I am the daughter of Sri Lalita Amba he is worshipping me." The war was destined and both began to fight. After defeating the opponents Bala Devi returned to her abode, Sripuri.

Folk Lore: According to the local folk lore the original abode of Bala Devi is in the South India. It is said that the saint of the temple had a dream in which she told him to visit Kashmir where he could have her darshana. The saint along with his devotees as per the divine blessing visited the village of Balahama which was a dense forest at that time. The goddess gave darshana to the saint in a spring. In order to keep the sanctity of the shrine she directed him to plant trees around the spring. The saint planted five saplings of Devdar trees around the spring which in the course of time grew to full size and covered the entire spring. The spring is no more visible today. The five Devdar trees are believed to be more than five thousand years old and are the principle object of veneration.

Bala Devi is the family deity of the Dogra rulers in the Valley. Dogra ruler, Maharaja Pratap Singh used to walk bare foot for about a kilometer to reach this shrine as a matter of respect and devotion towards this shrine. Devotees used to worship by reciting the hyms in the praise of goddess and the milk was offered.

Every year havan was performed in the month of Magh on the day of Tikchorum. Havan was also performed on other auspicious days especially on Haar Chorum. Late Pandit Jai Lal of Balahama was priest of this temple till his death in 1993.

Management of the Shrine: Till 1947 the Shrine was maintained by the Dogra regime and later it was taken over by the Dharmarth Trust. But it was not taken proper care of by the Trust authorities on the pretext that there was no income from this Shrine.

The local body named Bala Devi Asthapan Committee was formed in 1973 with Pandit Niranjan Nath as President, Pandit Omkar Nath as Secretary, Pandit Prithvinath and Pandit Radha Krishan as members. The first task the committee undertook was to fence the land around the shrine to prempt encroachment. Seeing the initiative taken by the villagers the Dharmarth Trust also came into to action and sanctioned one chowkidar for the shrine. The committee played a great role in renovating the temple and arranging the religious functions from time to time.

Under the present circumstances one can only hope that powers of Bala Devi will act as a shield against the forces of evil, ignorance and darkness till the dawn of a new era of peace and prosperity.

Amar Mahal Museum

Set in a picturesque setting of Himalayas, Amar Mahal Museum and Library, is an epitome of royal grandeur and magnificence. It is a repository of books and paintings and attracts art lovers and historians from all over the world. The museum building forms the major part of the majestic Amar Palace, which has a French touch in its architectural style. A veritable storehouse of historical documents, it has rich collection of exhibits, including sculptures, paintings, inscriptions and books. The Durbar Hall exhibits the paintings and artworks of the Dogra rulers and the Golden Throne, the highlight of the museum, is a symbol of great historic significance.

The books in the Library range from religion, philosophy and political science to fiction besides the various best-sellers international authors. Housed in the first and second floors of Amar Mahal, the library houses over twenty thousand books collected by Dr. Karan Singh over the last fifty years, including some rare volumes from the Library of Raja Amar Singh. Visitors are often attracted to the suite once occupied by Maharani (later Maharajmata) Tara Devi, which has been preserved almost exactly as it was when she resided there, complete with the silver bedspread, the period furniture and photographs, her personal items of clothing and the unique Victorian bathroom. The decoration Crown of India, which she received in 1945, is also displayed there.

The Art Galleries of the Amar Mahal aim to promote Indian art and artists and present a spectacular picture in informal surroundings. Endowed with ethnicity and a soft touch of contemporary art setting, the galleries exhibit the collection of paintings ranging over different styles. These include Kangra style of Indian miniatures paintings and also the contemporary collection including works of renowned artists like M.F. Hussain, J. Swaminathan, G. R. Santosh, Bikash Battacharjee, Ram Kumar, Laxman Pai and many others.

Hari Parbat—Symbol of our Cultural Heritage: As it is, Hari Parbat is the focal point in the Kashmir landscape, rising amongst historical ruins in its environs and commanding a panoramic view of the majestic and glistening hill tops griddling the extensive valley, the shimmering lakes which touch its boundaries as a mark of respect for its traditional associations and being a place of great sanctity in Kashmir. In ancient times, it was known as "Sharika Parvata", the hill of Sharika.

The crowning glory is the "Shrine of Cakreshvari", the Almighty Mother Sati, the controller of the titanic forces of nature. The cognoscenti have seen the mystical Shri Chakra represented in the shrine which structures her magic and mystery in the cubes, triangles, squares and circles represented therein. This then is a place of special veneration since the dawn of history. Besides, what is important is that all the important deities of the Hindu Pantheon have a traditional seat for themselves in and around "Sharika Parvata" as a mark of obeisance for Almighty Sati who had delivered the valley from the depredations of the demon "Jalodabhava" residing in the lakes.

Thus it is a shrine which has a unique place in the history of Kashmir, since millions of Kashmiris have been worshipping the related shrines since the day the valley became fit for habitation and life flourished. The legend adds that the deities in grateful memory of their deliverance took up their abode here, which accounts for the fact that every important individual stone or prominent rocky area is revered by the faithful.

At present important rocks depicting Jwala, Maha Ganesh are situated on the southwestern side of the Parvat. Further on, the rock known as "Sapta-Rishi", with which the earliest scientific calendar devised by Kashmiris and now 5078 years old is associated, is worshipped. Thereafter, we have the shrines of Mahakali and Siddha Laxmi. The resting place of Abhinava Gupta, the well known founder of Kashmiri Shaivism is also associated with Sharika Parvata.

The deliverance of the valley from the depredations of Jalodabhava enshrines a geological phenomenon which is duly substantiated on the basis of lacustrine deposits. The Kashmir valley is a boat-shaped basin, 140 km long on 40 km wide. It is an intermountain valley fill, comprising unconsolidated gravel-and-mud succession, which appear as plateaus above the present plain of the Jhelum and its tributaries. The plateau—like terraces are the present day Karewas or Uddars. Despite continuous erosion, still about half the valley is occupied by Karewa sediments.

The Wular and Dal lakes are the remains of a primeval lake known to the ancients as "Sati-Saras". There is a general consensus that due to the rise of the Pir-Panjal, the drainage got impounded and a lake about 5000 sq. kms. in area developed in the basin thus formed. To some of the earlier geologists, a nearly flat valley with steep hills all around appeared an ideal geomorphic setting for a lake to form. Due to further rise of the Pir-Panjal, the lake shifted to the Himalayan side.

This is the geological concept, but traditions associate the emergence of the habitable landscape due to the benign action of Mother Sharika who assumed the form of a bird (Maina) and taking a pebble in her beak dropped it at the spot where "Jalodabhava", the water demon was lying. The pebble swelled to gigantic proportions by virtue of her powers, crushing the demon by its weight. The pebble to this date survives as Hari Parbat and a depression in the ground outside *"Sangin Darwaza"* of Akbar's rampart indicates the place where he forced his way out as he was struggling under the crushing weight over him. The legend indicates that the Gods in grateful memory of their deliverance took up their abode in various pockets of Sharika Parvata.

As centuries rolled on, this area became the nerve centre of Pravarasena's "Pravarapura" in the 6th Century A.D. when he shifted his capital from Ashoka's "Pandrethan" (Puranadhisthana—the old capital), which clearly substantiates its growing importance. Close to the foot of the southern extremity of the hill is a rock which has from ancient times received worship as an embodiment of Ganesh. A legend related by Kalhana connects this Savyambhu image with Paravarasena's foundation of Pravarapura. It has to be emphasized that present Srinagar is ancient Pravarapura and as such the legend is doubly significant. From regard for the pious king, the god is said to have then turned his face from west to east so as to behold the new city.

A short distance to the southeast of the Bhimsvamin rock and just outside Akbar's rampart, lies the Ziarat of Bahauddin Sahib, built entirely with the materials of an ancient temple. It contains numerous Hindu remains, constructed with massive blocks of stones with extensive dimensions. Noteworthy among these at the southwest corner of this cemetery rises a ruined gateway, built of stone blocks of considerable size and still of considerable height. It is the precursor of the massive gateway of the ancient Martand temple built during the reign of Lalitaditya in the 8th Century A.D. This structure is traditionally believed to have belonged to the temple of "Shiva Pravaresvara" which Kalhana mentions as the first shrine erected by Pravarasena in his new capital.

An old legend related by Kalhana and before him by Bilhana who flourished in the 12th and 11th centuries A.D. respectively makes the king ascend bodily to heaven from the temple of Pravaresvara. Bilhana speaks of the temple as "showing to this day of gap above, resembling the gate of heaven, through which the king Pravara bodily ascended to heaven." Kalhana corroborates this by stating that he also saw in the temple of Pravaresvara a gate resembling the gate of heaven.

Its broken stone roof was supposed to mark the king's passage on his way to Shiva's abode. Architecturally it belongs to the earliest monuments of Srinagar. It owes its preservation probably to the exceptional solidity of its construction and the massiveness of its stones. Blocks measuring up to sixteen feet in length with a width and thickness equally imposing have been found.

The position of the remains is very central and might well have been chosen by the founder of Pravarapura for the prominent shrine in his new city. It also contains the graves of some of the most prominent personages of the Muslim period in Kashmir. What catches the eye is a tombstone which bears a bilingual Sanskrit and Arabic inscription which mentions the name of Muhammad Shah, the puppet ruler who was made king and dethroned not less than four times.

In the course of time many monasteries and Viharas were erected in its environs. One such vihara, called the "Amrit

Vihara" was built by the queen of Meghavahana at Vicharnagh. King Meghavahana was reported to be native of Gandhara and was invited by the nobles of Kashmir to rule the valley. Kashmir and Gandhara were in such close proximity to each other as to be deemed a single political unit, as is clear from the Greek records.

The Vihara at Vicharnagh (ancient Vanta-bhavana), a locality in close proximity was a flourishing area and was the terminal point of the Leh-Srinagar route. In its vicinity lies the suburb of "Sovura" (present day location of Sher-i-Kashmir Medical Institute) and is identified with king Surrendra who ruled the valley before king Ashoka.

In spite of the political upheavals during the early Muslim period, there were thriving settlements as is substantiated by exposed sections in "Malkhah area" outside Akbar's rampart, also indicating the density of habitation. In case some important sectors are properly excavated, it could throw a lot of light on the settlement patterns during the Sultanate period, and bridge a gap in the medieval history of Kashmir.

The importance of the area is further indicated by the construction of two very important and imposing monuments in the area. The earlier one is the mosque and Tomb of Madin Sahib in Zadibal area. Built in 1483 A.D., it is one of the most important Muslim buildings of the pre-Mughal period built in a characteristic style of the early Islamic period. The base is built entirely of materials belonging to the plinth of a medieval temple.

The architectural style is distinctive as it clearly indicates as to how remains of Hindu temples and shrines were utilized for construction of mosque and tombs. The architectural synthesis is distinctive and unique. Besides, the spandrels of the arches of the niches are decorated with beautiful tracery work. The wooden doorway is elaborately carved. The tomb of the saint is on the north of the mosque, and the wall surface is decorated with glazed tiles, a special architectural feature inducted into Kashmir in 15th century A.D.

Another important landmark in this thriving area was the Jama Masjid of Kashmir built in the characteristic wooden style, which developed in Kashmir and is also represented by the mosque of Shah Hamadan. The construction of the most imposing mosque in close proximity to Hari Parbat attests to its importance. Built initially by Sultan Sikandar But-shikan, who ruled Kashmir from 1390 A.D. to 1415 A.D., additions to the mosque were made by his illustrious son and successor, Zain-ul-Abidin. The later history of the mosque is the chequered one. It caught fire a number of times and was rebuilt with additions and alterations in later years. It is a mosque in the typical wooden style of the pre-Mughal period characterized by minarets and massive Deodaru pillars.

The importance of Hari Parbat area increased during the Mughal period. During Akbar's reign, in the 16th century A.D., an extensive rampart about 5 km in circumference was built. Although it is now in ruins, it requires protection as the only structure of its kind in the valley. It has been embellished with two imposing gates in chiselled stone—the *Kathi Darwaza* and the *Sangin Darwaza.* In the 16th and 17th centuries, the Mughals brought into the Kashmir valley their own style of stone architecture which contrasts with the typical Hindu Architecture developed in Kashmir as represented by the mosque of Shah-Hamadan and the Jama Masjid. The stone gateways of Kathi Darwaza and Sangin Darwaza have their own importance. The Mughals mostly lavished their attention on the famous gardens in Kashmir.

The Kathi Darwaza seems to have been the principal entrance, two inscriptions in Persian have been put up here. It is a simple structure, comprising a domed chamber in the middle with two side recesses. External decorations are marginal. On the spandrels of the main arch are two beautiful medallions prominently brought out and flanked by rectangular and arched panels. By way of comparison, the Sangin Darwaza, the stone gate which leads to "Cakreshvari shrine" is more ornate. The exterior is decorated by typical corbelled windows, and there are two stairs, one on each side, which give access to the roof.

Another conspicuous monument in the Mughal style just near the Kathi Darwaza on the scarp of Hari Parbat is the mosque of Akhun Mulla Shah, built by crown Prince Dara Shikoh, son of Shah Jahan, in 1649 A.D. It is built in beautiful grey lime stone. It was built by Dara Shikoh for his tutor Akhun Mulla Shah.

In modern times, both Muslims and Hindus have appropriated parts of the hill for their respective shrines. The Ziarat of Hazrat Makhdum Sahib revered by both Muslims and Hindus alike is situated on the southwestern side just above Maha Ganesh shrine referred to herein. People of all faiths offer their prayers here. Hazrat Sheikh Hamza Makhdum Sahib, meditated and lived till the end of the 15th Century A.D. and is buried here. He taught universal brotherhood and religious tolerance. Thousands of devotees, irrespective of caste, creed or colour, throng the mosque and offer their homage to him.

On the northeastern foot of this hill near Kathi Darwaza is situated, the chief religious centre of Sikhs, known as Gurudwara Chhatti Patshahi. Not only the Sikhs but people of other faiths also revere it as a shrine of religious sanctity. Hence the area in and around Hari Parbat bears a living testimony of religious tolerance, communal harmony and brotherhood where Hindus, Muslims and Sikhs flock around the Hill and offer their prayers without any acrimony and with complete accord. Religious tolerance is thus a living phenomenon and this is perhaps one of the few centres where there is complete harmony amongst different faiths.

This has considerably influenced the social ethos in Kashmir, as is evident in the Badamwari festival which is a typical feature of the social gatherings. During almond blossom time in the early spring when chills of the winter fade away, blossoms bloom in a riotous colour in some pockets in and around Hari Parbat. Kashmiris who get hemmed in during freezing winters find themselves flocking around early spring blossoms to give vent to their pent up emotions through folk songs and classical Sufiana Kalam.

It used to be a riot of colours, merry making and laughter on holidays and throughout the spring season, when gaily attired people would throng the blossom area especially in Hari Parbat which provided a fertile soil for almond saplings. It seemed as if the whole city had overflowed into the gardens and broken all the barriers of caste, creed and religion, enjoying the colours and the invigorating environment. Thus all Kashmiris cherished the past legacy in harmony with the enchanting environment. It was a spontaneous people's festival in the real sense of the term.

The Badamwari festival is now only a nostalgic reminiscence of the past. Blossoms do not bloom, for the trees have been felled and new constructions have sprung up. Akbar's rampart is crumbling, slums have sprung up all over and sacred stones which bear the imprint of divinity and history are being used in the construction of gutters and slums. Constructions have choked up access to some of the shrines which once throbbed with religious fervour.

The cultural, architectural and religious heritage of Hari Parbat is vanishing fast. The historical and religious traditions which have inspired and moulded the aspirations of Kashmiris are getting submerged under a false veneer of modernization. To maintain the physical remains in whatever form these still remain is a valuable and urgent undertaking and needs to be attended to on a priority basis. The environmental and religious heritage of the hallowed area has to be preserved.

Tradition makes it that the valley became habitable because of Hari Parbat. Hari Parbat became the focal point of "Pravarapura", which was the city of Srinagar when Pravarasena II shifted the capital, ignoring the claims of Ashoka's Pandrethan because of its difficult layout. The Sultans of Kashmir and later on the Mughals embellished it with structures of their own. The Hill reverberates with the deeply enshrined religious aspirations of the people of Kashmir of all faiths. Their heritage as such has to be preserved under all circumstances.

Some of the emergent steps that need to be taken by Central and State Governments are listed below :

(i) The Central Government should declare the whole of Hari Parbat, including the area and monuments between the rampart wall and the hillock and 500 meters area outside, as a protected area and a national heritage.

(ii) Mughal remains in the form of rampart wall, Akbar's Nagar—Nagar, Mosque of Akhun Mulla Shah, the two stone gates of Kathi Darwaza and Sangin Darwaza should receive attention for proper preservation.

(iii) All the vacant lands and slopes of Hari Parbat should be planted with almond trees, and the 'Sound and Light' show should be initiated to boost tourism and revival of interest of Kashmiris and outsiders in our secular traditions.

(iv) There should be a high-powered committee of dedicated and enlightened representatives of the three major communities for preservation of the religious and cultural traditions and development of the area on mutually agreed terms. Local trustees of the shrines in and around Hari Parbat could be included in such a committee so that there is a broad-based consensus relating to proper development of this area and removal of unauthorized constructions and encroachments.

(v) The Archaeological Survey of India along with the State Department of Archaeology and the Birbal Sahni Institute of Paleo—botany should be asked to survey thoroughly the area from "Thanedar Bag" to "Khoja Yarbal" which skirts Hari Parbat and touches `Nagin Lake' for possible prehistoric remains.

Temples of Historical Significant

The ancient sites of Ushkar, built by the Kushan king Huvishka approximately in the 3rd century A.D., and Harwan, a typical Buddhist settlement of the type that flourished in Gandhara kingdom, provide the earliest glimpse of the building-art in Kashmir. During the reign of the great king Lalitaditya, who ascended to the throne in 724 A.D., temples constructed using stone masonry sprang up in large numbers all over Kashmir. This building activity continued with the wave of religious emotion which swept over India about the same time, and resulted in a fever of temple building–Lalitaditya's triumphs in the realm of territorial expansion created a cultural climate, of which grandeur was an important ideal. The monumental

Buddhist shrine at Parihasapura, now a mass of sculptured stones, and the temple of the Sun at Martand show this quality, not only in their stupendous size but also by the bold confidence with which they were built.

The Martand temple has been often called "the materialized-spirit of a transcendent vision". Built on a plateau encircled by a range of eternal stones this temple represents an architectural expressiveness of the highest order, and forms the supreme model of a style to which a great number of later temples are subscribed. Instead of the Buddhist assembly hall, where congregational worship was held, the central structure here is a sanctuary for the divine symbol. This perhaps signifies a departure from the Buddhist influence and the acceptance of the Brahmanical creed by the people.

The shrine stands within a big courtyard surrounded by a pillared arcade and a series of cells. Certain features in the surface decoration of the Martand temple are of unique interest. The regularly spaced medallions, the frequent use of pilasters (cantilevers), and the pediment motif, all recall the architecture of the antique classical west. The capitals of the pillars that support cornices have something Doric about them, and their molded bases are of attic type.

The encircling colonnade is also reminiscent of the Greek style. However, experts are of the view that these influences are not deep-rooted and that the main composition is of indigenous inspiration, the product of the genius of Kashmir.

The mural sculpture on the walls displays unmistakably the influence of the art movement fostered by the Pala rulers of Bengal, which was apparently of such intensity that it made itself felt in regions far beyond its geographical boundaries.

As further evidence of the source of this influence, Percy Brown points out that the copper gilt image of the Sun-God installed in the cellar of the Martand temple must have been wrought in the very same foundry where expert Pala metal-workers shaped that of the famous copper image of the Buddha discovered at Sultanganj in Bengal (presently housed in the Birmingharn Art Gallery).

Avantivarman, who ascended to the throne of Kashmir in the latter half of the 9th century ushered in another memorable era of architecture. He built a group of temples at Avantipur, a township eighteen miles from Srinagar, among which that of Avantiswami, dedicated to Vishnu, still survives in part. It has been said that whereas the Martand temple is the expression of a "sudden glory", the Avantiswami temple shows greater maturity of experience and has therefore more sophistication and elegance. Graceful colonnades of pillars form an arcaded portico around the shrine and a monolithic pillar before the entrance bears a metal figure of Garuda, the king of birds and vehicle of Lord Vishnu.

Motifs borrowed from many sources, both foreign and indigenous, appear in the decorative carving, but these have been tastefully integrated into an ordered system with a recognizable unity. Designs reminiscent of Buddhist stone carvers of the Ashokan age and of the craftsmen of the Pala school are frequent, and symbols traceable to Byzantium, ancient Persia and Syria are also found. The conspicuously angular aspect of this temple is derived from the wooden houses of the valley where accumulation of heavy snow on roofs is prevented by their sloping character.

Two Shiva temples built at Pattan in the 10th century A.D., during the reign of Shankaravarman reveal that although the traditional mode established at Martand was still being followed two centuries later, the masonry tended to become more monolithic. The precision and skill with which the moldings are chiselled out of a huge stone is truly amazing.

Built in the 12th century A.D., the small, well preserved temple at Pandrethan, near Srinagar, gives a clear idea of the general plan of the temples in Kashmir at this time. The pyramidal structure of the roof, which is still intact, is a prominent characteristic of this style. The ceiling consists of beams laid on the angles, a technique obviously derived from wooden constructions. Wherever a tank is provided for ablutions, materials such as rock, brick, or stone are used for the construction of the tank. Two temples at Kiragrama or Baijnath in the Kangra valley, one dedicated to Shiva and the other to Jamadagni, are notable examples of Himalayan architecture of the early 13th century. Chamba, Kumaon and Kulu also have numerous temples of the same type. The famous Doongri temple, dedicated to Hirimba in Manali in the Kulu valley, is constructed of wood, and is a striking example.

Khanqah Mosque

Kashmir Hub offers you a unique opportunity to visit the ancient pilgrimage destination of Khanqah-e-moulah mosque. The Khanqah-e-moulah is popularly known as the Khanqah mosque or the Shah Hamdan Masjid. This mosque is located on the banks of the river Jhelum. Tours and travel to this pilgrimage destination gives you the thrill of watching this ancient monument on the banks of the river Jhelum in its complete rustic glory. This mosque was constructed by Sultan Shah Sikander in the year 1395 to honour Mir Sayyid Ali Hamdani, popularly known as Shah Hamdan who used to visit Kashmir for meditation. The word Khanqah basically means a lodge or resting place for Sufi saints.

Tours and travel to this pilgrimage gives you a chance to appreciate the most attractive feature of this mosque, and that is its intricate and characteristic woodwork and carvings. Cedar wood was used for the construction of this Khanqah. The medieval wooden style of Kashmir's Muslim architecture is best reflected in the Khanqah-e-moulah in Srinagar. There is a lot of papier machie work on the walls and ceilings of the mosque. The original structure of the mosque does not exist, in fact it has been rebuilt a number of times. The present structure is shaped like a cube with a pyramidal roof and was built by Sultan Hassan Shah. An inscription on the doorway of the shrine states 786 Hijrah as the year of death of the Sufi saint Shah Hamdan.

Kashmir Hub attempts to offer tourists comprehensive details on tour packages and travel options to the Khanqah mosque in Srinagar, Kashmir, India.

Pilgrimage Destinations—Amarnath: The pilgrimage destination of Amarnath shrine is located inside a cave in the Himalayas. The mythological and historical importance of this sacred place according to mythology is the fact that lord Shiva recounted the secret of creation and immortality to the Goddess Parvati in this cave. This secret is of immortality is known as the amar katha and according to legend lord Shiva made sure that no living being was around when he narrated this story to the Goddess Parvati.

According to common legend a shepherd called Buta Malik first discovered this holy cave at Amarnath and ever since, this cave became an important center of pilgrimage for the Hindus.

The Government of Jammu and Kashmir organize tours and travel to the Amarnath shrine in Jammu. There is an ice lingam of lord Shiva inside the Amarnath cave. This is supposed to represent the deity. Tours and travel to this shrine in Jammu can be undertaken only after being registered with the authorities.

Kashmir Hub offers details about tours and travel packages for the holy Amarnath yatra in Jammu, Kashmir, India. There are two different ways of reaching the Amarnath shrine. The traditional route passes via Pahalgam, Sheshnag and Panchtarni. The new route is via Baltal. If pilgrims opt to travel by the old route then it takes approximately four days to reach the holy Amarnath Dham. Those who choose to travel by the new route reach the place in a day's time. Most Hindus try to visit this shrine at least once in a lifetime.

Charar-e-sharif: The pilgrimage destination of Charar-e-sharief has one of the most sacred Muslim shrines, which is popularly known as the Hazrat Sheikh Noor-ud-Din Wali. This Muslim pilgrimage is dedicated to the memory of the Sufi saint Sheikh Noor-ud-Din Noorani, who was the patron saint of the Muslims in Kashmir. During the Sheikh's lifetime, he witnessed a cultural and religious transformation of those around him, from Hinduism to Islam. A number of historical events prompted the Sheikh to produce some valuable works of philosophy, in verses and poetry.

Tours and travel to the Charar-e-sharief shrine can be an educative experience. This pilgrimage is a 600 year-old wooden shrine. Most of the shrine and its surroundings were destroyed as a consequence of an armed battle between the Indian Army and the Pakistani Army. Later the shrine was rebuilt on the lines of central Asian architecture.

Charar-e-sharief is located on the way to Yusmarg, 40 kilometres from Srinagar. Tours and travel to this region is a little tricky as the region lies near Pakistan occupied Kashmir.

Kashmir Hub offers you details of tour and travel packages to the province of Charar-e-sharief and the sacred Muslim shrine.

In 1995 a major part of this 600 year-old shrine was destroyed. Tourists still have an opportunity to learn about the history of the sacred place of worship and Kashmir Hub attempts to introduce tours and travel options to this religious shrine to interested tourists.

Hazratbal: Kashmir Hub offers you an opportunity to explore the sacred Muslim pilgrimage destination of the Hazratbal shrine that is situated on the banks of the Dal Lake in Srinagar opposite Nishat Bagh. Tours and travel to this shrine can be a special experience as the Prophet Muhammad's hair, that is the Moi-e-Muqqadus, is preserved in this shrine. The history of this shrine dates back to the seventeenth century. The Hazratbal shrine is a marble structure that was specifically constructed by Muslim Auqaf Trust with the objective of preserving the Prophet's hair, this piece of hair arrived in Kashmir in the year 1699.

The Hazratbal shrine lies at a distance of 25 kilometres from the Badgam district in Srinagar, Kashmir. This pilgrimage destination is known by a number of names viz. the Assar-e-Sharif, Madinat-us-Sani and the Dargah Sharif. Mughal emperor Shahjahan's brother constructed the Ishrat Mahal at the site of the shrine sometime in the year 1623, later when the emperor himself visited the site he ordered the place to be converted into a prayer house. The shrine as such was built by the Muslim Auqaf trust. Before the Hazratbal shrine was constructed the sacred hair was placed in the shrine of Naqshband Sahib. The architecture of the shrine is a combination of Mughal and traditional Kashmiri.

The Moi-e-Muqqadus is usually on public display inside a glass casket on certain sacred and holy days. Tours and travel to the Hazratbal shrine gives you an opportunity to participate in the colourful and vibrant fairs that are held at Hazratbal every year, the most important among these is the Shab-e-Meraj. The Watul mela is also very popular among the tourists and the pilgrims.

Kheer Bhawani: Kashmir Hub offers tourists an opportunity to visit the holy temple of the Goddess Ragnya Devi. This pilgrimage destination is located in the village of Tulla Mulla, that is at a distance of 27 kilometres from Srinagar.

This temple is popularly known as the Kheer Bhawani temple. Devotees fast and gather here on the eighth day of the full moon in the month of May when, according to common belief, the goddess changes the colour of the spring's waters. The temple complex is known as Kheer Bhawani because of the thousands of devotees who offer milk and kheer, a form of Indian desert, to the sacred spring, which magically turns black to warn of impending disaster. Pilgrims who have faith in the divine powers of the goddess usually undertake tours and travel to this pilgrimage.

Travel and tours to the Kheer Bhawani pilgrimage during the annual festival can be the most thrilling experience. The festival of the Kheer Bhawani temple is extremely famous and devotees gather from far and wide to participate in the worship of the goddess Ragnya Devi. The festival ends with a maha yagnya. It has been a tradition among the Kashmiri pundits to visit the temple of Kheer Bhawani on all the nine days of the navratras. The tenth day of the festival is celebrated as Vijaya Dashami.

Kashmir Hub attempts to offer tourists relevant information on tours and travels to the Kheer Bhawani temple in Srinagar, Kashmir, India.

Shankaracharya Temple: Kashmir Hub offers you an opportunity to visit one of the most revered Hindu pilgrimage destinations, the sacred temple of Shankaracharya. This temple is located on the top of the hills, southeast of Srinagar and is commonly known as the Takht-i-Sulaiman. This temple is situated at a height of 1100 feet above the Srinagar city. The temple is devoted to the worship of lord Shiva. Tours and travel to this pilgrimage involves a trek to the top of the hills in the Srinagar region.

This ancient temple dates back to 250 B.C. It is believed that the saint Shankaracharya stayed here when he visited Kashmir ten centuries ago to preach the Sanatan Dharma. In the ancient times this temple was known as the Gopadri. The main shrine has a circular cell inside. An inscription in Persian inside the shrine indicates that the origin of this sacred place dates back to the reign of emperor Shah Jahan. The saint Adi Shankaracharya visited Kashmir in the first quarter of the ninth century with the basic aim of spreading the philosophy of Vedanta. The saint also popularized the worship of lord Shiva in Kashmir.

It seems before saint Shankaracharya came to this area, Buddhism was rampant in this region. The main aim of Kashmir Hub is to acquaint tourists with all the tours and travel options to the sacred Shankaracharya temple, Srinagar, Kashmir, India.

Gompas in Ladakh: Kashmir Hub offers you a unique opportunity to explore the Buddhist pilgrimages in Ladakh. Ladakh is basically a high altitude desert and is one of the most remote regions of the state of Jammu and Kashmir. There are more than 100 Gompas or monasteries in Ladakh. These Gompas are religious residences of Buddhist monks who stay here and adhere to the Buddhist way of life, meditate and pray. Tours and travel to these Gompas involves long mountain treks as these pilgrimage destinations are situated in remote places in the interiors of Ladakh.

Most of these Gompas are situated in remote areas, usually at great heights. Either the Mahayana or the Hinayana Buddhist sects built most monasteries in the Ladakh area of Kashmir. Monasteries in Ladakh are perched on high cliffs.

Tours and travel to these Gompas make you aware of the deep religious influence these monasteries have on the local people. The predominantly practised religion in Ladakh is the Mahayana Buddhism. Mahayana Buddhism is based on the eighth tenet of the concept of the eightfold part as propagated by Lord Buddha. This form of Buddhism stresses on meditation and concentration. One of the most innovative concepts introduced by the Mahayanists is that of the bodhisattvas.

The largest monastery in Ladakh is the Hemis Gompa that is located at a distance of 45 kilometres from Leh, the capital of Ladakh. The Namgyal Tsemo Gompa, which was built in the year 1430, houses a three-storyed statue of Lord Buddha. The Sankar Gompa is also an important monastery. The Dalai Lama inaugurated the Shanti Stupa in the year 1995. The Likhir monastery was built in the 11th century. There are huge clay images of Lord Buddha in this Gompa along with utensils and manuscripts from the olden days. Another old monastery is the Cave Gompa located at Shergole.

Vaishno Devi: The shrine of Mata Vaishno Devi is one of the most important pilgrimages of the Hindus. This sacred shrine is located at a height of 5, 300 feet above the sea level. The site is located inside a cave in the Trikuta Mountains in the state of Jammu and Kashmir, 62 kilometres from Jammu and 14 kilometres from Katra.

Mata Vaishno Devi is a form of the Hindu goddess Durga. According to legend a young girl Vaishno was created by the Gods to fight the demons in the Treta yug. According to common Hindu religious belief Mata Vaishno grants the four important boons of righteousness, material pursuits, contentment and enlightenment to all those who visit this sacred place of worship. Usually devotees offer coconuts, dry fruits and red net scarves as a token of worship to the deity.

The shrine as mentioned above is located in the Trikuta Mountains. Once at the entrance to the cave; the path turns into a narrow tunnel with a cold stream running through it. This stream is called the Charan Ganga. There are rock cut idols of three deities inside the cave, viz. Mahakali, Mahalakshmi and Mahasaraswati. These idols have crowns made of gold and silver. Kashmir Hub offers you all the relevant details regarding tour packages to Vaishno Devi, Kashmir, India.

Dal Lake: You will find your holiday in Kashmir incomplete without a stay on legendary floating hotels on Dal Lake. The houseboats are well appointed, built in Victorian style with every modern facility, they come complete with meals (Kashmiri/Indian/Continental) and several attendants. Shikaras (Kashmiri verse for a Gondola) are always available for crossings from the mainland and tours on the Dal Lake.

The scenic splendour of the Himalayas and coniferous forests add to the magical romance of Kashmir cruising.

Kashmiri cooking on the houseboats is based on the culinary art of the Mughals, Persians and the Pundits. The aroma of crushed saffron, packets of cumin, cardamom, cinnamom, cloves, red peppers being pounded, rice being steamed... the most elaborate meal "Wazwan", served on special occasions consists of 36 or more dishes (both veg. and non-veg). The 'wazas' or cooks pound the meat for hours and the finer the pounding indicates the waza's culinary art. Wazwan is a feast fit for an Emperor.

Wular and Manasbal Lake: Wular is Asia's largest fresh-water lake, formidable in its size is like a chameleon with every mile of its stretch. The calm waters of Manasbal Lake are retreat for bird watchers. Glide on a shikara on the lake with only gentle sound of the water and the birds to break the silence (2 hours round trip).

You can enjoy beautiful rides on shikaras; visiting Nehru park, Kabutur Khana, Charchinari, Floating Islands and typical vegetable farmer villages on the Dal Lake. The canals are spectacular.

Three Shrines of Khir Bhawani: The historical antecedents of Kshir-Bhawani, go back to very ancient times, as per the traditions. It is said that Ragniya Devi came to Kashmir from (Sri) Lanka in the era of Ramayana. Though Ragniya is a rupa of Durga, this one is a Vaishnav rupa in Kashmir Ragniya is also known as Tripura, while in (Sri) Lanka, the Mother Goddess was called Shayama. Sita too, is believed to have been an incarnation of Ragniya. Ragniya Mahatma has it that those who meditate on Panch Dashi Mantra during Nav-reh, Mother Ragniya grants their wish.

It is said that the night during which Mother Goddess came from (Sri) Lanka to Kashmir was Christened Ragniya Ratri In

Kashmir a number of shrines are decided to Mother Goddess at Tiker, Bhuvaneshvar, Manzgam (Noor-abad) Bheda, Loqraer-pur, Mani-gam, Rai-than and Baed-pur, but the Shrine at Tul-Mul is the most famous one and hence the focus of yatris. 360 springs (nagas) are said to have gathered there. Ragniya is a Sattavie form of Mother Goddess, i.e. the form of tranquility and bliss.

The first mention of Tula-Mula in Raj-Tarangni comes in Jaya Peda's reign when the Brahmins of Tula-Mula agitated against him. The protest of Brahmin fraternity indicates that Tula-Mula commanded much importance in Jaya Peda's time, because of which many Brahmins congregated there. The river on whose bank, Tula-Mul stands, has been called Chandra-Bhaga in Nilamat Purana. This Chandra-Bhaga is the branch of Indus which flows by Tula-Mula and finally merges in Veth (Jehlum).

Another tradition says that in the year 4041 Sapta Rishi over a thousand years ago, when the location of Tula-Mul Tirth had been lost to the people as the whole area of Tula-Mula had been inundated by water. Krishna Pandit, a devotee of the Devi, located it again, in that year. The reason for (Jesht) Ashtami being the day of fasting for Devi, is said to be the fact that its was in the night of (Jesht) Ashtami, that Devi came to Krishna Pandit in a dream and told him that she would lead him through water to the location of her asthapana, the next day. This is said to have happened exactly so and Krishna Pandit drone pegs around the place to demarcate it. Later when the flood ebbed the shrine was established a new.

Abul Fazl writes that Tula-Mula is an area of fifty kharwars which gets flooded in summer. About the marsh, he says, that when the waters recede, people catch ½ to 1 kg fish from under the mud.

Dara Shikoh's advisor, Maharishi Shyam Sunder Koul who was a Shakta-Margi, had a strange experience at Tula-Mula when his meat-dishes turned into vegetable ones. Devis' devotees have a firm belief that the waters of spring, in which Devi's shrine is located, changes colour.

Krishna Kar, attained spiritual height at this spring, during Aurangzeb's reigin (1659 AD).

Today the shrine is spread over an approximate area of 20 miles, which contains Dharam-salas etc. The area around the spring is floored in marble. Though there is a festival at Tula-Mula on every Ashtami of full-moon fortnight, the grand festival of the year is held on the Jesht Ashtami, in which people from Kashmir and outs-side take part.

The Devi temple of Tula-Mula is said to have been damaged in 14th or (and?) 15th centuries. The temple that was damaged (destroyed?), was also situated in the middle of the spring like the present temple. This came to light when the foundation for the new (today's) temple was being laid. The (ancient) temple had been built of beautifully carved flat stones, that were 9 feet in length and 3 feet in breadth. Besides a number of murtis were recovered which had great splendour and beauty. Maharaja Pratap Singh built a small marble temple in 1912 AD, on the foundation of that ancient temple. The small stone icon, adorning this temple is believed by experts to be more than 600 years old.

The original name of Main Gam is Maya Gram. The village is situated above Lar on the right-bank of Indus, a little to the interior, between 540-12(E) longitude and 340-17' (N) latitude, at a distance of 20 kilometres from Srinagar.

In the village proper, no ancient remains are found (now) but above the village on the foot of hill there is a heap of tiles, about which (M.Aurel) Stein writes that a temple existed there. On this path, enroute to Mahind Marg, there was a pond enclosed in stone-work with an in let in the north.

This spot is now called vata-shun. Haider Malik Chadoora calls this spring "Votur-Gang", and relates that its defiling, brought a fear of a snow-fall in Summer Hassan supported Haider Malik and has called it 'votur-nag'. Now this spring is used by the water-works department (PHE) as a water-source.

A mela is held at this spring, on the 12th of the bright-half of Shravana. It has been called Achha-ra-na Nag in Harmukh Mahatamya.

Raithan is to the North-West of Srinagar 32 km away. Near the village, between the Son-moi river and the road, there a very large stone which the Hindus have been worshipping since time immemorial as a form of Goddess Ragniya.

Till 1975, we were not aware of any historical significance of this place. In that year the people of the area decided to build a Dharamshala and a wall around the shrine and started digging near the Ragniya aakar. During this (digging) stone murti were found in two layers. The murtis in the upper layer related to the Hindu period and those below to the Buddhism. A specimen of wood-carving and a foundation of an ancient temple were also unearthed. Besides, charcoal mixed in earth was also found which indicated the destruction of the shrine by fire in some early time. The foundation of the small edifice is in front of the stone towards north.

Its lay-out points to a stupa having existed there. This is not surprising since the remains of a Boddh-Vihara existed, till only a short while ago in Arigam, just a little below Raithan. This indicates that Buddhist activities continued in the area for a long time. A little below Raithan, to the left of the road, there is a udara, which is even today called Raza-Geer (Raj Gadi-Capital). People say that coins of different period were found during ploughing.

Gh Ahmad Mahjoor, had collected many of these coins from the people. Mahjoor had been the patwari of Raithan, Ari-gam and Gra-veth, for a long time (before independence).

The murtis, that were excavated during digging, have got broken for the lack of caution. Most of the murtis are of soft-stone (lime-stone) which is not found in the vicinity. The murtis of Buddhist period are from the view point of craftsmanship and art much graceful, (but) those of the Hindu era do not possess that finesse and instead give the impression of crudity. It appears that these are related to the 11th and 12th centuries when the sculpture in Kashmir had decayed. However, the three-faced, green stone Vishnu, that has been found there is much graceful. Probably, it has been brought to the place from somewhere else. A similiar three-faced Vishnu has been found earlier at vont-i-pur (Avantipura).

Thus the Raithan shrine has have passed through three stages. First there had been a Buddhist shrine, then its became a Vishnu shrine and now it is a place for worship of Devi.

Prominent Holy Places in Kashmir: The happy valley of Kashmir is well known throughout the world for its Natural beauty. Here nature has been prodigal enough in crowning this ancient land with all its splendour and glory. Gulmarg, Pahalgam and Mughal gardens attract visitors from all over the world. Its lakes, green meadows, dancing and foaming streams, majestic forests full of fir and pine, snowcapped peaks are common attractions to the outsider as well as to the native.

Besides this, the valley being sacred and called Rishi wari till now, abounds in sacred places, Tirthas and Asthans. Long ago at the dawn of civilisation when the sons of Rishi Kashyapa from plains came to settle here they brought with them their traditions, religion, mythology etc. etc. These early settlers named the confluence of river Sindh and river Jhelum as Prayag, equal to holy Prayag at the confluence of the Ganga and the Jamna in India. They named the tallest mountain peaks here after their Gods and deities such as Brahma, Vishnoo and Mahadev.

These settlers must have felt surprised to see the hide and seek of water in the Spring of Trisandya; melting of snow around the spring of Bedaba Devi and other marvellous places. With the passage of time, these places became Tirthas or places of worship and has continued so upto the present time. The tradition being like this R. L. Stein who has translated Rajatarangini into English writes, "Kashmir is a country where there is not a place as large as a grain of seasam without a Tirtha. Time and conversion to Islam of greater portion of population has changed but little in this respect. "Pandit Kalhana while writing introduction to Rajatarangini names the miraculous springs of Trisandya Saraswati lake on the Bheda hillock, Self created fire at Soyambhu etc. etc."

One of the holy trinity, Shiva is a living god. The most sacred and most ancient book of India, the Rig Veda evokes his presence in its hymns. Vedic myths, ritual and even astronomy testify to his existence from the dawn of time. But Shiva, the destroyer, the mendicant, is undefinable: he is the great yogi, the guardian of the absolute. His actions are the themes of the myths in which his nature unfolds.

Lord Shiva: Shiva, he of the opposites and the absolute, is known to have made his home in the Himalayas. He built no house nor shelter, not for himself nor for his bride. He was an ascetic, and yet married; he could be both for "he was the wild god sporting in the forest or taking his ease on a cloud."

Legend has it that Shiva recounted to **Parvati** the secret of creation in a cave in Amarnath. Unknown to them, a pair of mating doves eavesdropped on this conversation and having learned the secret, are reborn again and again, and have made the cave their eternal abode. Many pilgrims report seeing the doves-pair when they trek the arduous route to pay obeisance before the ice-lingam (the phallic symbol of Shiva).

Along the Spectacular Sheshnag Lake: The trek to **Amarnath**, in the month of Shravan (July-August) has the devout flock to this incredible shrine, where the image of Shiva, in the form of a **Lingam**, is formed naturally of an ice-stalagmite, and which waxes and wanes with the moon. By its side are, fascinatingly, two more ice-lingams, that of Parvati, and of their son, **Ganesh**.

Shiva and Parvati with Ganesh: According to an ancient tale, there was once a Muslim shepherd named Buta Malik who was given a sack of coal by a sadhu. Upon reaching home he discovered that the sack, in fact, contained gold. Overjoyed and overcome, Buta Malik rushed back to look for the sadhu and thank him, but on the spot of their meeting discovered a cave, and eventually this became a place of pilgrimage for all believers. To date, a percentage of the donations made by pilgrims are given to the descendants of Malik and the remaining to the trust which manages the shrine.

Entrance to the Amarnath Cave: Yet another legend has it that when **Kashyap Rishi** drained the Kashmir valley of water (it was believed to have been a vast lake), the cave and the lingam were discovered by **Bregish Rishi** who was travelling the Himalayas. When people heard of the lingam,

Amarnath for them became Shiva's abode and a center of pilgrimage.

Whatever the legends and the history of Amarnath's discovery, it is today an extremely crucial centre of pilgrimage, and though the route is as difficult to trespass as it is exciting, every annum, millions of devotees from the subcontinent come to pay homage before Shiva in one of his Himalayan abodes.

The Shivalinga: Situated in a narrow gorge at the farther end of **Lidder** valley, Amarnath stands at 3,888 m and is 44.8 km from **Pahalgam** and 141 km from Srinagar. Though the original pilgrimage subscribes that the yatra be undertaken from Srinagar, the more common practise is to begin journey at Pahalgam, and cover the distance to Amarnath and back in five days. Pahalgam is 96 km from Srinagar.

The trek from Pahalgam to Amarnath cave is on an ancient peregrine route. The 45-km distance is covered in four days, with night halts at **Chandanwari, Sheshnag (Wawjan)** and **Panchtarni**. The distance from Pahalgam to Chandanwari (12.8 km) is covered in about five to six hours, and the trail runs alung the Lidder river. Pilgrims camp here on the first night out. A major attraction here is a bridge covered, year round, with ice even though the surroundings are free from it.

The next day's trek, of 13 km, is through spectacular, primeval countryside, and the main centre of attraction is Sheshnag, a mountain which derives its name from its seven peaks, resembling the heads of a mythical snake. The journey to Sheshnag follows steep inclines up the right bank of a cascading stream and wild scenery untouched by civilization. The second night's camp at Wawjan overlooks the deep blue waters of Sheshnag lake, and glaciers beyond it.

There are legends of love and revenge too associated with Sheshnag, and at the camp these are recounted by campfires, to the stillness of a pine-scented, Himalayan night.

The third day's 13 km trek steadily gains height, winding up across Mahagunas Pass at 4,600 m and then descending to the meadow-lands of Panchtarni, the last camp enroute to the holy cave.

From Panchtarni to Amarnath is only 6 km, but an early morning's start is recommended for there is a long queue awaiting entrance to the cave. The same day, following darshan, devotees can return to Panchtarni in time for lunch, and continue to Wawjan to spend the fourth night out; or continue further to Zojibal, returning to Pahalgam on the fifth day.

Entrance to the cave is regulated, and darshan a hasty affair for there are many others waiting outside to pay homage before the awesome Shivalinga. The devotees sing bhajans, chant incantations, and priests petform Aarti and puja, invoking the blessings of Shiva, the divine, the pure, the absolute. For those who journey with faith, it is a rewarding experience, this simple visitation to a cave-shrine, the home of the Himalayan mendicant who is both destroyer and healer, the greatest of the Hindu deities.

The Mysterious Cave of Amar Nath

Man's search after God began with the dawn of creation. This search has assumed various forms, some seekers have concentrated on the teachings of the great prophets of religions, and others have gone on pilgrimages to the birth places of saints and prophets and visited localities where the different gospels were preached. Thereby they seek inspiration to help them in their quest.

The grandeur of Northern India lies in its glorious mountain ranges. .. the Himalayas. It is on these ramparts of Nature that the prosperity of India depends. Shri Krishna says in the Bhagwat Gita, 'I am the Himalayas among mountains'. The Indians look upon them as the abode of celestial beings. It is said that in the caves of Himalayas live sages who have been in meditation for hundreds of years. They occasionally reveal themselves in disguise to pilgrims. Among the many holy places in the side-valleys of these mountains, two. .. Kidar Nath towards the south and Amar Nath in the interior of Kashmir Himdlaya's. .. stand out prominently. There art also a number of mountain peaks which are dedicated to certain gods or goddesses. The most sacred spots in Tibet on the further side of the Indian border are Mount Kailas and the Manasurwar lake where adepts in spiritual lore are supposed to be living in their subtle bodies. These Masters are ever ready to guide the travellers on the spiritual path. I think one of the reasons why men go to these places is to see the Hand of the Creation in scenes of Nature's impressive grandeur.

As these places are not easy of access, and as they are thousands of feet above the sea-level, beyond the dust and din of the world, man's soul gets elevated at the sight of their sublime beauty and thus he is brought closer to the object of his quest.

There are special days fixed according to the lunar calendar to visit these sacred places. The pilgrims assemble on a certain date in a certain place and start together. Such a rule is applicable only to those places which lie in mountains and the going is difficult. The Government provide facilities as far as possible everywhere for pilgrims.

The most famous of these pilgrimages is the Cave of Amar Nath which is an All-India Holy Place. People visit it from every corner of India. Mention of it occurs twice in the Raiatarangini (the history of Kashmir), first where the King Ram Deva is stated to have imprisoned the debauch King Sukh Deva and to have drowned him in the Lidder (Lambodheri) among the mountains of Amar Nath about 1,000 B.C., and a second time where King Sandimati (34 B.C. to 17 A.D.) is described as visiting the ice-lingam.

This shows that this sacred spot was known to the people in very early times. One can only guess as to how this cave was discovered. The villagers of the Kashmir Valley generally send their flocks under a shepherd's care to the pastures in summer. Each shepherd has his own pasture which he inherits from his father.

The word Pahalgam means 'a village of shepherds'. While grazing his flock round the pastures of Pantsatarni, some shepherd may have lost some members of his flock. In search of these he may have climbed the mountain and found this cave with the Shiva-lingam in it and communicated the news to his brothers who in turn must have made it known to others. The maliks as the guides to the cave are now called, have a share in the offerings to the deity. Formerly, in absence of tangas and lorries the whole journey from Srinagar was done on foot.

There were a large number of springs, places and streams in the way where the pilgrims had to bathe, and drink water. Since the introduction of wheeled conveyances many of these places have been abandoned being out of the way, and much time is thus saved. For the information of the reader I give a detailed list of places which a pilgrim is expected to visit for a bath and other ceremonial purposes.

Old Route: According to the Amar Nath Mahatma a pilgrim is expected to bathe or drink water at the following places before he enters the Holy Cave. As some of the places are not accessible to wheeled conveyance, they are not now visited by pilgrims.

Srinagar: Shudashi Khetor, the modern Shurahyar about 2.5 miles from Srinagar. It is said that in ancient times there was a stone staircase leading from this place to the top of the Shankarachar. Lately a temple has been built here.

Shivpor: There must have been a temple here, but there is no trace of it now.

Pandrenthan: The old Panthdreshti about 1.5 miles from Shurahyar. There is a temple in the middle of the spring built by Meru the Prime Minister of King Paratha (921-31 A.C.). Kak is of opinion that this is the temple of Shiv-Rilhanesvara erected by Rilhana, the Prime Minister of Jayasimha, about the year A.D. 1135.

Padampor: This was the favourite haunt of Rajank Acharyas the present Razdan family. It is 5.5 miles from Pandrethan. It was here that Shri Lalishwari lived. There is a spot here which is called Lalatrag.

Javati: The modern Zewan. It is 7 miles from Srinagar. The road is metalled. There is a spring here dedicated to Vasak Nag. There are regular buses running now.

Meshitoud: It means sweet water, the modern Petwan.

Avantiporika: It is known as Seda Khetor, the modern

Avantipor. There are at this place old temples built by King Avantivarman (855-883 A.C.).

Barsu: There is a stream flowing through the village called Rudara Ganga.

Jaubror: There must have been a temple here in olden times.

Mahawarishwarn: The old Mahawaras.

Haridrak Ganapati: Known as Hari Ganish.

Belihar: Known as Belyar. This was known as Lakhmi Khetor.

Wagahama: The place is known as Hastikaran.

Tsakrish: The modern Tsakodar. This is a plateau on the right bank of the Vetasta near Bijbihara. It is 28 miles from Srinagar.

Dewak Tirth: The modern Dewakivar.

Hari Tsander: It is the southern ghat of the Bijbihara stone temple. It contains a huge stone lingam.

Sthalwat: The modern Thajwor. It is 2.75 Miles from Bijbehara and here water drips from the southern side of the plateau through maiden-hair on the Shivlingam.

Suryi-Gohawati: The modern Sriguphvara. It is 4.75 miles from Thajwor.

Lambodari: A stream in which the pilgrims have to bathe.

Sirhom: Here is a spring called Surya Ganga where worship takes place.

Bodrus: The place is sacred to Ganpat whose worship removes all obstacles.

Tsatrus Bodrus: The place is now called Hayi.

Shirshi Ashram: The Woter Nag Ganga flows by this Spot. It is 2 miles from Sriguphvara.

Sallar: Here the people bathe in the stream. The place is 3.5 miles from Tsatrus Bodrus and is reached by a pony track.

Bala Khelyan: Known as Vishna Khetor, the modern Bala Khellan.

Canish Bal: 10.5 miles from Sallar. Here Ganish is worshipped. It is on the right bank of the Lidder below Pahalgam.

Mamalishwar (Shiva Lingam)

On the right bank of the Lidder is a spring and an old temple containing a Shiva Lingam at this place which is about a mile from Pahalgam. It is said that when Shiva removed His seat from Thojwara to Mamalishwar Ganish who was his door-keeper did not allow devas to visit Him. Hence the name of the village Mamal—don't go.

On one occasion Indra sought permission to visit Shiva. Ganish did not allow him. So there followed a quarrel, Ganish became furious and thirsty. He drank the river which became dry. Shiva while playing at his tabor poked the stomach of Ganish with it and out flowed the stream again, hence Lambodari.

In my opinion the source of the Lidder is the Kolahoi glacier. A stream joins it at Lidderwat which is the corrupt form of Lambodar wat-a rock dedicated to Ganish who is also named Lambodar and it is from here that the river was named Lambodari the modern Lidder. This must have been a place of pilgrimage in the olden times. An affluent from Tarsar enters the river at this place.

Bragapati Khetra: It is a spring in Pahalgam. It is said that Vishnu was pleased with the worship of Brago whom He embraced. Brago perspired, which gave rise to a spring. This spring is behind the village.

Nila Ganga: It is about 3 miles from Pahalgam. Close by the foot of Pisu Hill was the tirth of Sthanishwar where pilgrims had to bathe. One day Shiva kissed the eyes of Parvati to which antimony had been applied. He washed her eyes in water which turned dark-blue, hence Nila Ganga. There was a great fight between the Devas and the Daityas. The Devas did not allow the Daityas to see Shiva. The Daityas were defeated and ground down to tiny bits. Hence Pisu Hill.

Sheshiram Nag: A certain Daitya's body was entirely made of wind. He became very powerful. He troubled the Devas every way. They all entreated Shiva to rid them of the monster. Shiva told them that he was his disciple, and that they should approach Vishnu, which they did.

Vishnu sent his Wahan, Sheshi Nag who sucked all the wind from the Daitya's body and the Daitya was killed. Pilgrims bathe in the lake.

Vaovajen: Some of the Daityas still concealed themselves in the lakes around the place. These lakes, were dried and the Daityas were killed. Hence Hoka Sar (dried lake). The Deva's were told to build small houses of stones as a shelter against the wind. Hence pilgrims also make toy sheds of stones.

Pantsatarni: This is believed to represent plaited hair (jata) of Shiva from which the Ganga flows. It is said that Shiva told one of his Rudhragans to beat the drum every evening. He forgot to do so one evening. Thereupon he was cursed and turned into a mountain which is now known as Bairau Bal.

Garbagar: On the other side of the Bairau Bal is Garbagar popularly known as Garba Yatra. Nandi complained to Shiva that he could not stop the rush of Devas coming to visit him. He ordered Nandi to get a huge rock and make a hole through it, so that every one desirous of visiting him would have to pass through that hole while Nandi would be standing near the hole.

Amaravati: All living beings besought Shiva to disclose a method which would render them immortal. Thereupon Shiva rinsed His plaited hair (jata) and out flowed the Amaravati-the stream of immortality. Some of the drops fell here and there giving birth to some of the gods, while himself he turned into Sudhaling (immortal emblem) in a corner of the cave. Every one being satisfied praised Shiva.

Sangam: The confluence of the Amaravati with the Pantsatarni is the place where a pilgrim has to perform Shrada (a ceremony for the dead). He is required to make a pedestal of barley flour with four golden nails struck in the four corners and a pure pearl set in the middle which should be given in charity to a Brahman who is supposed to be Shiva's form. When returning from Pahalgam the pilgrims revisit Mamalishwar and bathe in the nine springs of Naudal.

Patal Ganga: This is the last place where a pilgrim has to bathe. This is a spring near Nishat Bagh.

Chhari Saheb

In the Bragish Sahita it is said that after Reshi Kashap Ji reclaimed the Kashmir Valley from the waters it became populated through the agency of Nag Raja Takhek. It so happened once that Bragish Reshi roaming through the Himalayas arrived here. It was he who gave a clue of the cave of Amar Nath Ji to the people. He gave them a detailed account of the Tirthas and the places on the route to the cave.

After some decades the Daityas had the upper hand here and this place fell into oblivion, and the people forgot all about the route. Thereupon Bragish ji reappeared. He told the people that he had propitiated Bhagwan Mahadiv from whom he had obtained a sceptre which he had entrusted to Nag Raj Takhek. They should go and get this sceptre from Nag Raj, and while ruler of the country shall make arrangements for the Pilgrims who should start in a body from Srinagar with the holy sceptre in front. There would be no hindrance nor any trouble on the way. The sceptre called the Chhari Sahib wielded at present by the Mahant under the supervision of the Dharmartha Department has led the procession of pilgrims ever since.

In 1819 A.C. Pandit Har Dass Tiku founded the Chhawani Amar Nath at Rambagh where the Sadhus from the plains assembled and where he gave them free rations for the journey, both ways from his own private resources. This cost him about two lakhs.

The Mahants who wield the divine command of holy place have always been the carriers of two holy sceptres which symbolise that command. Wherever a Mahant visits a place and takes his seat with ceremony a man holding one of the sceptres stands on his right and the other on his left.

The whole Amar Nath pilgrimage procession is conducted under the auspices of the Chhari Sahib. No pilgrim is allowed to go ahead of the Chhari, which is guarded by the Dharmartha Department, Kashmir. I am told that the Chhari in Srinagar was first wielded by Mahant Atwargir near the present Shital

Nath buildings. After some time Mahant Sarswatigir visited Kashmir and stayed at the spot Dashnami Akhara. He erected a platform and some buildings and began to entertain Sadhus who came from the plains to Amar Nath. He took the Chhari from Atwargir.

In the meantime Shivratananand Saraswati improved the Durga Nag Ashram to such an extent that most of the Sadhus bound for the pilgrimage stayed in his Ashram and were much cared for and warmly entertained. He put forth the plea that the Chhari must belong to his Ashram as he was the Shankarcharia of the place. Thereupon started a dispute over the Chhari. Shivratananand Saraswati marched to the Amar Nath pilgrimage. A compromise was made between the two claimants and Mahant Saraswatigir considered Shivratananand a Sadak chela.

The latter then naturally became the wielder of Chhari Sahib. Under his command the arrangements for the sadhus were excellent. There were enough tents and pilgrims were much cared for. But a section of the Sadhus of the place was not satisfied with the agreement. They protested to the Government and made demonstrations. After the demise of Shivratananand, the Chharipassed into the hands of a Chela of Saraswatigir who now wields it under the control of Dharmartha.

The Chhari generally leaves on the 4th day of the bright fortnight of Sawan. A state official is always present to perform puja at Dashnami Akhara on the eve of its departure. The carrier of this holy sceptre must walk on foot. They visit Hari Parbat and Shankarachar before departure.

They go by stages as pilgrims did of old but by a different route by-passing the places of interest mentioned in Amar Nath Mahatma. The first halt is, at Pampor. At Bijibehara all sadhus accompanying the Chhari are given a dinner by the pujari of the temple. Villagers call it 'Gosain Mela', the fair of hermits. Bijbehara to Anantnag-5 miles.

Anantnag: A great festival is celebrated for the townspeople who come to see the sadhus.

Anantnag-Bawan 4.5 Miles: Here is the famous spring of Martand where in the intercalary month or on vijaya saftami shradhas are performed.

The Lidder Valley

The Lidder valley forms the northeastern corner of the Kashmir vale. It has a pleasant and mild look and a calm and peaceful atmosphere is radiated from sober forest-covered slopes and woodlands which border this valley.

The word 'Lidder' is a corruption of lambo-dari which means a goddess 'long-bellied'. The main stream receives a number of tributaries from both banks. The first mountain torrent rises from Shisheram Nag and carving a deep gorge round the Pisu Hill, flows past Thanin or Tsandanwari on to Pahalgam. At Tsandanwari another tributary rising from Astan Marg—a stream of pure water mainly from springs—joins it on the right. Near Pahalgm a torrent rising from the snout of Kolahoi glacier, receives a tributary from the Sona Sar lake near the Kolahoi valley, the water from the Tar Sar lake joins it on the right at Lidderwat, and a stream from Katri Nag near Arau, enters it, the whole volume of water, swelling and flowing with rapidity to join another stream at Pahalgam.

It is this stream rising from the Kolahoi glacier, which is called Lambodari. It passes through Lidderwat which means Lambodarwat (Lambodar's stone) where in olden days the god Ganish must have been worshipped, and it is also here that the tributary from the sacred lake of Tar Sar joins the Lambodari.

The Lidder irrigates a large rich tract of alluvial soil and for miles from either of its banks one can see a green sea of rice-fields during the summer. Occasionally, the white wings of terns in the fields throw the greens of the fields into bold relief. The aqueducts full of glacial water infuse life everywhere and we hear the rush and flow of water all along. Acanal has been opened from the Lambodari at Ganishpor to water the Mattan Uder (plateau). This canal is called Shah Kol.

Picturesque villages are scattered all over the landscape. They are nestled among huge shady chinar, mulberry, poplar and willow trees. The walnut, apple and pear trees with drooping branches laden with fruits intercept the rays of the sun. Sometimes hay is stacked on trees for the winter fodder of animals.

The houses are generally two storeys high, the ground storey consisting of cattle-shed. A portion of the room is covered with a ceiling on which the children of the family and guests sleep in winter, the room being made comfortably warm by the breath of animals. Only a very small window opens from this part of the ground floor which is called 'Dangij'.

The second storey consists of a verandah and two or three rooms. In summer they sit and cook in the verandah and in winter in the rooms inside. Some have handlooms for weaving blankets or coarse cotton cloth. Here are also large earthenware cauldrons in which they store various kinds of seeds for their farms. In winter women are at work on the spinning wheel.

The roof is generally covered with rice grass. It is very steep so that rain and snow easily slip down. The loft is a store-room where grass from rice, ropes of dried turnips, with beans, knol khol and wild vegetables such as wopal hak (Dipsacus inermis) and hand (chicory) are kept hanging.

Abarn and a fowl-pen are generally found in the compound. The rich farmers have several barns wherein they store rape-seed, maize, linseed and other produce of their farms till their price rises to the maximum when they, dispose of their stocks. Thus they accumulate wealth which should not be the sole aim of man in this world. He has been taught from time to time by higher souls who have appeared on the world's stage in different epochs to be unselfish, and mitigate the sorrows of the destitutes. Unless we raise ourselves to that level, we are not true men and can only be a burden to society. Glimpses of the Great illumine our path here and there and this keeps the world from being engulfed in total darkness.

Trees round the village vibrate with the celestial music of their feathery denizens in the months of May and June. Out in the rice-fields on a solitary tree or on telegraph wires a roller (nila krosh) flaunting its blue-green plumage may be seen watching its prey. The paradise fly-catcher (phambaseer) in his angelic white and black garb opens the orchestra long before the break of dawn. It is followed by Tickell's thrush, with its yellow beak and grey body, incessantly singing at the top of its voice untiringly right on to sunrise.

The golden oriole in his royal bright yellow breast and pink beak sends forth his liquid note. Now the ringdoves from various quarters join the concert. The song is now in full swing. Later on the bulbul, the starling, the myna, the sparrow and occasionally the jackdaw, chirp and contribute., to the concord of the chorus. Some other birds too in their own way make a display of their musical talent. The rufous-backed shrike which is a mimic does not withhold its harsh note. The wryneck clinging to the willow harps on its fine sixnote chirp. The tree-creeper with its long curved beak and striped back scours the tree from stem to top for its food.

The tits with their white cheeks and white bars in their wing strike a creaking note. If the village happens to be near a mountain the gregarious black bulbuls make their appearance with their red beaks and legs and add a sweet whistle to the harsh noise and the streaked laughing thrush joins in with its delicious whistlelike note. The cuckoo and the hoopoe also string their harps. The kite screams from the top of a mulberry or chinar tree. The song gradually subsides as the orb of the day begins to flood our planet with his brilliance. What a blissful hour it is for him who keeps his ears open to receive this heavenly music and thereby merges his spirit with the universal soul that pervades the universe!

Attached to every house is a small croft where the farmers cultivate their vegetables—knol khol, egg plant, gourd, cucumbers, beans and pumpkins. A small rill diverted from the main canal passes through the croft and then enters their compound where they clean their utensils. The water rills wash the roots of the willows leaving them red and these are sometimes used by thrushes to build their nests on.

In the village there is always a mosque and a bathing house and sometimes a temple on a spring dedicated to some god or goddess. A village may also contain a ziarat or shrine sacred to some saint which sometimes has artistic lattice-windows and of which the roof is always covered with either red tulips, crown imperialis or iris.

The village graveyard is generally covered with white and mauve iris. At Aker there is a shiv-emblem bearing one thousand marks representing so many Shivic images, probably a remnant of those emblems which were made by the pious king Sandemati, (34 B.C.-A.D. 13) who renounced his throne and dedicated his later life to the service of the spiritual seminary at Sodura, in Wangat valley. The remains of this institution are still to be seen at the foot of Butsher at the head of the Wangat valley. There is also at this place a spring called Naran Nag where pilgrims on their return from Gangabal give away staves and grass shoes to Brahmans. Interesting sites en route from Srinagar to Pahalgam:

Pandrenthan

This place is about 4 miles from Srinagar. Here was the old capital of Kashmir, which was founded by king Ashoka of Buddhist fame. The word is a corrupt form of Purana-old, adhishthan-capital. There is now a cantonment at this pace. Not very far from the road there is a very low spring in the middle of which stands a beautiful stone temple. The roof of the temple consists of one stone artistically carved. This was erected by Meru, the minister of kinz Partha who ruled ashmir from 921-931 A.C. It was dedicated to Vishnu and was called Meru Vardhana Swami. It must have been a place of pilgrimage in the olden times. Mention of it has been made in the Amar Nath Mahatmva, but the place has now lost its sacred associations.

Pantachok

About six miles from Srinagar there is a stone quarry where towards the road side stands a stone image of Ganesh which is besmeared with red-lead. It is said that just opposite this image is a spring in the middle of the river. There is a myth that when the Vetasta flowed down the valley for the first time the whole of it was drunk by god Ganesh and for sometime the river disappeared till the god was appeased and the river flowed again.

On the other side of the road there is a mosque which was built by Haba Khotan the queen of the Epicurian king Yusuf Chak (1578-1584 A.D.). The mosque was exclusively made of wooden slabs, but now it has been rebuilt with stone in the modern style. Close by, another mountain spur also a quarry, a little out of the way towards Zewan village, contains fossils of marine animals and plants which testifies to the fact that the land was once under the sea. Last year when on excursion with my boys I found a piece of rock on one side of which was a shell fossil and on the other the form of a trilobite.

Pampor

This is a small town about nine miles from Srinagar. Its alluvial plateau has saffron beds which impart a glorious beauty colour to the place in late autumn. From the plateau we see a dharmasala (an inn) and a temple on a mountain spur in the north-cast built by Dr. Balkrishen Koul in memory of his mother. This spot is dedicated to goddess Jwala which points to the probability of the existence here in olden times of a volcanic strata or the occurrence of a slight volcanic eruption. Hence the place is considered sacred like Kangra. An annual fair is held here on Ashada Choturdashi when people offer the lungs of sheep and rice coloured yellow as a sacrifice to the goddess. Near the temple are sloping smooth slabs of stone down which children love to slide. At the foot of the hill is a spring round which a festival is held on the day. The spring is sacred to the Hindus, and is one of the guardian goddess of the pandits. The place is a fine resort for outing for the city people.

On the plateau there is a cedar round which there are stone images which are dedicated to goddess Bala. H. H. the late Maharaja Partap Singh used often to visit the place as a pilgrim.

The depression in the village is called Lall-trag. This place was the birth place of Lalla the saint. It was also the favourite haunt of the Razdan family, the famous votaries of the Shaiva cult. Here is also a beautiful Ziarat of Mir Muhammad Hamadani.

Awantipora

This is the site of the ancient city of that name founded king Avantivarman who ruled Kashmir from A.D. 855 to 883. The ruins of two temples which lie here about show that he dedicated one to Shiva and the other to Vishnu. The impressive architecture, are artistic carvings on the pillars, the magnificence of the design bewilder the onlooker.

This was a place of pilgrimage in olden times. When there was no wheeled traffic and people used to travel on foot from Srinagar to Anantnag, there were professional masseurs who used to massage people to remove their fatigue. This was done without using any kind of oil. They were called Motshah. People gathered round a huge hubble-bubble and smoked tobacco till sunset. This was called Wontpor (the hubble-bubble of Awantipor).

Bijbihara: The place is called Kashi of Kashmir. There existed a very grand and large temple just in the middle of the present town where a small temple has been lately erected by the people. It is said that the temple was so high that its shade at sunset rested on the Martand plateau. This Temple had a strong wall round it. This spot has been the target of numerous attacks by herds of hillmen during the Middle Ages.

Sikander Butshekan (A.D. 1394-1416) demolished the great temple and on one of its stones found an inscription which runs thus: 'Bismullehi mantrena nashanti vijayishwara' (by the incantation of Bismullah the temple of Vajishwara will be demolished). He is said to have been struck with remorse in later life for destroying those temples and incurring everlasting stigma for this vandalism. Sikander died in A.D. 1416. It is possible that the raised part of the town was built on the debris of this huge temple when in course of centuries earth covered and concealed the debris.

There is a stone temple built by Maharaja Ranbir Singh (1857-1885) outside the town on the bank of the Vetasta. There is a small ghat to the southeast of the temple. Here is a big Shivaling and the walls contain stone images. It is called Raja Hari Chandra's ghat and much sanctity is attached to it.

Tradition says that every day two souls who end their earthly sojourn here go to Nirwana. Just outside the temple there are huge chinars on both the banks of the river which were once joined by a bridge. There is a chinar on the left bank the trunk of which has a circumference of 56 feet the largest in Kashmir. This garden was planted by Mughal rulers.

In the town there is a mosque which has a stone in which there is imbedded an iron axe supposed to have been driven into wall of the mosque by a Hindu saint Shankar to give stability to the mosque. Hence it is now called 'Shankaran Makots' (Shankar's axe).

On the left bank there is a plateau called Tsakadar (Tsakara dhar a name given to Vishnu). In olden times this was a place of great importance, but no trace of any temple is to be found here now. The religiously minded people go round (prakram) it to gain merit.

On the plateau towards the town there are two spots where goddesses are worshipped. This was one of the stages on the old route to the Cave of Amar Nathji which led across the bridge to Pahalgam. Lately a new bridge has been constructed which will shorten the road to Pahalgam. Bijbihara is famous for wood carving and artistic lattice work.

Anantnag: This town is thirty-four miles from Srinagar. The road branches off to the right to a lovely place called Achhabal (Achha-peace, Bal-place). It is said that the garden at the place was laid out by a Hind king and remodelled by Mughal rulers. Water gushes forth from the mountain slopes which is covered with coniferous trees. The water is directed into canals and waterfalls to create an exquisite scenic effect. Here is also a trout-culture farm.

Closeby not more than two miles away is Nga Dandi Ashram founded by Swamiji—(popularly known as Sumbaluk Babaji). It is an excellent place for meditation. Refreshing breezes from the pines laden with fragrance, the cooing of turtle doves, the singing of orioles and thrushes the murmuring of the stream, add to the loveliness of the hermitage. An artificial lake with graceful water plants, the flowers such as Forget-me-nots,

Cranesbills, Strawberry and various alpine flowers beautify the surroundings.

In this part of the valley there are many charming springs Anantnag (Islamabad) is a great commercial town. Here is a large spring dedicated to Anant a satellite of Shiv. A fair is held on Aant Choterdashi when some Hindus keep a fast and particularly abstain from salt. Another fair is held when pilgrims to the Amar Nath Cave camp here. Close to the spring a beautiful garden has been laid out by the people. There is a Guru Dwara which commemorates the visit of Guru Nanak Dev. There are two important sulphur springs in the town, but they are not kept clean. The water supply of the town is plentiful. The Municipality should improve the drainage system.

The town is famous for wooden articles, toys and beautifully designed gabba work. The road turns towards the left among rice-fields. From Chinars, mulberries and poplars we hear the incessant song of Tickell's Thrush, orioles and doves. The aqueducts are range with Balsum, Milfoil and Senecio.

Bawan: This is a famous spring on the way to Pahalgam. It is full of fish. In the intercalary months and on the occasion of particular stellar dispositions in the heavens (Vejay Sapthami) the people from India and Kashmir come here to remember their dead. The spring is called the Martand (Mattan) spring dedicated to the sun who is believed to be the intermediary through whom good wishes are passed on to the departed relatives.

The Martand temple is situated on the plateau. This temple was built by the famous Lalitaditya who ruled Kashmir from A.D. 601-738.

'Of all the ruins in Kashmir the Martand ruins are both the most remarkable and the most characteristic. No temple was ever built on a finer site. It stands on an open plain, where it can be seen to full advantage. Behind it rises a range of snowy mountains. And away in the distance before it, first lies the smiling Kashmir valley, and then the whole length of the Pantsal Range, their snowy summits mingling softly with the azure of the sky. It is one of the most heavenly spots on earth, not too grand to be overpowering, nor too paltry to be lacking in strength, and it is easy to understand the impulse which led a people to raise here a temple to heaven.'

Bumazuv: Near the road is an interesting cave-temple with artistic carvings on the door pillars. There lived Boma Reshi (sage).

Aishimuquam: The Ziarat of Zain Shah Sahib—Perched high up on a mountain spur is the shrine of Zain Shah Sahib known among Hindus as Zanak Reshi. He is the guardian saint of the Lidder valley and is reputed to be one of the followers of Shiekh, Noor-Ud-Din the chief saint of the Kashmir valley.

The road now passes along the Shah Kul canal which has been taken out from the Lidder river from Ganishpor to irrigate the Mattan plateau. Here gradually the deciduous trees give place to coniferous ones. Bird-life here presents an interesting variety and laughing thrushes, black bulbuls, warblers, tits and woodpeckers and many more species cross one's path every now and then. Before we enter Pahalgam we see a rock in the stream on the right bank. It is dedicated to god Ganesh the supposed divine gate-keeper of the defile which contains Pahalgam.

Pahalgam: The hinterland of Pahalgam is in mythological parlance called Shiva Bhumi (the realm of peace). There is no lake, no meadow, no thountain peak which has not been named after a deity. In ancient times probably there existed in this place the hermitage of Reshi (sage). A spring* believed to be sacred to this sage can be seen here and the pilgrims to Amar Nath Ji are expected to visit it. In course of time a number of hamlets sprang up at the site near the bridge. To serve the dwellers in the hamlets a shop-keeper found his way here. These people began to live as shepherds. As this small village stands at the head of the Lidder valley the inhabitants of the lower village sent their flocks and cattle to be looked after by these shepherds who took them to various meadows for grazing. The place occupies a central position in relation to the side valleys crowned by high meadows which the shepherds distributed among themselves. Hence this village came to be named Pahalgam, the village of shepherds.

Recently this place has grown into a famous sanatorium where the people came to escape the sultry heat of the plains and enjoy the blissful breeze of the mountains. The Government has effected considerable improvements in the town. It has a Revenue Officer, a police station, a post and a telegraph office, a dispensary and a Health Officer. There are beautiful bungalows nestling among pines and hotels giving perfect comfort and satisfaction to the visitors. A church, a mosque and a temple are also there for people who seek to steep their souls in peace by communion with God.

It is thus that they develop a love for unselfish service to humanity which is true worship. The Lidder drains Pahalgam and a torrent from the Kolahoi glacier enters it just near Mamal. Flowing majestically among the pines like a fritte sheet of silver murmuring the sonorous song 'Men may come and men may go, but I go on for ever', the stream rushes in a hurry to irrigate the Valley below. This is the only charm-a silvery stream-in which Gulmarg lacks.

Modern conditions have turned the place into an active health resort. Rows of shops provide all kinds of amenities for the visitor. There is no dearth of hotels but any one wishing to enjoy tent-life can hire tent equipment from shop-keepers or contractors. Rajwas (place of Rajas) is a plateau on the right bank of the stream covered with pines and this is an ideal camping ground. A bungalow can also be hired by previous arrangement through the Director of Tourism or such arrangements can be made through some hotel-keepers.

In fact there is nothing wanting to a person who wishes to enjoy his holidays according to his own choice. The writer places a table and a chair under the shady and fragrance-emanating leaves of the pines and fills the pages of the book as his brain is refreshed by breezes from the mountains and flowery meadows.

The artist works at his brush and board to draw life-like sketches of natural scenes, of pine groves, old temples, cataracts, cliffs, hamlets, of people. The philosopher absorbed in thought on the various aspects of human life might reflect here on the ways and means for the betterment and unification of humanity.

The naturalist finds before him a wide field for research to keep himself busy. He can collect and examine wild flowers round about him, he can watch the itovemeiits of birds and discover their haunts. Men of all kinds of intellectual and artistic pursuits can find ample material for their purposes. The beauty of his surroundings overwhelms the beholder with wonder at this magnificent handiwork of Nature.

While we see Nature in perfect harmony, all peace and perfection, we cannot fail to observe her at her work of destruction which goes on unceasingly. We see woodpeckers eating hard against the bark of trees to take out grubs or insects which feed upon trees. We see treecreepers going from trunk to top to eat insects. We see pine needles falling on the earth and huge pines resting flat on the soil rotting and so enable saplings to incarnate. We see huge rocks reduced to sand and soil by the external agents of change on the surface of the earth. We see rushing torrents rolling boulders and stones and engaged in destruction and construction side by side.

We watch the trout going after the small fish and dippers diving deep in the rushing flow of the torrent to feast on water-insects, the redstarts keeping a sharp look-out for stray gnats and darting after them in the air and the sandpipers dashing with open mouth to catch an unfortunate insect. Vultures and kestrels hover about in the air to prey upon rodents, voles and other creatures which they can carry off. This aspect of Nature is inseparable from her role as the creative energy, for destruction and construction are interchangeable terms.

If, in our imagination, we stand in the ether outside our solar system we can watch the procession in which the stars, planets, star-cities, the earth and the sun rush ceaselessly to complete their circuits, of course, in perfect order and in strict obedience to cosmic law. Such are Nature's ways, as has been said by Utpala Deva Acharya:

'Pand shana prasadhana
Sambhukta samasta Vishwaya Shivaya
Pralayotsawa sarabhasaya
Dridham upagodham Shivam vanda'.

Translation: 'I merge myself in Shiv (peace) whom Shiva (Cosmic energy—Nature) embraces in all Her haste, after creating, protecting and destroying the universe'.

The Government has appointed energetic officers to improve this famous health resort and year after year new improvements are carried out for the comfort of visitors. As artificiality encroaches on this charming haunt of Nature, its Arcadian simplicity bears a retreat towards Aran, Astan Marz and other far away places where solitude reigns supreme and Nature stands alone in her virgin purity and serene grandeur. Pahalgam is the nearest health resort to New Delhi from where it can be reached within two or three days.

It is an ideal spot where to recoup one's health and to engage one's self in various healthy pastimes. Equipped with a staff and a nailed shoe or chappani, one can go for a mountain climb or to a glade right in the centre of a mountain slope surrounded by pines and fringed by ferns or maiden-hair plants such as Baisaran, Tulin or Shikargah. It is necessary to carry a good quantity of victuals. Walking sharpens appetite which calls for substantial nourishment. Water proofs are indispensable.

There are lovely pools formed by streams in which one can bathe, but the stones at bottom of the pools are slippery and care should be taken that one is not carried away towards the deeper parts of the stream where the water flows with irresistible force. Trout fishing is another interesting occupation. Permission should be obtained from Chief Game Warden. Muddy water is harmful to the trout. When the river rises in rains and gets filled with yellow mud many a trout die because of the turbid water.

The islets in the stream are beautifully fitted up with seats. Gay tea parties and lunch dishes are seen everywhere under the shady pine trees. Some seats project over the waterside to enable the holiday-makers enjoy the refreshing sight of water. There are badminton courts here and there and matches are played between parties previously arranged. Persons interested in bridge are seen busily carrying on the game. The islets are connected with each other by means of bridges and one can cross over from one to the other with ease. The glacial-water like a milky stream circumambulates the islets with its eddying currents. Roads are well kept and cars can easily reach the interior parts of the Rajawa's plateau.

The Pahalgam Club: The Pahalgam club is run by the Government. The secretary of the club is the Executive officer of the place. It maintains an office which is in the charge of a clerk of the department of Tourism. All enquiries regarding membership should be made from the office.

The club has a superb location. It is situated on an island surrounded by the branches of the Lidder. The rapid torrent with its milky glacial-water forming pools and whirls, encompasses the place with its cool breezes. The cluster of pines and firs which covers the premises casts a refreshing shade and fills the atmosphere with fragrance which enlivens the body and the mind.

The island stretches from south to north. There are a number of tanks built for women, children and non-swimmers for bathing purposes. It is dangerous to go out into the torrent, because the flow is rapid and the rocks of the beds are slippery. When once caught in the rapids, one cannot easily get back to the safety of dry land. For children there are trapezes to ride on. There is a lovely stretch of land attached to the club, but the pity is that round about the place acacia is being planted instead of pines. The place should have trees which harmonize with the plant life on the surrounding mountains.

There are a few Sunflowers, Zinnias, Crysanthemum and other garden varieties planted round the building. But there is a rich variety of wild flowers for a botanist to study. An expanse of Mentha sylvestris, with sweet scent, deep blue Delphinium and Erysimum altaicum. The club is the centre of activity. The Visitors' Association performs various games to entertain the public. One of their chief functions is the show which is given on Independence Day (15th August).

In the morning at 9 a.m., the Indian Union Flag is hoisted, lectures and talks are delivered, the purpose of which is to cultivate one's own character, to follow Gandhiji's footsteps, to serve humanity, be unselfish and let India lead the world in world peace.

Sweets are distributed among children and then sports are held for those between the ages of five to under sixty. After 9 p.m., a bonfire is lit by a group in the disguise of forest dwellers and comic dramas are performed on the stage, songs are sung and buffoons create in the audience an unbounded jubilation. The sparks from the fire rise higher to kiss the stars in the heaven. While, they in their turn shed lustre and effulgence from various quarters.

In the east a little above the eastern horizon is the Altair the first magnitude star of the Aquila, in the west near the horizon is the Arcturus the brightest star of Bootes, in the north lies the Polaris in the middle of Cassopiea and Ursa Major, in the south is the twisted tail of Scorpio with two horizontal stars, while on its neck shines the red star Antares. In the centre of the firmament, the Cygnus, Lyre, the Corona, and Cepheus are the principal constellations. The Galaxy spans the heaven from north to south.

In the dark forest covered mountains slopes, with red and white electric bulbs shedding light in tents, buildings and hotels, the whole place appears like a star-city.

On the 20th July 1963 at about 5 p.m. a cloud burst which dislodged boulders from the mountain side and columns of water rushed down making considerable loss of life and devastating the Pine View Hotel and some other buildings.

More on the Sharada Temple

The temple is approached from the lower slope of the hill in the west by an imposing stone staircase, now half decayed, which leads up in 63 steps to the main entrance of the quadrangular court enclosing the temple.

The staircase is about 10 feet wide and rises rather steeply in six flights between two flanking walls of massive construction. The entrance to the court is through a gateway with a double porch of Kashmiri design.

The court of the temple forms an oblong accurately oriented and enclosed by a massive wall 6 feet thick. The north side of the enclosure measures 142 feet whereas the east side measures 94 feet and 6 inches. Thus the quadrangle has proportion of 3:2. In the centre of the northern wall is a small recess 3 feet 3 inches square inside which opens by a trefoil arched door towards the interior of the court. This recess contained two ancient lingas.

In the centre of the quadrangle is the temple raised on a basement of 24 feet square and 5 feet 3 inches high. The entrance to this inner temple is from the west side and is approached by stairs five and a half feet wide with flanking side walls. The interior of the inner temple is a square of 12 feet and 3 inches and it has no decoration of any kind. The only conspicous object inside is a large slab which measures about 6 by 7 feet with a thickness of about half a foot. This slab is believed to cover a kunda, or spring, in which goddess Sharada appeared to the sage Shandilya. This kund is the object of the special veneration of the pilgrims.

The main Sharada temple rises in a prominent and commanding position above the right bank of the Madhumati on the terrace-like foot of a spur which descends from a high pine-clad peak to the east. Immediately below this terrace to the northwest is the spot where the waters of the Madhumati and Kishanganga mingle. The view from the staircase to the outer temple is magnificent. Not only can you see the valleys of Madhumati and the gorge of Kishanganga but also a stream now called Sargan that falls into Kishanganga.

The location of the Sharada temple in the village of Shardi is beyond the mountains, immediately surrounding the valley north northwest of Bandipur. It is beyond Lolab valley and beyond Drang so reaching it must take a few days. Although it is only about 35 miles or so from the northern reaches of the Wular, the journey in ancient times must have been carried out entirely on foot. I suppose now it should be possible to complete it rather quickly starting from Bandipur.

The Wonder that was Kashmir: Kashmir's geographical location partly explains is cultural history. It may be that its natural beauty and temperate climate are the reasons that Kashmiris have a strong tradition in the arts, literature, painting, drama, and dance. Its relative isolation, the security provided by the ring of mountains around it, and its distance from the heartland of Indian culture in the plains of North India, might explain the originality of Kashmiri thought. Its climate and the long winters may explain the Kashmiri fascination for philosophical speculation.

Kashmir is at the centre of the Puranic geography. In the Puranic conception, the earth's continents are arranged in the form of a lotus flower. Mt. Meru stands at the center of the world, the pericarp or seed-vessel of the flower, as it were, surrounded by circular ranges of mountains. Around Mt. Meru, like the petals of the lotus, are arranged four island-continents (*dvipas*), aligned to the four points of the compass: Uttarakuru to the north, Ketumala to the west, Bhadrashva to the east, and Bharata or Jambudvipa to the south.

The meeting point of the continents is the Meru mountain, which is the high Himalayan region around Kashmir, Uttarakuru represents Central Asia including Tocharia, Ketumala is Iran and lands beyond, Bhadrashva is China and the Far East. Kashmir's centrality in this scheme was a recognition that it was a meeting ground for trade and ideas for the four main parts of the Old World. In fact it became more than a meeting ground, it was the land where an attempt was made to reconcile opposites by deeper analysis and bold conception.

Kashmir's nearness to rich trade routes brought it considerable wealth and emboldened Kashmirs to take Sanskrit culture out of the country as missionaries. Kashmiris also became interpreters of the Indian civilization and they authored many fundamental synthesizing and expository works. Some of these works are anonymous encyclopaedias,

Kalhana's *Rajatarangini* (River of Kings), written in about 1150, provides a narrative of successive dynasties that ruled Kashmir. Kalhana claimed to have used eleven earlier works as well the Nilamata Purana. Of these earlier books only the Nilamata Purana survives. The narrative in the Rajatarangini becomes more than mere names with the accession of the Karkota dynasty in the early seventh century.

The political boundaries of Kashmir have on occasion extended much beyond the valley and the adjoining regions. According to Hiuen Tsang, the Chinese traveler, the adjacent territories to the west and south down to the plains were also under the direct control of the king of Kashmir. With Durlabhavardhana of the Karkota dynasty, the power of Kashmir extended to parts of Punjab and Afghanistan. It appears that during this period of Kashmiri expansion the ruling elite, if not the general population, of Gilgit, Baltistan, and West Tibet spoke Kashmiri-related languages. Later, as Kashmir's political power declined, these groups were displaced by Tibetan speaking people.

In the eighth century, Lalitaditya (reigned 725-761), conquered most of north India, Central Asia and Tibet. His vision and exertions mark a new phase of Indian empire-building. Kashmir had become an important player in the rivalries amongst the various kingdoms of north India.

The jostling of the Kashmiri State within the circle of the north Indian powers led to an important political innovation. The important *Vishnudharmottara Purana*, believed to have been written in Kashmir of the Karkota kings, recommends innovations regarding the *rajasuya* and the *ashvamedha* sacrifices, of which the latter in its medieval interpretations was responsible for much warfare amongst kings. In the medieval times the horse was left free to roam for a year and the king's soldiers tried to establish the rule of their king in all regions visited by the horse, leading to fighting.

This essay presents an overview of the most important Kashmiri contributions to Indian culture, emphasizing some of the lesser known aspects of these contributions. Specifically, we consider the contributions to the arts, sciences, literature, and philosophy. Our historical assessment of Kashmiri culture is hampered by the nature of our records. The texts and objects of art do not always indicate their provenance and the connections with Kashmir emerge only from indirect evidence. We are on sure ground when we come to Buddhist sources, the texts of the Kashmir Shaivism, and the names mentioned in the *Rajatarangini* and other early narratives.

Early Period: During the Vedic period, Kashmir appears to be an important region because it appears that the Mujavant mountain, the region where Soma grew, was located there. It is possible that in the Vedic era a large part of the valley was still under a lake. Kalhana's history begins with the Mahabharata War, but it is very hazy with regard to the events prior to the Mauryan Emperor Ashoka. The great grammarian Panini lived in northwest Punjab not too far from Kashmir and the university at Taxila (Takshashila) was also close to the valley. At the time of Hiuen Tsang, Takshashila was a tributary to Kashmir. It is generally accepted that Patanjali, the great author of the Mahabhashya commentary on Panini's Ashtadhyayi, was a Kashmiri, as were a host of other grammarians like Chandra. According to Bhartrihari and other early scholars, Patanjali also made contributions to Yoga (the yoga-sutras) and to Ayurveda.

It is believed that Patanjali's mother was named Gorika and he was born in Gonarda. He was educated in Takshashila and he taught in Pataliputra. From the textual references in his works, it can be safely said that he belonged to 2nd century BC. In any event, Kashmir of these early times was a part of the larger northwest Indian region of which Takshashila was a center of learning. The early levels of buildings in Takshashila have been traced to 800 BC. The first millennium BC was a period of great intellectual activity in this part of India and attitudes that later came to be termed Kashmiri were an important element of this activity. Amongst these attitudes was a characteristic approach to classification in the arts and the interest in grammar.

Panini's grammar remains one of the greatest achievements of the human intellect. It described the grammar of the Sanskrit language by a system of 4,000 algebraic rules, a feat that has not been equalled for any other language to this day. It also set the tone for scientific studies in India with their emphasis on algorithmic explanations. Patanjali's commentary on the Panini grammar was responsible for the exaltation of its reputation. It appears that Panini arose in the same intellectual climate that characterized Kashmir during its Classical period.

Drama and Music: The Natya Shastra: An early name seen as belonging to Kashmir is Bharata Muni of the Natyashastra. The indirect reasons for this identification are that the *rasa* idea of the Natyashastra was discussed by many scholars in Kashmir. Another reason is that the Natyashastra has a total of 36 chapters and it is suggested that this number may have been deliberately chosen to conform to the theory of 36 *tattvas* which is a part of the later Shaivite system of Kashmir. Many descriptions in this book seem especially true for Kashmir. The *bhana*,

It should be mentioned here parenthetically that a few scholars take Bharata to be a Southerner. It is also interesting that there exist some very close connections between Kashmir and South India in the cultural tradition like the worship of Shiva, Pancharatra, Tantra, and the arts. Recently, when I pointed this out to Vasundhara Filliozat, the art historian who has worked on Karnataka, she said that the inscriptional evidence indicates a continuing movement of teachers from Kashmir to the South and that Kashmir is likely to have been the original source of many of the early Shaivite, Tantric, and Sthapatya Agamas.

Bharata Muni's *Natya Shastra* not only presents the language of creative expression, it is the world's first book on stagecraft. It is so comprehensive that it lists 108 different postures that can be combined to give the various movements of dance. Bharata's ideas are the key to proper understanding of Indian arts, music and sculpture. They provide an insight into how different Indian arts are expressions of a celebratory attitude to the universe. Manomohan Ghosh, the modern translator of the Natya Shastra, believes that it belongs to the 5th century BC. He bases his assessment on the archaic pre-Paninian features of the language and the fact that Bharata mentions the arthashastra of Brihaspati and not that of the 4th century BC Kautilya.

The term *natya* is synonymous with drama. According to Bharata, the *natya* was created by taking elements from each of the four Vedas: recitation (*pathya*) from the Rigveda, song or melody (*gita*) from the Samaveda, acting (*abhinaya*) from the Yajurveda, and sentiments (*rasa*) from the Atharvaveda. By this synthesis, the Natya Shastra became the fifth Veda, meant to take the spirit of the Vedic vision to the common man. Elsewhere, Bharata says: "The entire nature of human beings as connected with the experiences of happiness and misery, and joy and sorrow, when presented through the process of histrionics (*abhinaya*) is called *natya*."

The concept of *rasa*, enduring sentiment, lies behind the aesthetics of the *Natya Shastra*. There are eight *rasas*: heroism, fury, wonder, love, mirth, compassion, disgust and terror. Bharata lists another 33 less permanent sentiments. The artist, through movement, voice, music or any other creative act, attempts to evoke them in the listener and the spectator. This evocation helps to plumb the depths of the soul, thereby facilitating self-knowledge. The algorithmic approach to knowledge became the model for scientific theories in the Indic world, extending from India to the east and Southeast Asia. The ideas of the *Natya Shastra* were in consonance with this tradition and they provided an overarching comprehensiveness to sculpture, temple architecture, performance, dance and story telling. But unlike other technical shastras that were written for the scholar, Bharata's work influenced millions directly. For these reasons alone, the *Natya Shastra* is one of the most important books ever written.

To appreciate the pervasive influence of the *Natya Shastra*, just consider music. The comprehensiveness of the *Natya Shastra* forged a tradition of tremendous pride and resilience that survived the westward movement of Indian musical imagination through the agency of itinerant musicians. Several thousand Indian musicians, of which Kashmiri musicians are likely to have been a part, were invited by the fifth century Persian king Behram Gaur. Turkish armies used Indians as professional musicians.

Bharata stresses the transformative power of creative art. He says, "It teaches duty to those who have no sense of duty, love to those who are eager for its fulfilment, and it chastises those who are ill-bred or unruly, promotes self-restraint in those who are disciplined, gives courage to cowards, energy to heroic persons, enlightens men of poor intellect and gives wisdom to the learned."

Cosmology and Science: The Yoga Vasishtha: Another book from Kashmir which has had enduring influence over Indian thought is the Yoga Vasishtha (YV). Professing to be a book of instruction on the nature of consciousness, it has many fascinating passages on time, space, matter and cognition. They are significant not only in telling us about thinking in Kashmir, they summarize Indian ideas of physics, available to us through a variety of sources, that are not widely known outside scholarly circles. Starting with a position that seeks to unify space, time, matter, and consciousness, an argument is made for relativity of space and time, cyclic and recursively defined universes, and a non-anthropocentric view.

Within the Indian tradition it is believed that reality transcends the separate categories of space, time, matter, and observation. In this function, called *Brahman*, inhere all categories including knowledge. The conditioned mind can, by "tuning" in to *Brahman*, obtain knowledge, although it can only be expressed in terms of the associations already experienced by the mind. In this tradition, scientific knowledge describes as much aspects of outer reality as the topography of the mindscape. Connections (*bandhu*) between the outer and the inner are assumed: we can comprehend reality only because we are already equipped to do so. In other words, innate, primitive, *a priori* ideas give rational organization to our fragmentary sensations.

The Yoga-Vasishtha (YV) is over 29,000 verses long, and it is traditionally attributed to Valmiki, author of the epic Ramayana, which is over two thousand years old. But scholars believe it was composed in the early centuries in Kashmir. The historian of philosophy Dasgupta dated it about the sixth century AD on the basis that one of its YV may be viewed as a book of philosophy or as a philosophical novel. It describes the instruction given by Vasishtha to Rama of the Ramayana. Its premise may be termed radical idealism and it is couched in a fashion that has many parallels with the notion of a participatory universe, where the actions of the conscious agents have a bearing on future evolution.

Its most interesting passages from the scientific point of view relate to the description of the nature of space, time, matter, and consciousness. It should be emphasized that the YV ideas do not stand in isolation. Similar ideas are to be found in the earlier Vedic books. At its deepest level the Vedic conception is to view reality in a unitary manner; at the next level one may speak of the dichotomy of mind and matter. Ideas similar to those found in YV are also encountered in the Puranic and Tantric literature. But the clarity and directness with which these ideas are described in YV is unique. Roughly speaking, the Vedic system speaks of an interconnectedness between the observer and the observed. The Vedic system of knowledge is based on a tripartite approach to the universe where connections exist in triples in categories of one group and across groups: sky, atmosphere, earth; object, medium, subject; future, present, past; and so on. Beyond the triples lies the transcendental "fourth".

Three kinds of motion are alluded to in the Vedic books: these are the translational motion, sound, and light which are taken to be "equivalent" to earth, air, and sky. The fourth motion is assigned to consciousness; and this is considered to be infinite in speed. It is most interesting that the books in this Indian tradition speak about the Universes defined recursively are described in the famous episode of Indra and the ants in Brahmavaivarta Purana, the Mahabharata, and elsewhere. These flights of imagination are to be traced to more than a straightforward generalization of the motions of the planets into a cyclic universe. They must be viewed in the background of an amazingly sophisticated tradition of cognitive and analytical thought.

The YV argues that whereas physical nature is taken to be analyzable it is defined only in relation to observers. Consciousness is considered a more fundamental category. But YV is not written as a systematic text. Its narrative jumps between various levels: psychological, biological, and physical, as is traditional in Indian texts. Not surprisingly, given the

Vedic emphasis on *rta*, YV accepts the idea that laws are intrinsic to the universe. But do these laws remain constant? There is some suggestion that the laws of nature in an unfolding universe also evolve.

According to YV, new information does not emerge out of the inanimate world but it is a result of the exchange between mind and matter. It accepts consciousness as a kind of fundamental field that pervades the whole universe. One might speculate that the parallels between YV and some recent ideas of physics are a result of the degree of abstraction that is common to both; or one might assert that the parallels are a reflection of the inherent structure of the mind.

It appears that the Kashmiri understanding of physics was informed not only by astronomy and terrestrial experiments but also by speculative thought and by meditation on the nature of consciousness. Unfettered by either geocentric or anthropocentric views, this understanding unified the physics of the small with that of the large within a framework that included metaphysics. YV ideas do not represent a break with the older Vedic thought; they are an amplification of the basic themes informed by advances in the unfolding understanding of the astronomy and other physical sciences.

Tantra: Shaivism and Vaishnavism: The Kashmiri approach to the world is uniquely positive. There is a celebration of nature and beauty for the objective world is also a representation of *Brahman* (Lord). This approach is part of the Kashmiri tantric thought in both its strands of Shaivism and Vaishnavism. The Tantras stress the equivalence of the universe and the body and look for divinity within the person.

Although the Vaishnavite Panchratra now survives only in South India, the earliest teachers looked to Kashmir as the seat of learning and spiritual culture. The Pancharatra ontology and ritual are described in the Kashmirian *Vishnudharmotta Purana*. According to this theology, the king was enjoined to build a temple for the rites to be performed to celebrate his victory over his opponents. These rites marked his union with Vishnu. This represented an important milestone in the conceptualization of the role of the king in Indic thought.

According to Kalhana, the worship of Shiva in Kashmir dates prior to the Mauryan King Ashoka. The Tantras were enshrined in texts known as the Agamas, most of which are now lost. The pinnacle of the Tantric Shaiva tradition is the Trika system. The great spiritual master and scholar Abhinavagupta (c. 975-1025) describes the goal of the Shaiva discipline is to find freedom. In this freedom, the adept becomes one with Shiva, transcending all oppositions and polarities. The *jivanamuka* (the liberated person) Two very interesting ideas in Kashmir Shaivism are that of *recognition* and of *vibration*. In the philosophy of Recognition, it is proposed that the ultimate experience of enlightenment consists of a profound and irreversible recognition that one's own true identity is Shiva himself. The doctrine of Vibration speaks of the importance of experiencing *spanda*, the vibration or pulse of consciousness. Every activity in the universe, as well as sensations, cognitions, emotions ebbs and flows as part of the universal rhythm of the one reality, Shiva.

Contributions to Buddhism: Kashmir became an early centre of Buddhist scholarship. In the first century, the Kushan emperor Kanishka chose Kashmir as the venue of a major Buddhist Council comprising of over 500 monks and scholars. At this meeting the previously uncodified portions of Buddha's discourses and the theoretical portions of the canon were codified. The entire canon (*the Tripitaka*) was inscribed on copper plates and deposited in a stupa. The Buddhist schools of Sarvastivada, Mahayana, Madhyamika, and Yogachara were all well developed in Kashmir. It also produced famous Buddhist logicians such as Dinnaga, Dharmakirti, Vinitadeva, and Dharmottara.

Kashmiris were tireless in the spread of Buddhist ideas to Central Asia. Attracted by Kashmir's reputation as a great centre of scholarship, many Buddhists came from distant lands to learn Sanskrit and train as translators and teachers. Amongst these was Kumarajiva (344-413), the son of the Kuchean princess who, when his mother became a nun, followed her into monastic life at the age of seven. He came to Kashmir in his youth to learn the Mahayana scriptures from Bandhudatta. Later he became a specialist in Madhyamika philosophy. In 383, Chinese forces seized Kucha and carried Kumarajiva off to China. From 401 he was at the Ch'in court in the capital Chang'an (the modern Xi'an), where he taught and translated Buddhist scriptures into Chinese. More than 100

Kumarajiva's contemporary, the Kashmiri Buddhabhadra also went to China to translate the Buddhist texts. The Kashmiri Buddhasena translated a major Yogachara text into Chinese. Hiuen Tsang, the famous Chinese pilgrim, came to Kashmir in 631, staying for two years. Many famous Buddhist Tantric teachers were associated with Kashmir. According to some Tibetan sources, Naropa and Padmasambhava (who introduced Tantric Buddhism into Tibet) were Kashmiris. The Tibetan script is derived from the Kashmiri Sharada script, It was brought into Tibet by Thonmi-Sambhota, who was sent to Kashmir during the reign of Duralabhavardhana (seventh century) to study with Devatitasimha.

Architecture and Painting: The uniqueness of the Kashmiri idiom in artistic expression has been recognized by historians. The ancient temple ruins in Kashmir are some of the oldest standing temples in India today (7th – 9th Centuries) and would have been among the most magnificent temples ever made in India. The sculptures found here are significant and exquisite. The Martanda temple, built by Lalitaditya, is one of the earliest and yet largest stone temples to have been built in Kashmir. The temple is rectangular in plan, consisting of a mandapa and a shrine. Two other shrines flank the mandapa. It is enclosed by a vast courtyard by a peristyle wall with 84 secondary shrines in it. The columns of the peristyle are fluted. Each of the 84 niches originally contained an image of a form of Surya.

The Lalitaditya also built an enormous chaitya in the town of Parihasapura which housed an enormous Buddha. Only the plinth of this huge monument survives, although one of the paintings at Alchi is believed to be its representation. There was also an enormous stupa in Parihasapura built by Lalitaditya's minister Chankuna, which may have even been larger than the chaitya. The Parihasapura monuments became models for Buddhist architecture from Afghanistan to Japan.

The Pandrethan temple as well as the Avantipur complex provide us further examples of the excellence of Kashmiri architecture and art. Kashmiri ivories and metal images are also outstanding, and are generally considered to be among the best anywhere in the world. Kashmir also had a flourishing tradition of painting, which must have been used to decorate the temples walls. The earliest surviving examples of these painting come from Gilgit and date from about 8th century. Representing a highly developed style, these paintings must be seen as belonging to a very old tradition. Kashmiri craftsmen were long famed for their work and their hand can be seen in many works of art in Central Asia and Tibet.

Although references to paintings in ancient Kashmiri literature are scattered, and because all records of painting in the Valley were destroyed after the advent of Islam, it is possible to piece together this tradition from the paintings that are preserved in the Buddhist temples of Ladakh and Tibet. The Tibetan scholar Rinchen Sangpo (950-1055) claimed to have visited Kashmir thrice to obtain the services of 75 Kashmiri craftsmen, painters and teachers to build and decorate one hundred and eight temples in Western Tibet. According to the 16th century Tibetan scholar Lama Taranath, author of a history of Buddhism in India, there existed in the 9th century India four principal school of art: eastern, middle country, Marwar, and the Kashmiri.

After Lalitaditya, Kashmiri style appears to have changed somewhat and it endured till 10-11th century. This phase is the most developed stage of Kashmiri art with its fame spreading into the remote Himalayas. The 9th century complex of Avantipura built by King Avantivarman (855-883 AD) is an amalgam of various earlier prevalent forms of India and regions beyond. The best example of this style is found in the bronzes dated to 9th to 11th century cast by Kashmiri craftsmen for Tibetan patrons. The style of such bronzes presents a remarkable affinity to the wall-paintings dating to 10-11th century decorated in the Buddhist temples of Western Tibet.

The wall paintings of Mang nang and manuscript painting of Thaling discovered in Western Tibet are generally accepted to have been created by Kashmiri painters. Stylistically, they are a pictorial translation of contemporary Kashmiri bronzes. In the treatment of costumes and ornaments, the artists have meticulously executed the finest details of diaphenous and embroidered garments and intricate design These wall paintings present a final stage of progression of the Kashmiri style which reminds something related to the distant Ajanta. One of the best sites to see the Kashmiri painting style is in the five temples comprising the *dharma-mandala* at Alchi in Ladakh, which escaped destruction that other Ladakhi temples suffered at the hands of a Ladakhi king who embraced Islam. The earliest of these buildings is the 'Du-khang where one can see astonishingly well preserved

The Sum-tsek, a three-level building next to the 'Du-khang presents the native architectural tradition, characterized by piled-up rock walls faced with mud plaster, decorated with delicate wood carvings of the Kashmiri style. Triangular forms are a part of the pillars and other architectural elements in a style that corresponds to the motifs found on the stone monuments of Kashmir. The plan of the building contains three extensions on the east, north, and west where gigantic two-storied images of Avalokiteshvara, Maitreya and Manjushri to remove impurities in speech, mind, and body were situated. Elsewhere in the building is a most interesting painting of Prajnaparamita, identified by the book and the rosary she holds. A tall structure depicted on her sides appears to be the famous chaitya built by Lalitaditya at Parihasapura.

According to the historian of art Susan Huntington, "Kashmir served as a source of imagery and influence for the northern and eastern movements of Buddhist art. The Yunkang caves in China, the wall paintings from several sites in Inner Asia, especially Qizil and Tun-huang, the paintings from the cache at Tun-huang, and some iconographic manuscripts from Japan, for example, should be evaluated with Kashmir in mind as a possible source. A full understanding of the transmission of Buddhist art through Asia is dependent on developing a greater knowledge of Kashmiri art."

2

Monuments of the Valley

Jammu & Kashmir has a good share of Indian historical and archaeological legacy. There has been a very unique and glorious tradition of the people of the State of preaching and worshipping of each other's religions and pilgrimage centres. There are well-renowned Hindu shrines coexisting with the equally famous Muslim pilgrimage centres that are held in highest esteem by the people of every faith. Buddhism, which is still followed in the Ladakh region of the State, has its origin in the valley and was preached and disseminated by the Kashmiri scholars in its earlier days. There are some wonderful examples of this communal harmony in pilgrimage centres like the one at Hari Parbat where monuments of all three religions—a temple, mosque and gurudwara are standing side by side. Some of the important shrines and monuments of the region have been covered below:

Hazratbal Mosque: Situated in a village on the western shores of the Dal Lake opposite Nishat Bagh, it is a pristine white marble edifice casting its reflection in the waters of the lake. It is revered for the fact that it houses a hair of the prophet Muhammad, which is displayed to the public on religious occasions. Fairs are held on such occasions. People throng to the place every Friday to offer their prayers. Unlike the other mosques in Srinagar, which have a pagoda like roof, Hazratbal is the only mosque to have a domed roof mosque in Srinagar; the others having distinct pagoda like roofs.

Jami Masjid: Situated in the heart of the old city of Srinagar, this huge mosque is visited by thousands of people who congregate here for the Friday prayers. The largest mosque in Kashmir, it is built around a courtyard with 370 wooden pillars to support it. Originally built by Sultan Sikandar in 1400, and enlarged by his son, Zain-ul-Abidin, it is a typical example of Indo-Saracenic architecture. Destroyed thrice by fire in 1479, 1620 and 1674 respectively and rebuilt each time, the mosque of today was repaired during the reign of Maharaja Pratap Singh. The principal features of the mosque are the four minars and eight wooden columns as support

Shankaracharya Temple: Believed to have been built at the auspicious site of Takht-e-Sulaiman, the sacred temple of Shankaracharya occupies the top of the hills in the southeast of Srinagar. Dating back to 250 BC, it is believed that it was the place where the great philosopher and saint Shankaracharya stayed when he visited Kashmir ten centuries ago to revive Sanatan Dharma. It was then that this place came to be known by his name instead of its former name Gopadri, an earlier edifice built on the same site by king Lalitaditya in the 6th century AD. Built on a high octagonal plinth and approached by a flight of steps, it has sidewalls that once bore inscriptions and the main surviving shrine consists of a circular cell. A modern ceiling covers the inner sanctum and an inscription in Persian traces its origin to the reign of Emperor Shah Jehan. The original ceiling was dome-shaped and the brick roof is not more than a century old.

Khanqah of Shah Hamadan: Situated on the banks of the River Jhelum, it is the first mosque ever built in Srinagar. The Shah Hamadan whose full name was Mir Sayed Ali Hamadni built the original mosque in 1395. Shah-i-Hamdan came from Persia in the 13th century and was responsible for the spread of Islam in Kashmir. Khanqah-i-Mualla was the place where he used to offer prayers. The Khanqah is a wooden structure whose chief aesthetic feature is its beautifully carved eaves and hanging bells. The interiors are richly carved and painted, and the antique chandeliers give it an air of magnificence.

Hari Parbat Fort & Temple of Sharika Devi: Built in the 18th century, atop the Sharika Hill, Atta Mohammed Khan constructed the fort from 1776 though the surrounding wall was built by Akbar in the 16th century and is much older. It has two gates, the Kathi and Sangin Darwaza. The Kathi is the main entrance with Persian commemorative inscriptions surrounding it while the Sangin is more ornate with sculptured windows on either side. Mow used as an arsenal, the fort contains a temple revered for its image of the Goddess Sharika, a form of Durga.

Makhdoom Sahib: The shrine, situated to the south of Hari Parbat, is dedicated to Makhdoom Sahib or Hazrat Sultan and is revered by Muslims and Hindus alike.

Chhatti Padshahi Gurudwara: Situated just outside the southern gate of Hari Parbat fort, Chatti Padshahi is one of the most important Sikh Gurudwaras in Kashmir. It is dedicated to the sixth guru of Sikhism who stopped here to preach occasionally while he was travelling through Kashmir.

Martand: The most memorable and beautiful work of Emperor Lalitaditya of Surya (meaning 'solar') dynasty is the construction of spacious Martand temple dedicated to the Sun god, Bhaskar. The style of the construction of the temple and the skill of the makers are rare in the history of the world. Now, in ruins, it is still appreciable for its design, beauty and art. Martand temple is a mirror of the art and skill of Kashmiri Hindus. In its backdrop are the snowcapped mountains and it is built with strong and square limestone. Its pillars have a Greek pattern that lends gorgeousness to this edifice.

Kheer Bhawani: Situated at Tullamulla in the Srinagar district, this spring is the most sacred place for Hindus in Kashmir. Hindus must abstain from meat on the days when they visit Kheer Bhavani or the milk goddess and offer her sugar, milk, rice and flowers. An annual festival is held here in May or June when a number of devotees visit the place to offer prayers and seek the blessings of the deity. The beautiful spring of clear water overshadowed by splendid shady trees and full of sacred fish adds an ethereal beauty to the place.

Awantipur: 29 km from Srinagar, the famous Awantipur temples are believed to have been built in honour of God Mahadev by Awanti Varman. The temples, although in ruins, are of great archaeological interest. King Avantivarman founded the city in the 9th century. There are two main temples, one of which is Shiva-Avantishvara, which is larger and marked by massive walls some half a mile beneath the town on the outskirts of village Jaubror.

Reduced to ruins now, the place almost lost its previous grandeur and has been reduced to ruins, though it is still visited by the devout. The sculptured reliefs principally found on the walls of the entrance and the flank walls of the stairs depict men and women in the acts of drinking, lovemaking and other such merriments. The base is either a plain square block with the upper edge rounded off or is elaborately molded. Half a mile up is Avantisvami-Vishnu, a better-preserved temple.

Kashmir proper is an irregularly oval valley 84 miles long from northeast to southwest by 20 to 25 miles broad. Its height above the sea level is everywhere over 5,000 feet. It is enclosed on all sides by ranges of snowcapped mountains, which vary at different points from 12,000 to 18,000 feet in height. The correctness of the local tradition regarding its lacustrine origin in remote prehistoric times has been demonstrated by the discovery of marine fossils and other characteristic features in the surrounding mountains and uplands. Politically it was, ordinarily, limited to its geographical frontiers, the mountain ramparts; but the neighbouring hill principalities of Prunts (Poonch) and Rajauri were often within its sphere of influence.

The extent of that influence usually depended upon the personality of the ruler for the time being. Some of its more energetic kings extended their sway to the north and northwest of the Panjab, and one king, Lalitaditya (in the middle of the eighth century), is credited with having effected the conquest of Kanauj.

The valley itself was divided into two great territorial divisions, Madavarajya, the southern half, and Kramarajya, the northern half; Srinagar, the capital, was included in the former. Madavarajya, modern Maraz, is represented by the present-day wazarat or district of Anantnag, and Kramarajya by the wazarat of Baramula. The large lateral valleys drained by the Sindh and the Lidar formed integral parts of their respective districts. The two rural divisions were in their turn subdivided into smaller areas—known in later times as parganas—which consisted of groups of villages ranging in number from a dozen to perhaps a hundred or more.

The capital, though forming part of Maraz, practically constituted an independent unit; and owing to its situation at the point of contact of the two main divisions, its compactness, the presence of the court, its large population, its organised public opinion, and the superior culture of its inhabitants, it was the most important of all. Its alliance or opposition almost always proved a decisive factor in determining the fortunes of war. Its position in the centre of a large, fertile, and populous valley, intersected by navigable rivers, canals and lakes, not only made it a point of vantage commercially, but also sufficiently accounts for the failure of all the attempts made from time to time to remove it from its present position to some other place.

The most striking features of the Kashmir landscape are its mighty mountain ramparts, its beautiful lakes and rivers, and its dry brown karewas. The former have largely determine the political fortunes of the little country they encircle. It is the inaccessibility and practical impregnability of these natural defences rather than the valour of Kashmiri troops that has so often turned the tide of invasion from the valley, when far more powerful kingdoms succumbed to it.

This inaccessibility, again, enabled Kashmir to preserve and consolidate its peculiar social and economic conditions up to very recent times. While, thus, the mountains long served as effectual barriers against foreign invasion, and as a sure means of conservation of indigenous culture, they do not appear to have proved equally effectual in preventing natives of the valley from seeing something of the world which lay beyond their circumscribed horizon. Kashmir played a notable part in the propagation of Buddhism in foreign lands, especially in China and Tibet. We may mention a single instance. Kumarajiva's distinguished scholarly labours in China during the regime of the later Chin dynasty (A.D. 384-417) gained for him the title of Tungsheo, which interpreted means that "although young in years he was ripe in the wisdom and virtues of old age." He is referred to as "one of the four suns of Buddhism," and is credited with the introduction of a new alphabet.

In mediaeval times when, according to the great Muslim scholar Alberuni, Kashmir had closed her gates to intercourse with foreign lands, her pandits lived as honoured guests at the courts of Indian princes; for instance, Bilhana, the well-known author of the Vikramankadevacharita, was the court poet of Vikramaditya VI (A.D. 1075-1126) of Kalyana in Southern India (modern Kalyani in the Nizam's Dominions). The numerous rivers and lakes, besides being invaluable as commercial waterways and producers of a variety of much prized foodstuffs, have from time immemorial been the means of innocent and inexpensive pleasure to the people. The former, specially the Vitasta, the largest of them all, have also been important in the physical history of the valley.

Indeed, with the exception of the uplands commonly called wudars or karewas, which date back to the lacustrine epoch, the whole of the valley owes its formation to deposits of river alluvium. This deposition of silt is still in progress, and consequently the level of the low-lying parts of the valley, particularly those where the Vitasta, carrying the drainage of the whole valley, debouches into the Wular lake, is year by year being slowly but steadily raised. According to Brahman tradition, every lake and river and spring of the valley has a divine origin and a sacred mission to fulfil—viz., washing away the sins of the faithful. The Vitasta is, above all, the sacred river, and is said to contain within its waters all that is holy in the world.

Indeed Kashmir itself is considered to be the holiest of all the Holy lands; it is called the Rishibhumi, "the land of sages," Saradapitha, "the eternally pure seat of the goddess Sarada." It has not only its own Prayagal (the Vitasta corresponding to the Jumna and the Sindh to the Ganges) and its own Kurukshetra, but it has also the replica of almost every other important river or spring that is held in reverence in India.

The uplands or wudars, officially known as karewas, range in height from 100 to 300 feet and in area from 5 or 6 square miles to over 50 square miles each. With one or two exceptions they are dependent for their productivity upon rainfall. In ancient times, when the population of the country was probably much larger than at present, not only these wudars, which are still for the most part under cultivation, but also the comparatively high mountain slopes, were cultivated, as is evidenced by the existence to this day of innumerable terraces surrounded and supported by cyclopean walls at Pandrethan, Avantipur, and almost everywhere. The chief crop and, therefore, the staple food of Kashmir is rice; though maize, barley, and wheat are sown in unirrigated uplands.

With the exception of a few Sikhs and Rajputs who have settled here during the last century, the whole of the valley is occupied by Kashmiri-speaking people, who are linguistically, and perhaps ethnologically also, distinct not only from the Indians of the plains, but also from Gujars, Khakhas, and Bombas, who inhabit the neighbouring hills. The substratum of their language, after its Sanskrit superstructure has been removed, appears to be akin to Dardic, which under various names and forms is spoken by the Kanjutis of Hunza and Nagar, Kafirs of the Karakoram, and other tribes inhabiting the great mountain barrier which separates North-western India from Central Asia.

The comparative immunity from fear of foreign domination, due to the strength of the country's natural defences and to the practical impregnability of the routes leading to it, the abundance and variety of wholesome and nutritious food, the mild and salubrious climate, the narrowness of the geographical horizon—the Kashmiri could see his whole world from the roof of his house—are largely responsible for moulding the character of the inhabitants of the Happy Valley, a character which has remained unaltered for many centuries.

Sources of Kashmir History

Our knowledge of the political, social, and economic conditions which prevailed in early Kashmir is exceptionally ample, and is derived from a variety of sources. References to the country and its people are found in the literature of the Greeks, the Chinese, and the Arabs, as well as in Indian literature. Incomparably the most authoritative and informative are, naturally, the indigenous writers of Kashmir.

Greek Notices: Speaking of the geographical position of the country, which he calls by the name of Kaspeiria, Ptolemy remarks that it is situated "below the sources of the Bidaspes (Vitasta) and of the Sandabal (Chandrabhaga) and of the Adris (Iravati)." He further states that it lies between the Daradrai or Darads on the Indus and Kylindrine or the land of the Kulindas on the Hyphasis (Bias) and eastwards. His definition of its territorial limits is considerably exaggerated.

The passage in the Bassarika of Dionysios of Samos, preserved by Stephanos of Byzantium, which makes mention of the Kaspeiroi as a tribe famous among the Indians for their fleetness of foot, probably refers to the Kashmiris, whose marching powers, owing to the mountainous nature of their country, are greater than those of the Indians of the plains.

Chinese Notices: The information which the Chinese records have left us is much more ample. The earliest reference which can with certainty be attributed to Kashmir is dated A.D. 541. It describes the northern part of India as a country "enveloped on all sides like a precious jewel by the snowy mountains, with a valley in the south which leads up to it and serves as the gate of the kingdom." But by far the greatest Chinese authority on Kashmir is the pilgrim Hsuan-tsang, who visited Kashmir in A.D. 631 and spent two years there studying "the Sutras and Sastras."

A fairly detailed description of the country is contained in the itinerary and life of Hsuan-tsang, who was accorded a princely welcome by the ruler of Kashmir. He entered Kashmir by way of Baramula. He found Buddhism flourishing though not predominant. On his nearing the capital the king came out to receive him, and invited him to a sumptuous feast at the palace. He gave him twenty scribes to copy the sacred books and Sastras, and also deputed five men to wait on him and to furnish him, free of expenses, with whatever he required.

Speaking of the state of learning in Kashmir, he says that "this country from remote times was distinguished for learning, and their priests were all of high religious merit and conspicuous virtue as well as marked talent and power of clear exposition of doctrine; and though the other priests (i.e., of other nations) were in their own way distinguished, yet they could not be compared with these, so different were they from the ordinary class."

Regarding the extent of the country, its products, and its people, he says that "it (Kashmir) was above 7,000 li (1,400 miles) in circuit, surrounded by high steep mountains over which were narrow, difficult passes, and the country had been always impregnable. The capital, which had a large river on its west side, was 12 or 13 li (about 2 1/2 miles) from north to south and 4 or 5 li (nearly a mile) from east to west. The district was a good agricultural one and produced abundant fruits and flowers; it yielded also horses of the dragon stock, saffron, and medicinal plants.

The climate was very cold in season with much snow and little wind. The people wear serge and cotton (pai-tieh). They were volatile and timid; being protected by a dragon they crowed over their neighbours; they were good-looking, but deceitful; they were fond of learning and had a faith which embraced orthodoxy and heterodoxy (i.e., Buddhism and other religions). Buddhist monasteries were above 100 in number, and there were 5,000 Buddhist brethren; and there were four Ashoka topes each containing above a pint (sheng) of the bodily relics of the Buddha."

The territories of Prunts and Rajauri were at the time of Hsuantsang's visit subject to the king of Kashmir. The next Chinese pilgrim who has left us an account of Kashmir is Ou-k'ong, who reached Kashmir in 759 A.D. Here he took his full vows as a regular monk. He resided in the country for four years, spending his time mainly in visiting holy places and in studying Sanskrit. He states that the number of Buddhist convents was more than three hundred; which shows that Buddhism was in a much more flourishing condition than in the preceding century when Hsuantsang visited Kashmir.

A somewhat earlier and more interesting reference is furnished by the annals of the T'ang dynasty of China. "These mention the arrival at the imperial court of the first embassy from Kashmir sent by king Tchen-t'o-lo-pi-li (in or shortly after A.D. 713), and that of another embassy sent by his brother and successor, Mu-to-pi." These kings are to be identified with Chandrapida and Muktapida Lalitaditya mentioned in the Rajatarangini. Besides the information that Hsuan-tsang gives, the only item of interest that this account furnishes is a reference to the Mo-ho-to-mo-loung or Mahapadma lake (present Wular lake), Po-lo-ou-lo-po lo, Pravarapura, the old and official name of Srinagar, and Mi-na-si-to, the Vitasta river, which flowed on the west of the capital.

From this last statement, as well as from the testimony of Hsuan-tsang, it may be inferred that in the seventh and eighth centuries the city of Srinagar lay only on the right bank of the river and had not yet extended to the left bank. This expansion must have taken place some time before the end of the tenth century A.D., as Alberuni (see below) speaks of the city being situated on both banks of the river.

Arab Notices: The above is practically all that the Chinese have to tell us about Kashmir. The next foreigner from whom we get information of real value is Alberuni, the great Muhammadan scholar who flourished at the court of Mahmud of Ghazni (A.D. 996-1031). He tells us that, owing to the victories of Mahmud over the Hindusj the Hindu sciences have retired far away from those parts of the country conquered by us and have fled to places where our hand cannot yet reach—Kashmir, Benares, and other places.

Notwithstanding the numerous difficulties which the contemporary political conditions of India placed in the way of his collecting accurate statistics of the remote valley, Alberuni seems to have succeeded in the attempt better than might have been expected; for his account of Kashmir is much fuller than that of other parts of India and appears to show that among his informants, if not among his actual teachers, there were Kashmiri scholars. Regarding the people and the country he remarks as follows:

The inhabitants of Kashmir are pedestrians, and they have no riding animals. The nobles among them ride in palankins called kati carried on the shoulders of men. They are especially anxious about the natural strength of the country, and therefore take always great care to keep a strong hold upon the entrances and routes leading into it. In consequence it is very difficult to trade with them. In former times they used to allow one or two foreigners, particularly Jews, to enter their country; but at present they do not allow any Hindu, whom they do not know personally, to enter, much less other people.

The best known entrance to Kashmir is from the town Babrahan (in the district of Hazara). The city of Kashmir covers a space of four farsakh, being built along both banks of the river Jailam, which are connected with each other by bridges and ferry-boats.

He adds that fourfarsakh below Addisthan, the capital, is a swamp of one square farsakh: that the people have plantations on its borders, and that Kashmir has no Varshakala (rainy season), but a snow-fall beginning with Magh up to the middle of Chaitra, when continual rains set in.

Kashmir holds the same rank among holy places as Benares, Kurukshetra, etc.

"The second of the month of Chaitra is a festival to the people of Kashmir called Agdus, and celebrated on account of a victory gained by their king Muttai over the Turks."

Alberuni counts five days' march "to the beginning of the ravine whence the river Jailam comes "—that is, to the entrance of the gorge through which the river flows immediately below Baramula. This estimate agrees closely with the actual road distance between Muzafferabad and Baramula, which is given by Mr. Drew as 84 miles. At the other or Kashmir end of the ravine, Alberuni places quite correctly the watch station Dvar (Skr. Dvara), the position of which, as we shall see below, is marked to this day by the site of the old gate known as Drang.

"Thence leaving the ravine you enter the plain, and reach in two more days Addishtan, the capital of Kashmir, passing on the road the village Ushkara." All this is perfectly accurate.

Adhisthana, the capital, is, of course, meant for Srinagara, and Ushkara for Ushkur opposite Baramula, the ancient Hushkapura already mentioned by Hsuan-tsang. Alberuni's mention of Ushkur, which is on the left river bank, shows that then as now the ordinary road from the "Gate of Varahamula" to Srinagar passed on the left or southern side of the valley. Two marches are still counted for this part of the journey.

"Marching on the right side (of the river), you pass through villages, one close to the other, south of the capital, and thence you reach the mountain Kularjak, which is like a cupola, similar to the mountain Dunbawand (Damawand). The snow there never melts. It is always visible from the region of Takeshar and Lauhawar (Lahore)."

Besides describing the valley with great accuracy, Alberuni makes mention of the adjacent hill territories of Bolor (Baltistan) and the Dard tracts of "Gilgit, Aswira, and Shiltas" (modern Gilgit, Hasor, and Chilas). He also speaks of the fortresses of Lauhur (Skr. Lohara), in the Loharin valley on the way to Poonch, and Rajagiri as the strongest places he had ever seen.

He closes his account with a reference to the town of Rajavari (Skr. Rajapuri), the modern Rajauri. In Hindu times it was the capital of a small hill state, situated immediately to the south of the Pir Pantsal range and often tributary to Kashmir. Alberuni distinctly names it as the farthest place to which the Muhammadan merchants of his time traded, and beyond which they never passed.

Indian Notices: The information that we can glean regarding Kashmir from the works of ancient Indian writers other than those of Kashmiri origin is extremely meagre. The great grammarian Panini and his commentator Patanjali make a bare mention of the name Kasmtra and its derivative Kosmira. The Mahabharata and the Puranas refer to the Kasmiras and their ruler, but in a fashion so general and vague that nothing but the situation of the country in the hill region to the north can be concluded therefrom.

Varahamihira, the well-known Indian astronomer, who probably lived about A.D. 500, had even more hazy notions regarding the location of Kashmir, inasmuch as he mentions it along with a number of purely mythical countries and people such as "the kingdom of the dead "(Nastarajya), "the gold region," "the one-footed people," etc. His mention of Abhisaras, Daradas, etc., who were undoubtedly living on the borders of Kashmir, does not help much in gaining knowledge of the valley as it existed at that time.

"Perhaps the most specific piece of information regarding Kashmir that Sanskrit literature outside the valley can furnish is conveyed in the term kasmira or kasmiraja, which designates the saffron, and also, according to the lexicographers, the root of the kustha, or Costus speciosus. As both saffron and kustha have been from early times famous products of Kashmir, the origin of the term is clear enough."

Kashmiri Authors: In strong contrast to the lack of definite geographical knowledge displayed by Indian authors is the refreshing abundance of historical and topographical detail in the works of Kashmiri authors. This splendid array of authoritative guides begins with the Nilamatapurana and continues practically without break to the present time. The age of the Nilamata is uncertain; but there is evidence to show that in one form or the other it was extant in the early middle ages.

Beginning with the legend regarding the lacustrine origin of the valley and its drainage after the death of Jalodbhava, the water demon, who infested the lake and made human habitation on its shores impossible, the Purana gives us a detailed list of the holy places of Kashmir. To each name it appends a more or less comprehensive topographical description, which is of great value in identification of the numerous places mentioned.

Analogous in nature, but far later in date, are the Mahatmyas of the different tirthas or places of pilgrimage. These works give lengthy accounts of the legendary origin of the holy places of Kashmir, and the religious merit accruing to the fortunate pilgrim who pays a visit to each sacred spot. They also furnish a complete survey of the sacred places of Kashmir.

By far the greatest amount of our information regarding ancient and mediaeval Kashmir is supplied by indigenous historians, of whom Kalhana is the oldest and most informative. He composed his Rajatarangini, the river of kings, in A.D. 1148-49. Born in a Brahman official family, and learned in the traditions of his country both from oral and written sources, Kalhana was specially fitted for his self-imposed task, which he has executed with conspicuous ability. His father, Champaka, was the minister of king Harsha (A.D. 1089-1101), but after the murder of his master in A.D. 1101 neither father nor son appears to have taken office under the succeeding rulers. With the characteristic reticence of ancient Indian authors he has left no information regarding his own life and pursuits.

The indirect evidence of his chronicle, however, compensates to some extent for his silence by revealing the character and intellectual equipment of the man. He had a keen, observant eye, considerable sense of humour, vivid poetic imagination, and extensive knowledge of human nature. His impartiality in according praise or blame to his royal contemporaries, no less than to the kings of the past, shows that he was no sycophant.

Though by birth he was a worshipper of Shiva, he respected other sects and religions almost as much as he did his own form of faith. His appreciation of the material conditions of his country, his topographical detail, his use of archaeological and numismatic evidence in the compilation of his history, give his work not only an absorbing interest in itself, but also an honourable place among histories of the mediaeval world.

It has, however, shortcomings which cannot be ignored. His chief defect is his want of critical acumen. He seldom quotes an opinion or a statement with a view to refute it. He is not able to distinguish between the legendary and genuine elements of tradition. Owing partly to this defect and partly, probably, to want of authentic sources, the first four books of his chronicles are little more than dynastic lists, interspersed here and there with anecdotes.

It is from the seventh century A.D. that history in the modern sense begins This does not mean that the earlier part of the chronicle is on that account without interest. On the contrary, it has very great value, not only because it mentions the great historic names of Ashoka, Kanishka, etc., but also because it presents us with a fairly detailed account of the general condition of the kingdom before we reach the centuries which immediately precede the time of Kalhana, and for which he had genuine oral and written information.

The latter consisted of a number of ancient histories written before Kalhana's time, of which he appears to have made extensive use. Unfortunately all of them are now lost. This makes it impossible to distinguish what is original from what is borrowed in Kalhana's Rajatarangini. Perhaps this work, which probably served as a convenient and comprehensive manual of Kashmir history for subsequent generations, was not a little responsible for the gradual disuse and final disappearance of the literary records which were available in his time.

The period which he knew personally or the knowledge of which he owed to living witnesses is treated by him with an exhaustiveness which leaves little to be desired, especially when we bear in mind that Kalhana regarded himself primarily as a poet, and composed the Rajatarangini as a didactic poem for the edification of his countrymen. Kalhana's chronicle has been published, with an excellent translation, exhaustive introduction, numerous explanatory notes, and a valuable monograph on the ancient geography and coinage, etc., of Kashmir, by Sir Aurel Stein. This monumental work is indispensable for the proper understanding of the social and political conditions of pre-Muslim Kashmir.

Exactly three centuries passed before a successor was found to continue Kalhana's work. He was another Kashmiri Brahman, Jonaraja, who was the contemporary and court historian of Zain-ulabidin (A.D. 1421-1472). His treatment of the centuries between him and his great predecessor is very superficial. The greater part of his work as well as of the history of Srivara, his pupil, who continued his master's task, is devoted to the reign of their patron Zain-ul-abidin. Prajyabhatta and Suka, two other historians who followed Srivara, bridge another century and terminate their labours with the conquest of the valley by Akbar in A.D. 1587. Thenceforward, Sanskrit chronicles ceased to be written; for, though Akbar tolerated and even encouraged Sanskrit learning, in such an out-of-the-way place as Kashmir it was no doubt at a discount, at any rate in an official sense. But with the decay of Sanskrit learning the Kashmiris' characteristic love of history and tradition did not wane and wither away.

Before bidding farewell to our Kashmiri Sanskrit writers, we must make mention of the poets from wkose works can be gleaned some useful information. The most important among them is Kshemendra, the well-known historian, whose books, composed in the second and third quarter of the eleventh century, form important landmarks in several fields of Indian literature. In the Samayamatrika, one of his most original poems, which is intended to describe the snares of courtesans, he gives us, among other stories, an amusing account of the wanderings of his chief heroine, Kankali, through the length and breadth of Kashmir.

The numerous places which form the scene of her exploits can all easily enough be traced on the map. More than once curious touches of true local colour impart additional interest to these references. To Kshemendra's poem we owe, for example, the earliest mention of the Pir Pantsal pass (Panchaladhara) and its hospice (matha). There too we get a glimpse of the ancient salt trade which until lately continued to follow that route.

Bilhana, the poet, who has been alluded to above, has also left in his Vikramankadevacharita a glowing picture of the beauties of Kashmir in general, besides giving a description of his rural home at Khunamusha, which is known today as the rakh (game preserve) of Khunamoh.

Mankha, the contemporary of Kalhana, has left a similar description of Kashmir and Srinagar. These accounts serve the additional purpose of enabling us to corroborate the statements of Kalhana from independent evidence. The book known as the Lokaprakasa is a curious mixture of the ordinary dictionary and a practical handbook dealing with various topics of administration and private life in Kashmir. Though much of the information given in it is decidedly old and probably from the hand of our well-known Kshemendra, there are unmistakable proofs in the form and contents of the book that it has undergone considerable alterations and additions down even to the seventeenth century. It supplies the earliest list of Kashmir parganas; and there are also the names of numerous localities insertsd in the forms for bonds, hundis, contracts, official reports, and the like, which form the bulk of Prakasas ii and iv.

In Mughal times and later, a host of Muslim and Hindu historians writing in the official Persian language recorded the events that occurred in their own lifetime, as well as the traditions which they heard from living witnesses. None of them, however, reached the standard of Kalhana.

What little they tell of the Hindu period they borrowed from him, and borrowed in a most perfunctory manner. The most important among these later historians are Haidar Malik of Tsodur, a contemporary of the emperor Jahangir; Narayan Kaul, who compiled his history in A.D. 1721; Hasan, who wrote in the last quarter of the eighteenth century; and Birbal Katsur, who is still more recent.

Besides the indigenous Sanskrit and Persian chronicles, we have notices of foreigners who collected information or visited Kashmir from time to time and recorded what they heard, or saw with their own eyes. Of these Mirza Haidar Doghlat of Kashgar, who conquered the valley in A.D. 1540 and ruled it in the name of Humayun till A.D. 1551, the historian Firishta, and Abul Fazl, the minister of Akbar, are the most instructive. Abul Fazl's account is specially interesting.

Besides supplying detailed information regarding the administration of the country, its products and industries, it furnishes an account of its chief places and objects of note, a list of thirty-eight parganas or administrative divisions with their respective land revenue figures in kind and in cash, and of the tribes residing in each. It also furnishes a short resume of the history of Kashmir, which Abul Fazl had got summarised from indigenous sources.

Among the European travellers who visited Kashmir before the valley became the fashionable summer resort of India, the earliest to contribute to our knowledge of it is the French physician Bernier, who accompanied Aurangzeb in his journey to Srinagar in A.D. 1664. He has left many interesting descriptions of the "merveilles," as he calls them, of Kashmir, as well as of the general condition of the country in Aurangzeb's time. The travels of Foster afford a peep into the state of tyranny that prevailed in the valley during the Pathan regime. Moorcroft, Vigne, Hugel, Honigberger, and Jacquemont are valuable for the Sikh times.

In addition to the numerous sources of Kashmir history above mentioned, we have to take into account the extraordinarily tenacious oral traditions, which have been handed down from generation to generation. They remove uncertainty in the identification of many ancient names given in the chronicles, and in certain cases they supplement the information furnished.

Architectural Styles

Early Buildings

No structural monuments which can, with certainty, be said to belong to the pre-Christian era have yet been discovered in Kashmir. Even the first six centuries A.D. are very meagrely represented; the only monuments which can with certainty be assigned to the Kushan period being the Buddhist structures at Harwan and Ushkar.

The abundance in which the coins of Indo-Greek, Parthian, and Saka kings of north-western India were found until recently in Kashmir points to the existence of considerable commercial intercourse, if not actual political connection, between the valley and the principalities of Peshawar and Kabul in the last two centuries B.C. and the first century A.D. It is also certain that in the second century A.D. Kashmir formed part of Kanishka's empire and that, for at least some generations after the death of that emperor, the country remained attached to the kingdom of Gandhara. This long connection with the northwest of India has left an indelible mark upon the character of the Buddhist and Hindu architecture of the valley. The early Buddhist religious edifices of Kashmir have practically the same plan, and probably had the same elevation, as the contemporary Buddhist buildings of Gandhara.

There was, however, a considerable difference in the materials used and in the modes of decoration. At Ushkar, for instance, the abundance of local quarries ensured a plentiful supply of stone chips, which the builders turned to excellent advantage. At Harwan, on the other hand, the most easily available building materials are the round boulders and pebbles brought down by the Dachigam Nala. Here accordingly we find the chip-masonry of Ushkar replaced by walls built of small pebbles (Plate XVII). The endeavour in each case seems to have been to employ building materials which were as small in size as possible. Probably it was thought that the merit accruing to the donor of a religious structure was commensurate with the amount of labour and care bestowed upon it.

But this method carried to excess was bound to lead to disaster. The masons of Harwan, at any rate, seem to have realised early that a pebble wall built in mud, each pebble being not more than one or two inches in diameter, even though it was covered by a coat of plaster, was not a durable structure. In fact, to keep it standing for even a short period was not easy without vigilant care and constant repairs, for every shower of rain was certain to peel off a part of its facing. They therefore adopted the practice of inserting large stones in the midst of pebbles, thereby giving it a somewhat more solid and certainly more picturesque appearance (Plate XIX).

This may be called the "diaper-pebble" style. The large apsidal temple at Harwan is built of this kind of masonry. It is, however, worthy of note that in this temple the diaper-pebble facing was covered with a revetment of beautiful and elaborately moulded bricks, some of which are still in situ on the enclosure wall.

This style was followed at Harwan by the diaper-rubble masonry (Plate XVI), which is represented by a large stupa, its surrounding walls, and chapels. The discovery of a coin of

Toramana underneath the stairs of the stupa fixes its date, and consequently also the style in which it is built, as that of the sixth century A.D. or later. This kind of masanry is also found in a building at Parihasapura, where it may possibly be nearly contemporary with the buildings of Lalitaditya (eighth century A.D.).

Mediaeval Architecture

Buddhist Buildings

We now come to the well-known and much described architecture of mediaeval Kashmir. It may be said with a fair amount of accuracy to begin at about the sixth to seventh centuries A.D. It ended with the transfer of the kingdom from Hindu to Muslim hands in A.D. 1337, though probably small monolithic shrines, such as those of Patan (Plate LVII) and Koil, continued to be consecrated even after that time. The buildings which represent this style may conveniently be divided into two classes—namely, the Buddhist and the Brahmanical.

In point of materials, ornament, and technique, there is practically no difference between the two, but the religious needs of the two communities being in certain essentials different, they differ widely in plan and elevation. The Buddhists, who inherited a long artistic tradition, naturally adhered to their old models, though they employed better materials and somewhat elaborated the decoration. The material brought into use was a beautiful grey limestone, which was easy to carve, and presented a very smooth surface when properly dressed.

The plinth of the old stupa, which was a simple rectangular structure with a single flight of steps, was now elaborated into a square with one or more offsets on each side projecting far into the courtyard (Plate LV), and flanked on either hand by side walls adorned with sculptural reliefs. The plinth in the larger buildings consisted of a double terrace, each comprising five courses of finely chiselled stone blocks of great size. The two lowest courses and the fourth course were plain, the third was fashioned into a round torus moulding, and the topmost into a filleted torus or cyma recta. The re-entering angles of the offsets afforded a pleasing contrast of light and shade.

As there is not a single stupa of which the drum remains intact, it is difficult to say precisely what its external decorations were?

Of the monasteries there is little to be said, as only one example survives—namely, the Rajavihara of Parihasapura. In plan it is a cellular quadrangle facing a rcctangular courtyard. The cells were preceded by an open verandah. In the middle of one side was the flight of steps which afforded an entrance and exit. The central cell on this side served as the vestibule. In the range of cells on the opposite side are a set of more spacious rooms which served either as a refectory or as the abbot's private apartments. Externally, and probably internally also, the walls were plain. The roof was probably sloping, and gabled like modern roofs in Kashmir.

Parihasapura has also bequeathed to us the only surviving example of a Buddhist chaitya, or temple. It is a square chamber built upon a square base similar to that of the stupa, save for the offsets and three stairs, and is enclosed by a plain wall, with entrance facing the temple stairs. The stairs lead up to the portico which gave admission to the sanctum. The latter was an open chamber surrounded on all sides by a narrow corridor which served as a circumambulatory path. At the four corners of the sanctum are bases of pillars which no doubt held some sort of screen designed partly to conceal the Holy of Holies from profane eyes. As the external wall of the corridor has been almost razed to the ground, it is very difficult to say whether there were openings in it for admission of light and air; probably there were.

The portico was covered by a massive trefoil arch, which in its turn might have been surmounted by a pedimental roof. The roof of the shrine was probably pyramidal like that of contemporary Hindu temples. At any rate, its plan would easily admit of such a roof.

Hindu Buildings

The second and far most numerous group of buildings belonging to this style are Hindu temples. The earliest example of this class, the date of which can be fixed through archaeological as well as literary evidence, is the temple of Martand (Plate LIII), which is also the greatest and one of the most finished of all the Kashmir temples. From this, however, it must not be inferred that the mediaeval Hindu architecture of Kashmir was born like Athene in panoply fully accoutred and complete to the last detail; that, in other words, it was evolved by a single brain or set of brains at a specified point of time.

It is true that, owing to the remarkable dearth of early dated examples, we are reduced to mere conjecture as to what was the prototype, and what were the stages of evolution which resulted in such magnificent products of the builder's art as the Martand and Avantisvami temples (Plates LIII, XLVIII, and XLIX). But it seems reasonable to presume that the earlier examples were simpler, and that art progressed step by step, up to a certain point, from the simple to the more elaborate.

We have briefly noticed above the extent and depth of the influence of the Buddhist art of Gandhara on that of Kashmir. So great was it that it would be more correct to say that, excepting the natural and unavoidable difference in the material used, the two are practically identical. Though the religious needs of the Hindus did not necessitate their borrowing stupas and sangharamas from the Buddhists, such considerations did not lie in the way of their taking advantage of the experience the latter had gained in temple-building.

The needs of the two communities were the same in two respects: a chamber was required for installation of a divine image (whether of the Buddha and the Bodhisattva or of Vishnu and any other Hindu deity is of little importance), and accommodation was required for worshippers. It is of course not impossible for a new religion to commence an architecture of its own, but the chances are overwhelming in favour of its utilising, at least in the initial stages, the older models, and adapting them to its purposes.

This may not always hold good in the case where the new religion follows in the wake of foreign conquest and the conquerors have already evolved a style of their own, which they naturally wish to impose upon the vanquished. But when the new religion, like the old, is indigenous; when both live in mutual amity and exchange of good offices; and, lastly, when the mode of worship of both is practically the same, it becomes almost inevitable that the sacred buildings of the new religion should follow the style of those of the older one. This, at any rate, has happened twice in Kashmir, once when Buddhism slowly and gradually gave way to Hinduism, and again when, with the accession of Shah Mir, Islam, at first imperceptibly, but with increasing speed, supplanted Hinduism in the valley.

Regarding the first transformation, the similarity pointed out by Foucher between the "angular roofed" vihara (le Vihara d toit anguleux)' of Gandhara and the temples of Kashmir, particularly the larger temple at Loduv (Plate XLVII), is specially interesting and instructive. The latter is an extremely plain structure, circular in plan internally, square externally, very simple in construction, and almost devoid of decoration. It has a single opening, the entrance, which is arched at the top. The arch is semicircular and built of horizontal projecting courses. The few stones of the roof which still exist prove that it was steep, straight, and sloped.

The stones of which it is built are comparatively small in size. This is a curious feature, considering that the quarry which probably supplied the gigantic blocks of the Avantipur temple, and from which stones of immense size are still taken, is little more than a stone's throw from the shrine. This may be merely coincidence; but, taking it in conjunction with the simplicity of its design, it seems probable that the temple belongs to the time when the great possibilities of ashlar-dressed limestone began first to dawn upon the architects of Kashmir—that is, to the sixth or seventh century A.D.

This hypothesis is strengthened by the striking resemblance of the Loduv (Plate XLVII) temple to the vihara of Guniyar in the Swat valley. The dcscription of the former which has been given above would literally apply to the latter but for a few minor differences, which are: in the Guniyar example the plainness of the cella is relieved internally by four recesses placed diagonally; the row of projecting brackets which support the eaves of the roof are replaced at Loduv by a simple cornice consisting of three courses of projecting filleted blocks; on the other hand, there is no trace of a pediment over the entrance of the vihara. These details, however, do not impair the analogy between the two. Now the Guniyar structure cannot possibly be later than the fifth century A.D., and unless there is something positive to prove the lateness of the Loduv temple (to my knowledge there is nothing), we must on the strength of the reasons adduced above consider it either contemporaneous with the former, or at most a century or so later.

A structure of which the date has caused much controversy is the Sankaracharya temple (Plate V) on the Takht-i-Sulaiman hill. General Cunningham, relying mainly upon local tradition, assigned it to Jalauka, son of Ashoka, whom he puts about 220 B.C. Professor Buhler denies the existence of this tradition, but does not himself give any definite opinion. Mr. Fergusson rejected Cunningham's view chiefly on grounds of style. He remarks: "At the bottom of the steps is a round-headed doorway, not, it is true, such as is universal in the Hindu imitations of Muslim architecture in the seventeenth and eighteenth centuries.

The same is the case in the small temples alongside, which are evidently of the same age. The one most like it that I am acquainted with is that erected by Chait Singh of Benares (1770-1781) at Ramnagar at the end of the eighteenth century. I know of no straight lined pyramid of much older date than that, and no temple with a polygonal plan combined with a circular cell, as is the case here, that is of ancient date. The ceil itself with the linga is undoubtedly modern, and the four pillars in the cell with the Persian inscriptions upon them are avowedly of the seventeenth century.

It is suggested, moreover, that they belong to a repair. My own conviction, however, is that the temple, as it now stands, was commenced by some nameless Hindus in honour of Shiva during the tolerant reign of Jahangir and that the building was stopped at the date engraved on the staircase, A.H. 1069 (A.D. 1659), the first year of Aurangzeb. It was then unfinished, and has remained a ruin, and this may have given it an ancient appearance, but not such as to justify putting its date back 1870 years."

Sir Aurel Stein is inclined to accept the opinion of Fergusson, at least so far as the superstructure is concerned. He states that "the circular cella, which contains a modern linga, was undoubtedly built in Muslim times. The imposing polygonal base, consisting of remarkably massive blocks and without mortar, must belong to a much earlier period (Plate LXXIV). Whatever may be the date and origin of the temple on the Takht hill, its connection with the worship of Jyestharudra is highly probable."

Cunningham's theory, which was based on the traditional identity of the temple with the temple of Jalauka, lost all basis when the existence of that tradition was questioned and disproved. Fergusson's arguments in support, on the one hand, of his rejection of Cunningham's view and, on the other, of the plausibility of his own, are equally untenable for the following reasons:

1. True round-headed arches of the early Hindu times are known in India; and the existence, therefore, of a horizontal round-headed arch in a Hindu temple does not necessarily imply its late date and imitation from Muslim models. At Loduv we have a similar arch.
2. Whatever the value of his assertion that he did not know of any straight-lined pyramid much older than the eighteenth century, nor any "temple with a polygonal plan combined with a circular cella," his deduction from it is invalidated by the fact that the Sankaracharya temple is not a straight-lined pyramid in the sense which his words seemingly imply, and that its plan is not polygonal. Its walls rise straight up to the eaves, and its roof, the lowest course only of which is extant, was triangular in section like the roofs of other ancient temples in Kashmir. In plan the cella is externally square, with a couple of offsets on each side.
3. Though the pillars in the sanctum bearing Persian inscriptions are modern and were probably put up in Shah Jahan's time, it does not seem that they alter the

position in any way, for the ancient domical ceiling built of concentric circles of kanjur masonry is still in existence above the modern ceiling.

4. Lastly, his conviction that it was begun by some nameless Hindus in Jahangir's time and was left incomplete after the accession of Aurangzeb in A.D. 1659, "which gives it its ancient look," is flatly contradicted by Bernier, who saw it in A.D. 1664, only five years later, and states that it was in ruins and desuetude. Catrou, whose General History of the Mughal Empire was published in 1708, only one year after Aurangzeb's death, ascribes it to Solomon. This shows that its origin was even then unknown, which would scarcely be the case if its construction had been taken in hand in the time of Jahangir and stopped by Aurangzeb's order.

Rai Bahadur Daya Ram Sahni states that "the temple belongs to the same mediaeval period as all the other buildings of this class," which is probably correct. But his further remark, "that the enclosure wall of this temple represents a decadent form of the cellular peristyle," seems to imply that the smallness (that is what he probably means by decadence) of the peristyle necessarily connotes a late date, and that consequently the Sankaracharya temple is later than those temples which have larger peristyles.

Now there are several temples in Kashmir whose date admits of no doubt—e.g., the Martand, the Avantipur, the Patan, the Kother temples. The first belongs to the beginning of the eighth century A.D. and the last to the end of the eleventh century. But the lapse of the three centuries and more does not appear to have in any way influenced the dimensions of the peristyle, except of course in cases where the reduced size of the central shrine itself necessitated proportionate reduction in the dimensions of the peristyle also, and secondly where the nature of the site chosen for the erection of the temple did not permit of the construction of a large, or for the matter of that any, peristyle. The first, for instance, is the case in the two Patan temples which were built by Sankaravarman and his queen Sugandha at one and the same time. The Pandrethan temple which, I believe, belongs to the middle of the twelfth century A.D., but which according to Rai Bahadur Daya Ram Sahni "is certainly quite 200 years older," has a surrounding wall, but no cellular peristyle; this would be very strange indeed in a temple which so closely followed the Avantisvami temple (A.D. 852-855), if the peristyle were an indispensable adjunct to the early Hindu temples.

As a matter of fact we know from extant examples that it was not. It has been established that the two larger temples, at Wangath were built by Lalitaditya, who built the Martand temple also. Of these three temples erected by the same king, one (Martand) has the largest peristyle known to exist in Kashmir, the second (Jyeshthesa at Wangath) has a comparatively small one, and the third (Bhutesa at Wangath) has none at all. Thus it seems to me that the smallness—the so-called decadence—of the peristyle, or its very absence, does not in itself afford any indication of the age of the temples.

From the foregoing remarks it will have been observed that though it may be indisputable that the Sankaracharya temple "belongs to the same mediaval period as all the buildings of this class," its proper position in the sequence of Kashmir monuments is by no means well established. Fortunately in this matter the temple itself comes to our aid. The salient features of the central shrine are the following: (1) externally it is square in plan with two offsets on each side; (2) internally it is circular; (3) the cella is absolutely without decoration both internally and externally; (4) it is pierced by a single narrow opening (the entrance) semicircular at the top and surmounted by a very shallow and steep pediment; (5) it stands in a narrow octagonal court which is enclosed by a low parapet wall adorned with rows of small niches.

Of all the temples in Kashmir that to which it bears the closest resemblance, both in disposition of parts and in ornament (or rather the want of it), is the one at Loduv. Apart from the enclosure wall and the base, which are submerged in the swamps formed by the spring at Loduv, and which therefore are not available for comparison, the only difference between the two shrines is that the Sankaracharya has two offsets on each side externally, while the other has none. This certainly is an innovation and an improvement, since the light and shade of the re-entering angles of the offsets compares favourably with the baldness of the exterior of the Loduv temple. But it must be noticed that the offsets are severely plain.

In this respect they stand in very marked contrast with other examples of mediaeval Hindu architecture. Not only do such undoubtedly late temples as those of Mamal and Kother possess more or less ornate trefoiled recesses on each side, but even the very latest miniature monolithic shrines, which were probably erected at the time when Hindu rule and Hindu art were at a low level, display these decorative features, sometimes actually carved out of the stone, as in the structural examples, or merely traced in outline.

It seems, therefore, clear that the absence of such decorative features as attained currency in the eighth century is, in case of the Sankaracharya temple, an indication of its older age, and not a sign of decadence. In other words, though the Sankaracharya temple is somewhat later than the Loduv temple, it cannot be less than a century older than the Martand temple; that is to say, its approximate date is probably A.D. 700.

The octagonal enclosure is more a matter of accident than of design. It is due to the situation of the temple, which precluded the possibility of a larger enclosure of any other type without immense expenditure. But notwithstanding the fact that it is a great improvement upon the Loduv temple, there is a considerable gap from the Sankaracharya to the Martand which must have taken a good deal of time and invention to bridge over.

In accelerating progress, however, Lalitaditya's large resources and even-handed generosity to the Hindus and the Buddhists effectively came to the aid of the Kashmir architect. To the Buddhist the king's bounty brought no change. All that he did was to use better and more massive materials. He built a monastery of gigantic ashlar—dressed limestone blocks exactly as he would have built it of rubble stone and timber. The Hindu, on the other hand, used both his hands and his brain, with what result is evident to every one who has seen the wonderful ruins of the Martand temple. He did not invent many new forms of design and decoration. He simply re-arranged the motifs he had ready at hand into a new artistic combination which was so beautiful and at the same time so dignified that it fixed for all succeeding centuries of Hindu rule the ideal of what a temple of the Gods should be.

He had already adapted a Buddhist temple for his purpose at Loduv; he had improved it by the addition of offsets at Sankaracharya; he had pierced the offsets with trefoiled niches at Narastan (Plate LII), which probably follows gankaracharya in date. The most important feature that still remained to be added was the cellular quadrangle. This he achieved at Martand.

Regarding the origin of the cellular quadrangle there can be little doubt. The Buddhist monastery from very early times consisted of a quadrangular block of rooms facing a common courtyard, in which usually stood a small private chapel. If the chapel was a large one and placed in the centre of the court, the plan would exactly correspond with that of the Martand or the Avantisvami temple, the former of which is contemporary with the Buddhist structures of Parihasapura.

Of course, in the Hindu temples the size of the cells was considerably reduced, as they were no longer required for residential purposes, but merely for the accommodation of the images; the width of the promenade in front of the cells was also reduced in the temple; the columns which supported its roofs were now used for a purely decorative purpose, and sometimes, when the resources of the builders failed, were altogether given up; the unpretentious flight of steps, quite suitable for a congregation of religious mendicants, was replaced by a magnificent double-chambered entrance, almost equal in size to the temple, to make it a fit portal for an abode of the Gods.

These and other details, as the necessity or the fancy of the artist dictated, were gradually added; but the broad outline of the ordinary Hindu temple of the best period remained the same—namely, a chaitya built in the middle of a monastic courtyard.

Later, when the Hindu rule lost its early vigour and the country was constantly torn by intestine warfare, the religious buildings of Kashmir gradually lost much of their impressive grandeur. Architectural features, such as the trefoil arch and the detached column, lost their original purpose and became mere decorative motifs. The dimensions of the temple gradually dwindled until they became small monolithic miniatures not more than 2 feet each way. The column was altogether given up. The arch became shallower and shallower. At Payar (Plate LI) it is merely a sculptured niche over the lintel of a rectangular doorway; at the Bumazu cave-temple only its outline has been shown; the small shrine in the Patan (Plate LVII) spring does not show it at all, though it still reproduces the elaborate double pediment and the moulded bases and capitals of the jambs.

Thus, curiously enough, the principal features of both the beginning and the end of the mediaeval Hindu architecture of Kashmir are the absence of the structural trefoil arch and the colonnade, which would for the purpose of fixing their chronological sequences be confusing enough, were it not that other characteristics—such as the design, decoration, mouldings, etc., render it possible to distinguish one from the other.

The mediaeval architecture of Kashmir depended for its effect upon (1) the simplicity and unity of its design, (2) the masslveness of the blocks of limestone and granite that were used, (3) the finish of dressing, and (4) last but not least, the natural beauty of the site chosen for erection of the temple. Its main feature is a happy combination of the column and the arch.

(1) The temple was conceived as a single whole, and after its construction afforded little or no scope for subsequent additions. Its plan and disposition were apparent at a single glance. In this characteristic it differed essentially from the majority of Indian temples, which, whatever their beauty in detail, present when viewed as a whole a rather confused appearance.

(2) and (3). All the temples of Kashmir, except those of Wangath (Plate LXII) and Buniar (Plate LX), in which

the material used is granite, are built of limestone, which the quarries of Loduv, Zewan, and Ajas plentifully supply. The blocks used are extraordinarily massive, often measuring 10 feet and more in length. The floor of the chaitya at Parihasapura consists of a single block approximately 14 x 12 x 6 feet. The blocks, before being placed in their proper position, were-only roughly dressed, the architectural decoration and sculptured reliefs being merely blocked out; the final dressing was done in situ. It was an inconvenient and somewhat circuitous method, but it was necessary, as otherwise the delicate carving, if not done in situ, might sustain grievous damage in handling. Lime mortar was undoubtedly used; but the stability of the masonry was sufficiently assured by the massiveness of the blocks, which had only vertical pressure to resist, there being no lateral thrust, owing to the absence of voussoir arches and the frequent use of iron clamps. There is reason to believe that this wealth of stone carving was covered by a coat of gypsum plaster, which was probably painted, and in which the more delicate details of sculpture and other decoration were finished off.

(4) A natural result of the pantheistic tendencies of early Brahmanism is the extraordinary reverence in which both the Buddhists and the Hindus have always held Nature. To them the wide prospect over the rolling plains, as at Ellura, or the wild grandeur of glaciers and eternal snows, as at Amarnath, or the view of a magnificent sunset over the hills, as at Martand, not only made a general aesthetic appeal, but had a special religious significance; for they viewed Nature as the multifold manifestation of the Almighty. It was for this reason that they invariably chose the most naturally beautiful spots for their sanctuaries. Much of the charm which the religious buildings of Kashmir undoubtedly possess is due to this fact. To take only one example: as the site of a temple, the conical summit of the Takht-i-Sulaiman hill, rising a thousand feet vertically above the surrounding plains and commanding a panoramic

view of the entire mountain-griddled valley, would be difficult to rival anywhere. The temple seems the natural apex of the pyramidal hill. The steep sombre lines of the barren slopes blend insensibly with the still more sombre, grey, and vertical lines of the temple walls. Art has not only advantageously utilised, but also emphasised, the natural characteristics of the situation (Plate IV and Plate V).

Plan: In plan the Kashmirian temple (Plates LXVIII, LXXIII, and LXXV) is a rectangular quadrangle pierced with cells facing the courtyard. The temple usually consists of a single chamber with a portico, and is, as a rule, at the point of intersection of the diagonals of the courtyard. The entrance, which is almost equal in dimensions to the main shrine, is a double-chambered structure, and is built in the middle of a shorter side of the peristyle. The chambers are divided by a partition wall, which is open in the middle and was probably closed by wooden doors. The entrance has a double flight of steps, one external and the other facing the temple. The stairs are flanked with plain stone rails and sculptured sidewalls.

The main shrine consists, as has been stated above, of a single square chamber, preceded by a small portico (Plate LXV). Externally a facet is added on each side, which is hollowed out into a trefoil-arched niche; the front one, being open, serves as entrance to the sanctum. The temple stands on a single or double base which consists usually of five ashlar-dressed courses, the first, the second, and the fourth of which are plain and the remaining two moulded (Plate LXXIV, A, B, C, and D).

The cells of the peristyle also stand on a plinth which is similar to the base of the temple. The central cell on each of three sides is slightly larger than the rest, and is somewhat advanced beyond the line of the peristyle.

Some of the temples possess subsidiary shrines. They are usually built in an angle of the courtyard and are similar in plan to the main shrine (Plate LXVIII).

Variations in Plan: The Loduv and the Sankaracharya temples are circular in plan internally. The former does not possess any facets externally, and in the latter they have not yet developed into trefoiled niches. The Payar and some other temples do not possess any cellular peristyle. The Narastan temple has a plain enclosure wall with a gateway of the conventional type. It has a small tank in front, and a bath chamber in one of the corners of the enclosure wall. The Sankaracharya temple has an octagonal range of miniature cells in its surrounding wall.

Walls: The walls are built of finely dressed and massive blocks of limestone. Mortar was used, though not in considerable quantities, as the stones were secured by iron clamps. The joints are usually very thin. The surface was often carved with sculptured reliefs, geometrical and floral patterns, but the internal surface of the walls of the cella was generally kept plain. The walls were surmounted by a sloping cornice, usually decorated with rows of geese alternating with rosettes and kirtimukhas (Plate LXX). Externally, the walls of the peristyle are plain, except in certain cases where a series of shallow projections marks the position of the crosswalls of the cells. Internally the pilasters of the cells are decorated with half-engaged columns carved in low relief (Plate LXXII).

Openings: Curiously enough there exist no traces whatever of any windows or skylights in any of the known temples of the valley. This is probably due mainly to the fact that the light and air entering through a single large doorway was enough for a small square cella. Still less was there any need for such apertures in the case of the cells of the peristyle. The only openings, therefore, that are found in the walls of the Kashmirian temples are the doorways. They were rectangular, surmounted by trefoil arches, and were usually preceded by trefoiled and pedimented porticoes. In the Loduv and gankaracharya temples, the entrances are round-headed.

Temples of the mandapa, or "bower" type, like the Pandrethan (Plate XLIV) and Payar (Plate LI) temples, being open on all four sides, have naturally four doorways; while temples of the vimana type, such as the Avantisvami temple, have only one entrance.

A large temple (Bhutesa) in the group A at Wangath has two doorways facing each other.

Ceilings: Ceilings of Kashmiri temples were of four types, or rather three only, the third being merely a variety of the second type.

1. The ceiling of superimposed diminishing squares. The plan of the cells being square, the architect chose the method of cutting off the angles as the easiest means of spanning it. The second square thus formed was further reduced by another series of four stone beams which rested upon the first four. This process was repeated until a single square stone of sufficient dimensions was found to span the whole gap at the top. The triangular spaces resulting from this construction were filled with carved figures of flying Yakshas, and the apex was usually decorated with a full-blown lotus flower. The best example of this kind of ceiling is in the temple at Pandrethan (Plate LXVI).
2. The domical ceiling. The dome rested upon a projecting string-course, and was built of kañjur or kanait, a light and porous limestone which burns into excellent lime. It was not built on the radiating principle, but consisted of a series of concentric circles of small blocks of kanjur held together by mortar of extraordinarily adhesive properties. The stability of the dome, in fact, depended entirely upon the tenacity of the mortar. The ancient architects probably constructed this dome much as a modern engineer would construct an arch of cement concrete. The two largest temples at Wangath have ceilings of this type.
3. The corbelled ceiling seems to have been a variety of the domical ceiling, the only difference being that in this case the dome instead of rising direct from the string-course is supported on an elaborate system of corbelled pendentives. The corbels could have also been used with great advantage in the ceilings of the first type, inasmuch as they were capable of sustaining a greater weight than the unsupported stone beams, and could more easily reduce the span of the space to be covered.

4. The fourth type may aptly be described as the "no-ceiling "type. The best known, perhaps the only, examples of this class are the buildings at Narastan and Naranthal. The walls of the cella are carried up vertically until they reach the level of the eaves. Therefrom the pyramidal roof itself forms the ceiling.
5. A small temple at Wangath and the detached room to the northwest of the Sankaracharya temple have flat ceilings of rectangular stone slabs resting on transverse stone beams supported by columns.

Roofs: The roofs are invariably pyramidal. In the examples which have survived—e.g.., the Pandrethan (Plate XLIV), Payar (Plate LI), and Manasbal (Plate LXI) temples, not to mention the miniature shrines at Patan (Plate LVII), Koil, etc.—the pyramid is a double one, the lower storey being truncated at about the middle of the roof, and a second one built on a projecting string-course. The apex of the pediments of the porches reaches up to the upper edge of the lower storey, and produces a pleasing effect of light and shade. The plainness of the upper pyramid is sometimes relieved by a miniature gabled trefoil niche (Plate XLIV) in the middle of each of the four sides. The apex of the roof, as well as that of the four pediments, was crowned with a ribbed melon-like finial. Two of these are extant at Payar (Plate LI).

The roof of the small temple at Naranthal consists of a single plain pyramid.

Columns: Perhaps the most striking feature of the Kashmiri temple is the majestic colonnade (Plates XLVIII, LIII, and LX) which surrounds it on all sides. The columns are either smooth or fluted, and at the angles of the peristyle they are square. They are composed of three separate parts: the base, the shaft, and the capital. The base is either a plain square block with the upper edge rounded off, as at Avantipur (Plate XLIX), or is elaborately moulded, as at Martand (Plate LIII) and elsewhere. The latter has been described by Cunningham thus: "The upper member is an ovolo with a straight fillet above, and the apophyge below. The next is a filleted torus, with a fillet above and below and surmounting the straight face or neck of the pillar. In the large Martand pillar the torus is plain. Beneath this is a quirked ovolo with a straight fillet above and below, and the last is the plinth. In all these the upper and lower members are of the same height; that is, the ovolo and the apophyge are equal to the plinth."

When the shafts are fluted the flutes are sometimes so shallow as to have scarcely any concavity. In some cases—for example, at Avantipur—the central portion of the flute is roughly chiselled, and is in strong contrast to the edges, which are finely dressed. In the columns of the Patan temples the flutes are well accentuated. The number of flutes in different examples is twelve, sixteen, twenty, and twenty-four; but never less than twelve nor more than twenty-four.

It is difficult to say whether or not the diameter of the columns was a factor in determining its height.

The capitals are square, voluted, or bracketed, and rest upon a ribbed astragal (Plate LXVII). The height of the capital is usually equal to the upper diameter of the column. The bracket capital is sometimes adorned with figures of Yakshas.

The inter-columniation of the Kashmir colonnade was about two-thirds of the height of the column itself.

The entablature consists of the architrave and the cornice. In the case of the peristyle, the architrave returns, connecting the pillar with the pilaster of the cell behind. Both the architrave and the cornice are decorated with rows of rosettes alternating with Kirtimukhas or grinning lions' heads (Plates LXX, A, and LXXIV, E).

Ornaments: This consists of sculptured figures and geometrical and floral patterns which are mostly intermingled (Plates LXVII, LXX, LXXI, and LXXII). The most common motif of the former is the figure of a god or goddess standing in a pedimented niche (Plate LI and Plate LXIV). At Avantipur there are groups of figures of both sexes, engaged in drinking, making love, or other occupations (Plate L). The sculptured reliefs are principally found on the walls of the entrance and the flank walls of the stairs. It is probable, as stated above, that not only the plain wall surfaces but also the reliefs were covered with a fine coat of lime plaster, on which the addition of colour defined the more delicate details of decoration.

The principal mouldings (Plate LXXIV) employed are (1) cyma recta, (2) torus, (3) filleted torus, (4) ovolo, (5) echinus, and (6) fillet. None of these was enriched by any surface decoration, except in the case of the second, which was in a few examples adorned with broad, plain, slanting bands carved in bold relief.

Muslim Architecture

It will have been remarked, from the short account of Kashmir history given above, that the transfer of the sceptre from the Hindus to the Muslims was a purely domestic matter, and had nothing to do with the great Pan-Islamic conquests of the twelfth and thirteenth centuries. It was, moreover, an entirely secular affair. Rinchana, who was the first non-Hindu to occupy the Kashmir throne, was a Tibetan, and became a Muslim by accident. Shah Mir's usurpation was a coup d'etat and not a conquest. He and his immediate successors depended upon the support of the indigenous nobles, who were mostly Hindus, for the stability of their rule. The absence from Kashmir of the regular Saracenic mosques with cloisters and domes is not therefore surprising.

The Muslims in Kashmir were in the beginning far too few to initiate an architecture of their own. All that they did was to utilise the materials of disused Hindu temples for construction of their mosques. The result was peculiar. The most characteristic examples of this style are the mosque of Madin Sahib, outside the Sangin Darwaza of the Hari Parbat fort and its adjacent ruins, the ruins of the mosques on the roadside at Vitsarnag, and Zain-ul-abidin's mosque on the island in the Wular lake. All these will be described in detail below.

Another structure belonging to this period, and fundamentally different from all other buildings in Kashmir, is the tomb of Zainul-abidin's mother (Plate VIII). The plinth originally belonged to a Hindu or Buddhist shrine, and does not seem to have been tampered with by the Muslim architect, who simply followed the lines laid down by his Hindu predecessor. A peculiar feature of the brick buildings of this period (there are only three: the tomb of Zain-ul-abidin's mother, Madin Sahib's tomb, and the anonymous tomb on the island in the Wular) is the glazed tile-work with which they were decorated.

The mosques and tombs of the modern Kashmiri style are so similar that their features need not be separately discussed. The tombs are square in plan. The mosques are either self-contained, square buildings like the tombs: such are the mosques of Madani, Shah Hamadan (where the cloisters were added later) (Plate VI), and the Jama' Masjid at Pampur (Plate XLVI); or else they consist of a group of square-planned buildings connected together by a colonnade like the Jama Masjid in Srinagar.

The walls are constructed sometimes of bricks and mortar, sometimes of logs laid across each other, the space between logs being in some cases filled with brick-work. Piers are constructed of timber in the same way. In large chambers where the timbers of the roof or ceiling require intermediate support, modern columns are used with very good effect. Sometimes these columns are elaborately ornamented, and there is a tendency in modern restoration, as, for instance, at the mosque of Naqshband, to cover the bases with coarse and unsuitable ornament. Timber trusses do not seem to have been understood by ancient builders, but they are now employed in restoration.

The old method of supporting the rafters was by building up piers formed of logs laid horizontally—a very extravagant arrangement. The typical roof covering consists of turf laid in birch bark, which retains waterproof properties for a great number of years. The birch bark is laid on boards, and these in turn are supported on rafters. The roof is usually surmounted by a steeple, the finial of which is moulded, the largest moulding being sometimes in the shape of an outspread umbrella usually covered with metal. All the older buildings appear either to have lost their steeples and finials, or to have had them restored. The oldest umbrella mouldings are probably some of those on the Jama' Masjid (Plate IX and Plate X) at Srinagar, erected in the reign of Aurangzeb.

A remarkable feature in the steeple is the sloping gable which projects from the sides. Window openings and balustrades are commonly filled with elaborate jali screens, the patterns of which are formed by little pieces of wood fitted together so as to form geometrical patterns (Plate X).

"The angles of the eaves are generally ornamented with wooden pendants suspended from the corners, carved like small bells and shaped like cactus leaves. The cornices are very heavy, and are formed of logs corbelled out from the wall face on timbers laid crosswise. The butt ends of the cross timbers form a dentil course, and the space between them is filled with elaborate carving. The best examples are at the mosques of Madani at Srinagar and of Amir at Pampur.

The interior of the mosque of Shah Hamadan is entirely covered with panelling consisting of geometrical patterns.

The mouldings are as a rule flat, not deeply recessed, and curved and hollow members seem to be avoided. They generally consist of flat fillets, each of which is differently carved.

The carved ornament is generally Saracenic in character. In older buildings the patterns are conventional. In some later restorations realistic flowers are carved, bearing much resemblance to the stone-work of Shah Jahan in the Taj at Agra and elsewhere.

Of the Mughal style as exemplified by buildings in Kashmir it is not necessary to say much, because the style is practically the same as that with which we are familiar at Agra, Delhi, and Lahore.

The Pathar Masjid (Plate VII), the mosque of Akhun Mulla Shah (Plate XII), and the largest barahdari in Shalimar Bagh (Plate XIV) are unsurpassed in purity of style and perfection of detail by any buildings in Agra or Delhi.

Another important branch of architecture in which the Mughals excelled, and in which they left their mark upon Srinagar, is gardening. These gardens conform strictly to the style of Shalimar Bagh at Lahore and Delhi, and other gardens of the same period in India; but nowhere is there to be found a group comprising so many examples as at Srinagar."

3

Monuments of the Upper Valley

The small village of Pandrethan is situated 3 miles above Srinagar on the Anantnag cart-road. At present its only attraction, excepting the newly built military barracks, is the well-preserved mediaeval temple behind the willow grove on the left-hand side of the cart-road (Plates XLIV, LXIII, LXIV, LXV and LXVI). The temple measures 17 feet 6 inches square externally, and belongs to the mandapa type—i.e., it is open on all the four sides.

The unusually bold projection of the pilasters which support the pediments of the porches is "a great improvement upon the earlier stage, as the boldness of the projection and the retirement of the connecting walls afford a great and pleasing variety of light and shade which is altogether wanting in some parts of the more ancient buildings." The roof is of the usual pyramidal type, but its monotony is relieved by an ornamental band of dentils which divides it horizontally into two storeys. In the upper section of the pyramid are four trefoiled ventilation apertures which remind one forcibly of similar niches in the architecture of Gandhara.

The interior of the cella is plain, except for the ceiling (Plate LXVI), which is one of the best examples of carving on stone extant in Kashmir. It consists of nine stones arranged in three overlapping squares, each of which cuts off the angles of the square below it, and thus reduces the extent of the space to be covered. The twelve triangles so formed have been utilised for figure decoration. Each triangle in the lowest square contains a pair of flying Yakshas, facing each other and holding a garland in their hands, which falls in swags about their bodies and between their knees.

The second group of triangles contains only four figures, each holding a disc in his right hand and a lotus stalk in his left. Underneath his right arm is seen the outstretched end of flying drapery. The uppermost set of triangles contains a similar group of flying figures. The whole is crowned by a square slab decorated with an exquisitely carved full-blown lotus within a beaded circle. The convention by which the peculiarly graceful floating motion of the body, somewhat similar to that of a swimmer, is made to represent the flight of human figures without the appendage of wings, is noteworthy. The floor of the cella is paved with stone flags. In the centre is the depression about 7 feet square which must have held the pedestal of the image worshipped in the temple.

The plinth of the temple remains submerged for the greater part of the year, but it is certain that it is well preserved. A remarkable feature of it is the string-course of elephants which runs round the temple and upon which the walls of the sanctum rest. The springs which have arisen round the structure do not seem to have been there when the temple was originally built, for it is impossible to believe, now that Cunningham's theory of "the Kashmirian temple being placed in the centre of a tank "no longer holds good, that the temple was built in the midst of an extensive marsh, which has only lately been drained.

Cunningham, and after him Cowie, Cole, etc., believed that the temple was "Vishnu-meruvardhanasvami," built by Meruvardhana, the minister of Partha who flourished in the beginning of the tenth century A.D. He bases his identification on the statement of the Rajatarangini coupled with absence of other temples in Pandrethan.

But this theory is considerably weakened by the presence, in the trefoiled niche above the northern entrance, of a seated figure which is believed to be the Lakulis'a form of Shiva, and by the internal arrangement of the floor of the cella which "can only admit of a Shiva image." The Rajatarangini mentions in another passage the erection of the temple of Shiva-Rilhanesvara by Rilhana, the minister of Jayasimha, about the year A.D. 1135. There is nothing in the architectural style against the identification of our temple with Rilhana's foundation. Around this site a number of late Brahmanical images have been found.

Buddhist Structure

But the history of Pandrethan goes much farther back than the twelfth century A.D. The name is a corruption of Puranadhisthana, which means "Old Capital." It was founded under the name of grinagari by the emperor Ashoka in the third century B.C. But eight hundred years after, Pravarasena II removed the site of his capital farther down the river. Gradually the younger city not only deprived its older rival of all its importance, but usurped its name also, and Ashoka's city came to be known simply by the appellation of Puranadhishthana (old city).

This name was in use as early as the time of Hsuan-tsang (seventh century A.D.). The only remains that now exist of the ancient Pandrethan are the ruins of level terraces, long lines of loose rubble walls, and innumerable mounds of stone debris, which thickly dot the mountain slopes from Pantchhok to the Sankaracharya hill—an extent of about a miles. Not all these heaps of debris, however, are expected to conceal ancient remains.

In fact, a considerable number of them appear to have been collected together for the purpose of bringing all available land under cultivation in olden times, when the population of the country seems to have been larger than it is now. But there are a good manythe excavation of which will undoubtedly yield interesting results. Three such mounds have been tapped and have revealed two Buddhist stupas and the courtyard of a monastery. They are situated on the mountain slope about half a mile to the east of the temple.

The stupa known in the records of the Archaeological Department of the State as "Stupa A "is the larger of the two.

It was surrounded by a dressed stone wall, only the lowest course of which exists in places. The entrance to the compound seems to have been in the middle of the south wall.

The stupa has lost its outer dressed stone casing, except in one or two places. These, however, are sufficient to show that it was in plan a square of 72' with offsets on each side, the re-entering angles of which must have afforded a pleasing contrast of light and shade. Almost all that exists at present is the circular rubble stone core of the structure.

To the west of it is another stupa, but it has been so carefully demolished that nothing remains of it except a few stones, and a rail of its western stair. With the exception of a few fragmentary sculptures which may be assigned to about the seventh century A.D. or perhaps a little earlier, nothing of importance was found at these sites.

The sculptures are, however, very interesting inasmuch as they show that the influence of the art of the Imperial Guptas had penetrated into Kashmir and left a permanent mark upon the local craftsmanship. These sculptures are now in the Srinagar Museum. Plate XLV illustrates a life-size image of a Bodhisattva excavated at Pandrethan.

While digging for the foundations of the military buildings in the new cantonment near by, nearly a dozen beautiful sculptures, more than life-size, representing Indrani, Chamunda, Varahi, and other goddesses, known as the Ashtamatrika (eight mothers) were discovered. These too are now preserved in the Srinagar Museum.

The ruins mentioned above and the Shiva temple show that the old capital, though eclipsed by its younger rival, was not entirely deserted even in the later centuries of the mediaeval epoch. Another ancient relic is the beautifully carved stone capital (Plate LXVII) built into a late Muslim platform, situated on the hill slope towards the east of the temple.

The carving consists of a pair of geese with highly ornamental foliated tails and crests, facing each other and pecking at what looks like a bunch of grapes placed upon a decorative stand.

Loduv

Three miles and a half above Pandrethan, the road branches off to the sulphur springs at Wuyan and the Khruv game preserves. The branch road skirts the foot of the hills, and after describing a wide sweep of nearly 10 miles, joins the main road at Barus. The village of Loduv is situated on this road at a distance of 3 miles from the last-mentioned place. It contains two temples, the larger one (Plate XLVII) of which stands in the middle of a shallow tank of water which is fed by a spring in its northeast corner. The temple is a very simple structure 24' square externally.

It differs from every other temple of Kashmir both in plan and in appearance. Externally the walls are without decoration, their bareness being only partially relieved by a cornice which consists of three courses of stone adorned with projecting fillets. There is a torus course at the base. The corner pilasters are quite plain, and project only very slightly from the walls. The entrance, which is on the southwest side, is headed by a semicircular, almost horseshoe-shaped, arch surmounted by a single-storied pediment of very slight projection.

Internally the temple is circular with a diameter of 17' 6". In this respect it resembles the Sankaracharya temple on the Takht-i-Sulaiman hill. The wall surfaces are quite plain. At a height of nearly 10 feet from the ground level is a plain projecting string-course over which springs the domical ceiling. The dome was built of projecting courses of kanjur in lime, and must have been similar to the ceiling of the larger temples at Wangath. The holes and mortices in the walls seem to have been intended for scaffolding while the temple was under construction.

The simplicity of its plan and decoration seems to point to its being, perhaps, the oldest example of Kashmiri mediaeval architecture and the prototype of the elaborate style which culminated at Martand and Avantipur.

The water of the tank is nowhere more than a few inches deep, and a number of green fish of a remarkably light and transparent tinge may always be seen swimming gracefully in it.

A few yards behind this temple, higher up the hill and immediately at the back of the mosque, is a smaller temple which externally presents nearly the same appearance as the larger temple, the only difference being that the projecting pediment which enclosed the round-headed doorway has here developed into a well-defined portico with a trefoil niche. From this arrangement there is but a single easy step to the full trefoil-headed recess or entrance enclosed in a steep pediment which is so universal a feature of the mediaeval religious edifices of Kashmir. As a matter of fact the portico of this same temple had a true trefoiled arch, of which the lower courses are still extant. Internally the temple is only 6 feet square. The ceiling consists of three courses of overlapping stones. There is a base for the image in the centre. The corner pilasters project not more than 2 inches. They are surmounted by rectangular capitals, which seem to have originally borne in relief the figures of some animals, probably lions, standing back to back. The capitals of the pilasters of the portico are carved with floral scrolls.

Pampur

The flourishing town of Pampur was founded in the beginning of the ninth century A.D. by Padma, who, though the son of a spirit distiller, had through the influence of his sister, a concubine of King Lalitaditya and mother of the minor Chippata-Jayapida, risen to the position of an all-powerful minister. He consecrated the temple of Padmasvami-Vishnu at Pampur, ancient Padmapura. Remains of the cella of a temple are still in existence near the shrine of Shah Hamadan, which has appropriated two of its fluted columns and other carved stones. Probably these fragments are all that remain of Padma's temple. The mosque of Pampur is an inferior imitation of the ziarat (shrine) of Shah Hamadan in Srinagar (Plate XLVI).

Avantipur

Narastan

This is a village situated a little over 20 miles from Avantipur and reached by a rough bridle-path. The road branches off from the Avantipur-Tral road and, skirting the barren hills on the left, debouches into the Arpal valley. From Arpal village Narastan is only 6 miles distant.

The temple (Plate LII), with the exception of the roof, is very well preserved, and possesses several interesting features. It is built on a single base which, unlike other examples of its kind, consists of only four instead of five courses of stones. The cornice is a plain, straightlined, filleted course, of which only the topmost fillet is rounded off into a cyma recta moulding. The base is, as usual, square. The corner pilasters project very slightly from the temple walls. In the middle of each wall is a trefoiled recess surmounted by a highpitched double pediment. This in turn is enclosed by a very shallow closed trefoiled arch, surmounted by a two-storied pediment. The capitals from which the pediments spring are crowned by human—headed birds, facing each other; they are very similar to those of Avantipur. The apex of the pediments is decorated with a squat human figure, which may represent Garuda.

An interesting feature of the temple is the novel treatment of the trefoil arches on the exterior of the shrine walls; the lower trefoil arch is usually shallow or closed, but the upper trefoil is deeply recessed. At Narastan the process has been reversed; the lower trefoil encloses a deeply recessed niche, whereas the upper arch is so shallow that it projects only 2 inches from the plain wall surface. Another remarkable feature is the absence of a circumambulatory path on top of the base, which is a universal feature in temple bases of this size in Kashmir.

The shrine is reached from the courtyard by a flight of four steps. The pilasters of the side-walls of the staircase are adorned with shallow trefoil arches from the apex of which hang two swags of beaded garlands.

The portico projects about 4 feet from the temple wall. Its outer surface is plain except for two pairs of human-headed birds which adorn the capitals. The inner walls of the pilasters are decorated with two pedimental niches, each of which contains the six-armed figure of a goddess. The upper two hands hold a pitcher and a full-blown lotus; the middle two were probably crossed over the breast; and the lower two hang downwards, but the objects they hold are too defaced to be identified. There are miniature fluted columns, standing on bases and surmounted by capitals like those of Avantipur, on each side of the niche. Underneath them are three similar niches containing atlantes.

Internally the temple cell is 8 feet 6 inches square. It faces south and contained a Shiva-linga. Its walls are quite plain except for a string—course at a height of 7 feet 6 inches from the floor, which resembles somewhat the cornice of the plinth outside, and a small double-pedimented niche on the east wall, the upper pediment of which is decorated with the carved figure of a kneeling human being. The left pilaster of the niche is only half-carved, which is another illustration of the method of work of the ancient sculptors who were accustomed to carving large stone blocks in situ. Unlike most of the other temples, this one does not possess a ceiling. The walls rise perpendicularly until the level of the eaves is reached. From this point they begin to contract. Each course is made to project slightly beyond the one below it, until at last the space became so narrow as to be spanned by one square stone, upon which doubtless was placed a finial.

The courtyard is 70 feet square. It is surrounded by a wall which is unornamented except for a plain filleted string-course at about 2 feet from the ground, a pedimental trefoiled niche in the west wall, and a recess 3 feet square. It is roofed over by a coping of sloping stones which rest on a cornice similar to the string-course below. There is a small side entrance near the southwestern angle of the enclosure wall. In front of the temple stairs is a square tank about 8' square and over 2 feet deep.

An elaborate stone conduit poured water into it. The spout of the conduit is carved in front with a full-blown Iotus through the centre of which the water flows; its sides are decorated with grinning makara heads. Above the spout is a stone platform 12 feet by 6 feet 3 inches, which probably served as a bathing place, and in summer would be an admirable place for an afternoon siesta, the more so as the water-conduit runs through its centre. From the tank a drain conducts the water to a chamber in the southeastern corner of the enclosure wall, whence it makes its final exit from the temple yard. This chamber is 9 feet 6 inches by 12 feet 3 inches, and is entered through a narrow doorway 5 feet 8 inches by 1 feet 6 inches. It has a small trefoiled pedimented window 1 feet 3 inches by 1 feet pierced in the wall at a height of 3 feet 1 inches above the ground. It probably served as the bathroom of female worshippers.

Only a few feet to the north of this chamber is a small shrine 2 feet 10 inches square internally. It has a sloping roof and its ceiling was of superimposed squares like that of the Pandrethan temple.

Exactly opposite the sanctum in the middle of the south wall is the gateway. It consists as usual of a double chamber, each measuring 7 feet by 4 inches, connected by a doorway. Each of the chambers was faced by a pair of half-engaged round columns. The lintel of the doorway was, on the outside, carved with a row of crenellations alternating with squares surmounted by lozenges.

The temple is built of greyish limestone and was originally covered with a thick coat of lime plaster, traces of which still exist.

Avantisvara Temple

The village of Avantipur, situated at a distance of 18 miles from Srinagar on the Anantnag cart-road, represents the town of Avantipura, founded by Avantivarman, who reigned from A.D. 855 to 883. Its chief interest centres in two magnificent temples with which its founder embellished it. The first and larger is the temple of Shiva-Avantisvara, whose massive walls rise in forlorn grandeur outside the village of Jaubror, half a mile below Avantipur. The temple, which has been sadly mutilated, is situated in a courtyard enclosed by a massive stone wall, the western face of which is adorned externally with a row of fluted columns, but without any recesses behind. The gateway is in the middle of this wall, and is divided into two chambers by a cross wall. Its walls are not decorated with figure sculpture. The niches and the panels are quite plain.

The base on which the shrine in the centre of the courtyard stands is 57 feet 4 inches square and 10 feet high. To each of its corners was attached a platform about 16' square, which must originally have supported a small subsidiary shrine. It has a stair on each of its four sides like the temple of Pandrethan. The stairs have a width of 28.5 feet, and are supported on either side by flank walls 17.5 feet in length. The sanctum has been reduced to a "confused mass of ruins."

The platforms seem to have originally been attached to the plinth of the temple at one point only, but afterwards they were completely joined with it by means of a connecting wall built of architectural fragments which had fallen from the temple. This arrangement can best be seen at the southeastern corner of the base.

The sole exterior decoration of the temple base, the only part of the building that exists, is a series of projecting facets, the larger of which were originally surmounted by plain rectangular capitals.

In the two rear corners of the courtyard are two subsidiary shrines.

There is a large assortment of architectural fragments strewn about in the courtyard, the most interesting of which are (1) the spandrel of an arch in front of the southern stair, (2) the flower-and-vase capital of a dodecagonal pilaster, (3) the spandrel of another arch by its side, and (4) the base of a pilaster decorated with two seated rams and a dancing girl who plays upon a damaru (small hand-drum) standing on a throne ornamented with two lions at the sides and an elephant, facing, in the middle.

Avantisvami Temple

Half a mile farther up is the small but much more ornate and better preserved temple of Avantisvami-Vishnu. It is the work of Avantivarman's youth, before he came to the throne. It has been reclaimed by the removal of an enormous mass of silt and debris which during a thousand years of neglect (for the temple had already silted up when it suffered from the iconoclasts) had accumulated to a height of about 15 feet and buried the whole structure except the upper part of the walls of the gateway and a shapeless heap of stones in the centre.

The edifice comprises a colonnaded peristyle (Plates XI, VIII and XLIX) enclosing a paved courtyard 174 feet by 148 feet 8 inches, in the centre of which is the main shrine, built on a double base with four smaller shrines at the four corners. The peristyle is comparatively plain externally except on the west side, which has a row of fluted columns. The only decoration on the other three sides is a rectangular string-course and pilasters enclosing rectangular spaces, corresponding respectively with the cyma recta cornice of the plinth and the cells inside.

The entrance, which is in the middle of the west wall, is divided by a cross-wall into two chambers, and is approached by a flight of steps bounded on either side by a plain rail and a side-wall. The front pilasters of the side-walls bear figures of Vishnu and of his consorts carved in relief. On either side of it was a portico supported on tall massive advanced columns, one of which exists to this day, though in a precarious condition.

The wall surface of the entrance is both externally and internally ornamented profusely with sculptured reliefs (Plate L). The larger female figures on the right and left hand walls of the outer chamber represent the goddesses Ganga and Yamuna, easily recognised by their respective vehicles, the crocodile (makara) and the tortoise. The scenes in the rectangular panel on the right-hand pilaster of the wall represent probably a king and his two queens seated in "sportive fashion" on a simhasana (lion throne), here symbolised by two lions facing, one on each side of the panel.

On the two external sides of this pilaster the scenes are the same with slight variations. In the scene in front the lions have been replaced by two standing females. In the southern panel the king has his right hand in the abhayamudra (attitude of granting immunity from fear), and the lady on his right is admiring her own charms, reflected in a round pocket-mirror which she holds in her right hand. In the other two panels the figures are seated on separate cushions; here all three occupy a single long cushion.

Three rectangular panels are carved on the huge block which forms the lowest course of the left wall of the gateway. The largest panel is in the middle and contains a bas-relief. In the centre are three figures, a male and two female chauri-bearers; but much more interesting are the highly caparisoned elephants who are fighting with horned birds of monstrous size.

It is evident that the elephant is fighting at a disadvantage. (Perhaps the scene syrnbolises the fight of Garuda with the Nagas, the latter here being represented by the elephants and not the usual snake gods. Naga means both snake and elephant.) The other two scenes contain each a male figure standing with folded hands between two human-headed birds. Above this is a row of kirtimukhas, or lions' heads, surmounted by a line of rosettes. Higher still is another row of circular panels, eack containing a Garuda. The rectangular panel in the left cross-wall contains a male and two female figures seated on a cushioned sofa in a grove of trees.

They seem to be in a joyous mood. The man is offering the lady at his left hand what seems to be a cup of wine, while the doves at their feet are billing and cooing in sympathy. Above the group is a pedimental niche which contains a smaller representation of the goddess Ganga. On the narrow facets on either side of this niche is a vertical row of standing pairs of male and female figures. This row starts from a rectangular panel which contains the figure of a four-armed Atlas wearing a cushion-like head-dress. The walls were decorated with numerous groups of figures, but unfortunately most of them are now too defaced to be distinguished, much less identified.

The view of the courtyard from the inner chamber of the gateway is charming. In place of the bald monotony of the external surface of the peristyle, the eye feasts on all sides on the picturesque ruins of a beautiful range of cells, preceded by a noble row of fluted columns. Another flight of steps similar to that on the outside leads down to the stone-paved courtyard. The side-walls of this stair are plain, but the pilasters are covered with sculptured reliefs. Each of the smaller panels facing the courtyard depicts an erotic scene.

In the middle of the space between the gateway and the main shrine is a stepped stone which appears to be the base of a Garudadhvaja. It will be remembered that Garuda, the divine eagle, is the vehicle of Vishnu, and also forms the emblem on the banner of his Master. Thus the Garuda-dhvaja column is always an indispensable adjunct of Vaishnava temples.

The central shrine is built on a double base, the only decoration of which is a torus moulding and a cyma recta cornice (Plate LXXIV). The base is intact, but the sanctum which measured 33 feet square externally, has almost disappeared. In fact the only fragments remaining are some parts of the lowest courses and a few stones of the north wall.

Unlike its sister temple lower down the road, this edifice has only one stair. But that apparent deficiency is more than rectified by the sculptured reliefs on its pilasters. The two scenes facing the gateway represent Vishnu, the deity worshipped in the temple, seated in an easy attitude between his two consorts, Lakshmi and Bhumi (?). Lakshmi in the northern group (Plate L) is distinguished by the cornucopia which, even in the late ninth century, to which this temple belongs, was retained as the special emblem of the goddess, who traces her descent, through Gandhara, from the Greek Athene.

Vishnu in the northern relief possesses six arms, two of which, in impartial affection, encircle the bodies of his two consorts, while the remaining four hold his distinctive emblems, the bow, the mace, and the lotus, etc. Below the throne are two pairs of parrots, and the same bird crowns the capitals of the square pilasters from which springs the cusped arch which canopies the divine group. The panel is surmounted by a dentil course consisting of conventional lions' heads (kirtimukhas) alternating with geese and flowers. This again is surmounted by a border of square rosettes (Plate L and Plate LXX, A).

The group on the opposite pilaster is similar to that described above, the main difference being that the god, instead of having six has only four arms. The goddesses in every case have only two arms. Both the god and the goddesses are elaborately ornamented. The former has his hair brushed neatly back and arranged in braids which are tied in knots on the top. Two roses are inserted in the braids just above the ears. Besides the necklace and armlets he wears the mandaramala (garland of celestial flowers). An enormous circular ornamental disc adorns his right ear, while a smaller jewelled pendant is suspended from his left ear. The goddesses, whose exaggerated breasts and attenuated waists are even more profusely ornamented, are crowned with three-peaked tiaras. Their ear-lobes are unusually elongated by the weight of their heavy circular ear ornaments.

The relief on the inner surface of the southern pilaster represents a group of ten figures, the central and the largest pair consisting of a male and a female wearing dhotis. The male wears an ornamental band across his breast (over his right shoulder and under his left arm). The whole group seems to breathe a spirit of profound devotion to some undefined object. It probably represents the major and minor gods coming to worship the image of Vishnu in the temple.

The group opposite also comprises ten persons. The principal figures are those of a bearded and crowned male, probably representing the donor, and a lady, perhaps the princess, who wears a scarf over her head which kangs low down her shoulders, a fashion which the women of Kashmir have preserved to this day. The lady is followed by a female attendant. Above her is a male, who wears a curiously knotted and twisted head-dress.

The courtyard is paved with stone flags, and measures 174 feet east to west by 148 feet 8 inches north to south. The five shrines in the courtyard, arranged in a quincunx, show that the group was intended to belong to the pancharatna (five jewels) class. The shrine in the northeast corner seems to have been dedicated to the river goddess Ganga, as the spout of the pedestal of the image which it contained has been carved in the shape of a makara, or crocodile, which is the vehicle of that goddess. The water trough in the courtyard on the north side of the main shrine was intended to hold the sacred washings of the deity inside the sanctum.

But the chief beauty of the temple lies in its cellular colonnade (Plates XLVIII, LXVIII, and LXIX). It comprises sixty-nine cells, each of which measures on the average 3 feet 8 inches by 4 feet 10 inches, the cell in the centre on each side being larger than the rest and advanced slightly forwards. All of them are preceded by twenty-four-sided columns on plain square bases which have for the most part suffered severely at the hands of the destroyer. The only wall decoration of the peristyle is the range of 138 half-engaged columns (Plate LXXI and Plate LXXII) on the pilasters on both sides of the trefoiled entrance of the cells. The latter were intended to contain replicas of the main image which the temple enshrined. In one or two of them in the eastern wall of the peristyle the pedestals of these images are still found in situ.

A large assortment of antiquities has been unearthed during the excavation of this temple. The most valuable are a series of sculptures which have been placed in the Srinagar Museum. The large jars arranged in a row on the lawn above the excavations were, doubtless, used for the storage of grain and foodstuffs. Among those that have been brought to the Museum is one which bears an inscription mentioning the name of Avantivarman. This record is of interest as being the only independent evidence of the correct identification of the site.

Kalhana states that the Avantisvami temple was occasionally subjected to sacrilegious treatment even in Hindu times. The tyrannical Kalasa (A.D. 1081-1089) confiscated the villages which formed its endowments. Its military possibilities do not seem to have escaped the notice of the ancients, for "its courtyard served as a fortification when, shortly after the accession of King Jayasimha (A.D. 1128), Bhasa, a commander of the royal troops, was besieged at Avantipur by the rebel Damaras of the Holada (Vular) district." In the fourteenth century Sikandar But-shikan completed the destruction which had already begun in the troublous times which followed the reign of Avantivarman.

Martand

The temple of Martand (Plate LIII and Plate LXXIII) is situated at a distance of 5 miles from the town of Anantnag. Being on the top of a lofty plateau, at whose feet stretch the broad verdant plains of Kashmir intersected by a network of rivers, lakes, arid canals, thickly dotted with clusters of busy villages nestling like beehives in closely planted groves of trees, and encircled by snow-clad mountain ramparts—the temple of the Sun, as Martand originally was, commands a superb view, such as the eye rarely lights upon. It is this beauty of situation that contributes so largely to the sense of grandeur with which the sight of these ruins always inspires even the most unimaginative visitors.

Like most mediaeval temples of Kashmir, Martand consists of a courtyard with the principal shrine in the middle and a colonnaded peristyle. The latter is 220 feet long by 142 feet broad and contains eighty-four fluted columns facing the courtyard. The peristyle is externally plain, except on the west side, which originally had a row of columns similar to that of the Avantipur temples.

"The entrance, or gateway, stands in the middle of the western side of the quadrangle, and is of the same width as the temple itself. This proportion is in accordance with the ideas of Hindu architectural grandeur; for the rules laid down by them, as quoted by Ram Raz, give different proportions from six-sevenths to ten-elevenths of the width of the temple, for each different style of gateway from the most simple to the most magnificent. Outwardly the Martand gateway resembles the temple itself in the disposition of its parts and in the decoration of its pediments and pilasters.

It was open to west and east, and was divided into distinct portions forming an inner and outer portico, by a cross wall with a doorway in the centre, which was no doubt closed with a wooden door. On each flank of the gateway the pediment was supported by massive fluted pillars, 17.5 feet in height, or 8 feet higher than those in the quadrangle.

One of these is still standing to the south of the entrance; and the style of the architrave and entablature which connected these pillars with the gateway must have been the same as that of the architrave in the Avantisvami temple described above. I surmise that the front and back pediments of the gateway were supported on similar large pillars; but it is possible that the square foundations, which I observed in the front, may have been only the remains of the wing-walls of a flight of steps. The roof was no doubt pyramidal; for a portion of the sloping mouldings of its pediment was still to be seen on one side." The walls of the gateway are profusely decorated internally and externally, the chief motif of decoration being rows of double pedimented niches alternating with rectangular panels. Most of the pedimented niches contained single standing figures of gods; occasionally they also contained an amorous group similar to those at Avantipur.

The rectangular panels contained sitting groups, floral scrolls, pairs of geese, etc. Each of the two large niches in the side-walls of the inner chamber of the gateway contains the tall figure of a three-headed Vishnu standing between two attendants. Immediately below is the long rectangular panel decorated with a row of dancing urchins striking a variety of attitudes. The temple proper "is 63 feet in length by 36 feet in width at the eastern end and only 27 feet in width at the western or entrance end.

It contains three distinct chambers, of which the outermost, named ardkamandapa or 'half temple,' answering to the front porch of classical fanes, is 18 feet 10 inches square; the middle one, called antarala or 'mid temple,' corresponding to the pronaos of the Greeks, is 18 feet by 4 inches; and the innermost, named garbhagriha, or 'womb of the edifice,' the naos of the Greeks and the cella of the Romans, is 18 feet 5 inches by 13 feet 10 inches. The first is open and highly decorated in accordance with its name, mandapa, meaning literally ' ornamented.' The middle chamber is decorated in the same style; but the inner chamber is plain and is closed on three sides. The walls of the temple itself are 9 feet thick and of its entrance chamber only 4.5 feet thick, being respectively one half and one fourth of the interior width of the building."

"Among the images carved on the walls of the antarala and the antechamber, we notice on the left wall of the former a well executed image of the river-goddess Ganga, standing upon her vehicle, the crocodile, which is looking up towards her. A female attendant on her right holds an umbrella over her head, and a chaurt-bearer is on her left. She holds her usual emblems, a water pot in her left hand and the stalk of a lotus flower in her right. (She is crowned with a double conical tiara.) On the opposite side of the antarala is the river-goddess Yamuna, with her vehicle, the tortoise. Above the niche in the north wall is a relief consisting of a pair of Gandharvas in flight with an umbrella over them.

The statues on the western walls of the antechamber are undoubtedly representations of Vishnu, and what Mr. Fergusson mistook for hoods of snakes are in reality points of their coronets. Each of them is three-faced, like the Vishnu image found in the Avantisvami temple, the left face being that of a boar (Varaha) and the right one that of a man-lion (Narasimha). Both are eight-armed, and their lower hands are placed on the heads of chauri-bearers, as in other images of Vishnu found in the valley. Furthermore, they wear the garland (vanamala) and we also notice the bust of the earth-goddess (Prithivi) between the feet of the statue on the north wall.

Most of the hands of the images are unfortunately broken and weather-worn, and the emblems they hold can no longer be identified. Nor can the fourteen seated figures which occur on the walls of the antechamber below the cornice be identified with certainty. Twelve of them occur in the north and south walls—i.e., six on each, and two on the east wall.

Of the two panels on the east wall, the one on the right seems to represent Aruna, the charioteer of Surya, holding the reins of his seven horses. The pilasters of the great trefoil arch of the antechamber contain images which cannot yet be identified." "The chapels to the north and south of the antechamber each contain two niches 5' 9" by 4' internally, which face to the east and west respectively, possibly an allusion to the rising and setting of the sun."

The roof seems to have been of the pyramidal type common in the temples of Kashmir.

Such was once the magnificent mass of building dedicated to the worship of the Sun, a mass 75' in height, 33' in length, and the same in width including the wings. Entrance was gained by a wide flight of steps which are now covered by ruins.

On each of the other sides was a closed doorway surmounted by a trefoiled arch, and covered by a pediment which rose to a height of 60'. At the angles of the buildings on each side of the doorway were stout pilasters, which were divided into panels, each decorated with a miniature representation of the Aryan style of temple.

These pilasters sustained the entablature, and gave a look of strength and solidity to the walls which was fully needed for the support of the vast and massive roof. This lofty pyramid of stone was itself rendered lighter and more elegant in appearance by being broken into two portions separated by an ornamental band, and by the addition of small niches with pointed roofs and trefoiled recesses, all of which were in strict keeping with the general character of the building.

The peristyle is the largest example of its kind in Kashmir. In the middle of its larger sides there are a pair of large fluted pillars, 13' in height and 8 3/4' apart, somewhat advanced beyond the line of the other cells. "The quadrangle itself contained seventy round, fluted pillars, and ten square parallel pillars which with the four pillars of the central porches make up the number of 84, that was sacred to the sun. Of these about one-half, all more or less imperfect, now remain standing.. .. Each pillar was 9 1/2' in height, and 21 1/2" in diameter, with an intercolumniation of 6' 9 1/2".... The imposts (behind) were surmounted by human-headed birds facing each other, and a smaller bird, looking to the front, ornamented the horizontal mouldings of the pediments ....

About one-third of this entablature still exists, principally on the northeastern side of the quadrangle.

"The other walls of the quadrangle are ornamented by a succession of trefoil-headed panels similar in shape and size to the recessed openings of the interior." As suggested above, it is probable that its western outer facade was adorned by a series of columns similar to that of the two temples at Avantipur.

There is some uncertainty regarding the exact ascription of this temple, owing to the ambiguity of Kalhana's statement. But the most probable assumption, which is strengthened by the architectural style, is that the temple as it exists today was built by King Lalitaditya in the middle of the eighth century A.D.

The courtyard of the temple was excavated recently, and a vast quantity of debris and stones was removed. Among other movable antiquities which the excavations yielded, the most noteworthy are a number of large earthen jars which were found embedded in the floor of the courtyard. Removal of the accumulated debris of centuries from the base of the temple has also brought to light a very important fact—viz., that previous to the construction of the present temple there existed another temple of somewhat smaller dimensions at this site. When the new temple was built, the older temple base was not demolished, but was enveloped by a new base of larger dimensions, as is borne out by the existence of both bases, side by side, one within the other, on the east side of the temple. The older temple was probably the one built on this site by Ranaditya.

Payar

Three miles farther, and situated at the foot of the karewa on the opposite side of the rivulet, is the village of Payar, which contains a very elegant little temple (Plate LI and Plate LXIII). The name Payach, which has obtained currency through Vigne and Cunningham, is not known locally. The identification of the temple with the temple of Narendrasvami, built by Narendraditya circa A.D. 483-490, proposed by General Cunningham, is in keeping neither with the style of architecture according to which it could be assigned to about the eleventh century A.D. nor with its dedication to Shiva, as the name Narendrasvami would presuppose its dedication to Vishnu.

This temple, in spite of, or perhaps more correctly on account of, the feeble attempt that has been made to dismantle it—the top stone of the roof is still out of position—is by far the best preserved example of a mediaeval Kashmiri shrine. It is 8 feet square internally and 21 feet high, including the base, the chief mouldings of which are a plain torus in the middle and a filleted torus on the top. The sanctum is open on all sides, but is reached only by a single flight of steps on the east side. The doorways are rectangular, and are surmounted by a trefoil arch, which in turn is enclosed by a pediment. The pilasters on which the pediments rest are surmounted by capitals bearing pairs of geese with long foliate tails, and the pilasters from which the trefoiled arch springs are crowned by recumbent bull capitals.

The bulls have scarves tied to their humps. The eastern trefoil itself encloses a relief, in which Shiva is seen seated cross-legged on a throne under the canopy of an overhanging tree, surmounted by votaries, two of whom are seated, European fashion, with legs hanging down. On the north side the relief represents Bhairava, the terrible manifestation of Shiva, pursuing a human being, who turns towards him in an attitude of supplication. Behind the Bhairava is a long elephant's trunk. On the west side is the very animated figure of six-armed dancing Shiva.

The upper two arms are raised aloft, holding the two ends of a scarf. The middle two hands are gesticulating, the lowest left hand holds a flower and the right the trident, the special emblem of Shiva. In the left lower corner of the group is a musician playing on a vina (lute); on the right is another beating a drum in accompaniment.

The southern relief represents a three-headed Shiva seated cross-legged on a wicker-work pedestal. The god is only two-armed and wears the Brahmanical thread. In the left lower corner is a seated female, probably his consort, Parvati. The remaining three figures are emaciated, and are perhaps those of ascetics. Over the god's head is seen the flying figure of a Yakhsha. The corner pilasters are crowned by very beautiful floral capitals.

The roof is pyramidal, and is divided into two sections by an ornamental band, consisting of square spaces alternately projecting and receding. "The latter are occupied by flowers, but the projecting ends are carved into three upright mouldings slightly rounded at the top and surmounted by a straight and horizontal band." The resemblance of these triglyph ornaments to the dentils of classical architecture is remarkably striking.

The blank sides of the upper pyramid are relieved by gabled niches which are replicas of the doorways, the only difference being that the trefoil of the latter is replaced by a semicircular top, and the tympanum is filled by a flower-ornament.

The four pediments as well as the apex of the roof were crowned by ribbed melon-like ornaments, two of which are still in existence.

The superstructure is built of ten stones only. "In the interior the walls are plain, but the roof is hollowed out into a hemispherical dome of which the centre is decorated by an expanded lotus flower. The lower edge of the dome is ornamented by three straight-edged fillets and by a beaded circle.

The spandrels are filled by single undraped and winged figures (of rather spirited execution), who with outstretched arms and legs appear to be supporting the roof .... They are probably Yakhshas. The dome itself rests upon the cornice, which is formed of six plain straight-lined mouldings." The ceiling of the Pandrethan temple is a copy of this on a larger scale. The cult image of the temple is a giva-linga, which has an octagonal base.

Malangpura

Halfway between Avantipur and Payar, about 3 miles from each, is the village of Malangpura, partly hidden from the highroad by the projecting spur of the karewa. On the top of this spur are the ruins of a mediaeval stupa, the only part of which that is in position being the base.

The stupa follows the usual plan of other similar structures of its age in Kashmir in that it is square, with two projections on either side and large staircases each of which faces a cardinal point. The most interesting feature of the ruins are the sculptured reliefs which adorn the exterior of the flank walls of the stairs.

Each of them is only partly preserved, but the complete group seems to have represented a furious monster pursuing a man, who is flying precipitately before it. The creature, half-brute and half-reptile, is beaked, horned, and winged, with huge protruding eyes. The artist has represented the climax of the struggle, when the monster overtakes his unfortunate victim; its raised paw crushes the left leg of the fleeing man; the terrible beak opens wide and is about to devour his head. The latter in his desperation raises his left arm and thrusts a dagger into the throat of his enemy.

This is the scene as depicted on the left flank wall of the southern staircase. On the right flank wall of the western stair, the monster and the ornamental wheels behind are much better preserved, though unfortunately the forepart of the relief containing the man is missing.

The monster here has a curly mane, an ornamental necklace, and foliated wings. Its rear paw has five toes, four of which—three in front and one behind—are visible. Behind are two highly decorated discs.

4

Monuments in Srinagar

Khanqah of Shah Hamadan

The city of Srinagar can best and most conveniently be seen from the river. The streets are narrow and often muddy. The river and the canals, on the other hand, form a very pleasant means of communication. As the visitor floats down the sluggish streams many objects attract his attention.

The large and imposing palaces, the modern temples with tin-plated spires glittering in the sun, the brawny, loquacious boatmen plying their little airy craft, their pretty rosy-cheeked babies sprawling in the bottom, heedless of the shrill warnings of the distracted mothers, the curious cantilever bridges which span the river at short intervals—with these and the multifarious other objects of interest and amusement which usually appeal to the newcomer in Kashmir, the present monograph is not concerned. The attention of the reader is therefore specially invited to the extremely large number of architectural stones belonging to ancient Hindu temples which have now been built into the retaining walls of the river banks.

Between the third and fourth bridges on the right bank stands the Khanqah of Shah Hamadan, or, to give him his proper name, Mir Sayyid Ali Hamadani (Plate VI). Tradition ascribes his origin to the city of Hamadan in Persia. Legend further adds that Timur "was one night wandering in disguise about the streets of his capital, Samarkand, and overheard an old man and his wife talking over the prospects of starvation; upon which he took off an armlet, threw it to them, and departed unseen. A pretender Syud, or descendant of the prophet, asked them how they came by the armlet, and accused them of having stolen it.

The matter was made known to Timur, who sagaciously decreed that the owner must be the person who could produce the fellow armlet. He then displayed it in his own possession, and ordered the accuser to undergo the ordeal of hot iron, which he refused, and was put to death in consequence. Timur, moreover, put to death all the other pretender Syuds in the country.

One, named Syud Ali or Shah Hamadan, who really was a descendant of the prophet, accused Timur of impiety, and told him that he would not remain in his country; and by virtue of his sanctity he was able to transport himself through the air to Kashmir. He descended where the Masjid now stands, and told the Hindu fakir to depart. He refused, upon which Shah Hamadan said that if he would bring him news from heaven, he would then believe that he was a great man.

The fakir, who had the care of numerous images, immediately despatched one of them to heaven, upon which Shah Hamadan kicked his slipper after it with such force that the image fell to the ground. He then asked the fakir how he became so great a man; he replied, by doing charitable actions; upon which Shah Hamadan thought him worthy of being made a convert to Islam; and in a few days so many more followed his example that two and a half kirwahs [kharwar = nearly two maunds] of Juneos, or sacred strings worn by the Brahmans, were delivered up by the Hindu proselytes.

The converted fakir himself was called Shyk Baba Wuli [Shaikh Baba Wali], and a penance of forty days performed at his shrine is considered the ne plus ultra of the meritorious." Whatever the religious value of this story, it is certain that the Sayyid must have been a personage of great importance, inasmuch as a number of shrines throughout the valley have been dedicated to his memory.

It is difficult to determine the date of the present structure, but it is practically certain that it does not belong to the time traditionally ascribed to the migration of Sayyid Ali Hamadani to Kashmir. Baron von Hugel, who visited Kashmir in 1835, speaks of it as a modern-looking building. But there is no doubt that a mosque or some such religious edifice stood here at least as early as the reign of Akbar; for Abul Fazl in his Ain-i-Akbari says that "Mir Sayyid Ali Hamadani resided for some time in this city (Srinagar), and a monastery founded by him still preserves his name."

Apart from the cloisters, which have been added later, and the additions and alterations that are being carried on by its present-day caretakers, the original building is a square structure. Its chief structural peculiarity is that it is for the most part built of wooden balks. The spaces between the balks are filled by very small and carefully dressed bricks. Some of the doors and windows are beautiful examples of wood carving, and the wooden cornice of the plinth is an exquisite piece of workmanship.

The interior consists of a single large hall 63' by 43'. On the southern and northern sides are fourteen chambers which now serve the purpose of godowns. The one in the northwest corner contains the tomb of the saint. The only decoration in the interior is the very beautiful panelled wood-work on the walls, to which age has imparted a rich brown colour. The dado consists of a number of panels decorated with carved floral patterns. The larger panels in the walls bear carved on them the names of God, which have been painted in gold. A strong contrast with the sombre hue of the walls is furnished by the glass and glazed work which decorates the external surface of the chamber containing the mausoleum.

The ceiling is supported in the centre on four wooden columns, covered with pieces of wood arranged in fish-bone patterns which originally bore painted inscriptions. Their bases have been carved with lotus leaves, and their capitals, which are sixteen-sided, are adorned with acanthus (?) Ieaf decoration.

Two ladders at the sides give access to the balconies above. The upper floor does not possess any points of interest.

Over the doorway of the shrine is carved an inscription which gives 786 Hijra as the year of Shah Hamadan's death. This date corresponds to A. D. 1384.

Patthar Masjid

"Of the Mughal style as exemplified by buildings in Kashmir it is not necessary to say much, because the style is practically the same as that at Agra, Delhi, and Lahore. The only differences which suggest themselves are that a local grey limestone was generally used in Kashmir for face work; and white marble, owing no doubt to the difficulties of transport, is hardly ever seen." This stone is an excellent material for mouldings and for carving, and is capable of receiving a very high polish, as is testified by the pillars in the pavilion at Shalimar.

Of the Mughal mosques in Kashmir, the Patthar Masjid, "The Stone Mosque," so called in contradistinction to the indigenous wooden mosques of the valley, is the largest surviving example (Plate VII). The facade consists of nine arches, including the large arched portico in the centre. The arched openings are enclosed in shallow decorative cusped arches, which in their turn are enclosed in rectangular frames. The horizontal construction of these arches is remarkable. All of them have recently been closed up with rubble stone masonry.

The half-attached "bedpost "columns in the two outer angles of the jambs of the entrance are noteworthy. The plinth, which is now mostly underground, is surmounted by a lotus-leaf coping. The frieze between the projecting cornice and the eaves is decorated with a series of large lotus leaves, carved in relief, some of which have been pierced, and thus made to serve the purpose of ventilation apertures. A flight of steps in each jamb of the entrance gives access to the roof, which is, as usual in Kashmir, sloping, except in the centre, where there was originally a dome which was later dismantled by the Sikhs. The roof consists of twenty-seven domes, the central one of which is the largest. The domes are mostly ribbed inside, though there are some which are flat or waggon-vaulted.

The roof is supported internally on eighteen extraordinarily massive square columns having projections on two sides. The lower portion of the columns is built of stone and the upper of brick covered by a thick coat of buff-coloured lime plaster.

The enclosure wall is built of brick masonry, with a coat of lime plaster, adorned by a range of shallow arched niches.

The mosque is said to have been built in A.D. 1623 by the Empress Nur Jahan. There is a tradition that, being once questioned regarding the cost of its construction, she pointed to her jewelled slippers and replied, "As much as that." The jest was reported to the mullahs, who unanimously decreed that by this sacrilegious allusion the mosque had become desecrated, and was unfit for religious use. For this reason the Patthar Masjid has never been used as a place of prayer.

Jama' Masjid

The history of the Jama' Masjid of Srinagar is a singularly chequered one. Its original conception and erection are ascribed to Sikandar But-shikan, who reigned in Kashmir from A.D. 1390-91 to 1414-15. He is said to have laid its foundation in A.D. 1398 and completed it in 1402. His illustrious son Zain-ul-abidin is reported to have greatly exerted himself in adding to its aesthetic attractions. He also established an Islamic school as an appendage to the mosque, and endowed it with estates to enable it to defray the cost of maintenance. In A.D. 1479 a large conflagration reduced it to ashes, and the then reigning sovereign, Sultan Hasan Shah, set about its reconstruction with greater splendour.

Unfortunately the king died before completing his task, which was brought to a successful end in A.D. 1503 by Ibrahim Magre, Commander-in-Chief of the Kashmir forces, in the reigns of Muhammad Shah and Fateh Shah. In the year 1620, in the reign of Jahangir, a severe conflagration again broke out in Srinagar and destroyed twelve thousand buildings, among them the Jama' Masjid.

The emperor, who is stated to have been in Kashmir at the time, immediately directed its reconstruction, which was taken in hand and completed in the space of seventeen years. Malik Haidar of Tsodur, the historian of Kashmir, was entrusted with the execution of the work. The inscription on the southern entrance, which was erected about this time, gives the history of the mosque up to this date. In addition to restoration of the mosque the emperor bestowed munificent grants of land, not only for its upkeep, but also to provide subsistence allowance for the caretakers. I'taqad Khan, a provincial governor of Kashmir during the reign of Shah Jahan, was a gross tyrant.

The emperor on a visit to Kashmir dismissed him, and appointed Zafar Khan, the son of the Prime Minister, Asaf Khan, as his successor. The latter drew up a list of the irregularities practised in Kashmir by his predecessor, and submitted it to the emperor, who in a royal farman, or decree, directed remission of all the petty exactions which the former local governors had inflicted upon the inhabitants of the valley. The royal farman was engraved on a block of black marble and set up on the right wall of the southern gateway of the Jama' Masjid, for the benefit of the public.

The document is of extraordinary interest, not only because it illustrates the ways and means to which some unscrupulous governors, gifted with more ingenuity than conscience, had recourse in their haste to amass a fortune, but also as an honourable testimony to the emperor's solicitude for the welfare of his distant Himalayan dependency.

In A.D. 1674 the mosque was for the third time destroyed by fire. It is stated that when the emperor Aurangzeb heard of the accident, his first enquiry was whether the chinars were safe; for he said "the mosque could be rebuilt in a short time; a full-grown chinar can never be quickly replaced." He impressed all the bricklayers and masons of the city into his service, and had the mosque completed within the short period of three years. In his restoration it is evident, both from the building itself and on the authority of history, that the Mughal strictly adhered to the plan of the original mosque of Sikandar Butshikan. Aurangzeb seems to have spent a considerable sum of money on gilding and other evanescent embellishment of— the mosque.

From the time of Aurangzeb down to 1914 the structural history of the mosque is a record of steady decay. The fitful repairs by the Afghan governors did not arrest its downward progress to ruin. In the earlier part of the Sikh regime in Kashmir the mosque was closed and its doors were blocked up. After a period of twenty-one years, it was reopened by Ghulam Muhi-ud-din, the Sikh Governor, who spent nearly a lakh and a half of rupees on its repair.

In Dogra times attempts were more than once made to put it into repair, but they do not seem to have led to any appreciable result. Since the year 1913, however, the Muslims of Kashmir, substantially aided by a grant from His Highness's Government, have put forth their best energies for the achievement of the difficult task, and it has recently been brought to a successful conclusion.

The mosque is a quadrangle and roughly square in plan, its northern and southern sides being 384' in length. Its principal features are the four minars, one in the middle of each side (Plate IX). They are covered by a series of pyramidal roofs, which terminate in an open turret crowned by a high pinnacle (Plate X). All these minars, except that to the west, which contains the pulpit, cover spacious arched entrances which are plain but very imposing.

The southern entrance seems, as now, to have always been the one most commonly used. This is borne out by the fact that the inscriptions—among them Shah Jahan's farman, which would naturally be placed at the most frequented spot in the mosque—have been built into the wall of this entrance. The roof of each minar was supported on eight wooden columns, 50' in height and over 6' in girth, whose modern substitutes still stand on the original square limestone bases. The columns are plain and unornamented. The minars are connected by spacious halls, the principal feature of which is the vast array of 378 wooden columns which support the roof.

The western minar differs from its companions of the other three sides in having slightly larger dimensions and two stairs, one in each jamb of the arch, giving access to the roof and each surmounted by a small brick dome. The gachh (gypsum) plaster is inartistic and of recent date.

The compound is bisected by two broad paths, planned after the manner of a formal Mughal garden. At the point of their intersection has been built a small and insignificant barahdari.

Formerly a small canal which entered through the eastern entrance used to feed the large, but now dilapidated, tank in the compound. The canal fell into disuse when the Srinagar waterworks system was instituted. Its place is now taken by an ordinary P.W.D. water-supply. The water from the tank flows down a small ornamental stone chute, and passing out of the channel leaves the mosque by an underground passage in the west wall. After a meandering course of a quarter of a mile the pretty little rill, now replaced by the usual gutters, emptied itself into the Mar canal. The streamlet was in existence as recently as thirty years ago, and bore the name of Lachhma-kul. It was originally brought from the Sindh by King Zain-ul-abidin, and its first name was Zaina-Ganga.

The most charming feature of the compound, apart from the singularly imposing aspect of the arcaded front of the halls, is a group of shady chinars, which tradition assigns variously to Zain-ul-abidin's and Hasan Shah's reigns. But there seems to be little doubt that some, if not all of them, are of more recent growth.

Sankaracharya Temple

The Sankaracharya temple is situated on the summit of the Takht-i-Sulaiman hill, to the southeast of Srinagar (Plate IV). Neither the hill nor the temple preserves its ancient name; in Hindu times the former bore the name of Gopadri, and the latter—or more probably some earlier structure which occupied its place—that of Jyeshthegvara. But the modern name of the hill seems to be of fairly long standing, as it is mentioned by Catrou, and in a slightly altered form (Koh-i-Sulaiman) by Abul Fazl.

The temple is built on a high octagonal plinth approached by a long flight of steps enclosed by two side-walls which originally bore two Persian inscriptions. One of these was dated A.H. 1069 =A.D. 1659. Both inscriptions disappeared some time in the last few decades. The plinth is surmounted by a low parapet wall 23' 6" long on each side, the inner surface of which was originally adorned by a range of eighty-four round-headed recesses enclosed in rectangular panels. The greater part of the wall has now fallen. The shrine consists of a cell, circular inside, with a diameter of 13' 2". Externally it is square with two projecting facets on each side (Plate V). The surface is plain, except for the salient and re-entering angles of the facets.

The maximum thickness of the walls in the middle of each facet is 8' 2". The interior of the sanctum is covered by a modern ceiling "composed of flat stone slabs and wooden boards, which rest on two lintels of the same material, themselves supported on four columns in the centre of the room. The southwest column bears two Persian inscriptions, one of which states that the column on which it is engraved was carved by a mason named Bihishti in the year 54—i.e., A.H. 1054, corresponding to A.D. 1644. The date falls in the reign of Shah Jahan. It is obvious, therefore, that this ceiling with its columns was erected in the time of that king."

The original ceiling, which this modern addition has hidden from view, is dome-shaped and built of horizontal courses of kanait or kanjur (a kind of light and porous limestone). The absence of the trefoiled entrance to the sanctum, and similar niches on the other three sides, is remarkable. In this respect, as in the circular interior plan, this temple is similar to the larger temple at Loduv. The brick roof seems to have been constructed within the last century.

The date of this temple has been a source of controversy among archaeologists. General Cunningham and, after him, Lieut. Cole assigned it to the times of Jalauka (whom they date 220 B.C.) on the strength of local tradition. This theory has been rejected, firstly on architectural grounds, and secondly because of the doubtful character of the tradition.

Another theory, advanced by Fergusson, is that the temple was built in the reign of Jahangir. He says that "the temple as it now stands was commenced by some nameless Hindus, in honour of Shiva, during the tolerant reign of Jahangir; and that the building was stopped at the date engraved at the staircase, A.H. 1069 (A.D. 1659), the first year of the reign of the bigoted Aurangzeb. It was then unfinished, and has consequently remained a ruin ever since, which may give it an ancient look." But Fergusson's conclusion was based on arguments which appear to have little foundation. Among other things the Jesuit Catrou, who published his History of the Mughal Empire in 1708 A.D., only one year after Aurangzeb's death, says that the Kashmiris are descended from the Jews. "Moses is a very common name there; and some Ancient Monuments still to be seen discover 'em to be a People come out of Israel.

For instance the ruins of an Edifice built on a high mountain is called at this Day the Throne of Solomon." Again, Bernier, who accompanied Aurangzeb to Kashmir in 1665, writes of the existence of an "extremely ancient building, which bears evident marks of having been a temple for idols, although named Tact-Souliman, the Throne of Solomon."

These statements show that as early as the beginning of the reign of Aurangzeb the origin and authorship of the temple were lost in the mists of antiquity. They also prove that the temple had already fallen into disuse and ruin; and its construction, therefore, could not have been begun in the reign of Jahangir and stopped by Aurangzeb.

Kalhana, in his Rajatarangini (i, verse 341), definitely states that king Gopaditya built a shrine of Jyeshthesvara on the Gopadri (modern Takht-i-Sulaiman), but it cannot be asserted with certainty that the present temple is the same as that which was built by Gopaditya. It appears, however, probable that that shrine occupied the same position. Gopadityais date, and consequently that of his buildings, is uncertain. But the conjecture that the present temple must be at least a century or so earlier than that highly finished example of Kashmir architecture, the Martand temple, seems plausible.

To the north of the base is a low cell 10' 8" square, entered through a plain and nearly circular-headed low doorway. The ceiling is flat and built of plain stone slabs placed on long stone joists, which rest on remarkably long beams supported on two octagonal columns.

To the southeast of the temple base, slightly lower down the hill, is a tank 10' 1" square.

In the area in front of the temple are the ruins of two Muslim structures, probably the remains of the small mosque and garden mentioned by Bernier, and belonging perhaps to the reign of Shah Jahan, when the Persian and Arabic inscriptions in the temple were put up.

The temple of Sankaracharya commands one of the finest views in the whole of Kashmir. The view of the city with its green, turfed roofs, covered in the spring with iris, tulip, and a variety of other flowers, is without a doubt unique.

Tomb of Zain-ul-abidin's Mother

A couple of furlongs lower down the river, between the fourth and the fifth bridges, is the Sri Ranbir Ganj, the busiest and most important trading mart in Kashmir. Near it are seen the high and massive domes of the tomb of the mother of Zain-ul-abidin, towering far above the gabled roofs of the surrounding houses (Plate VIII).

The most attractive chapter in the history of the Muslim rule in Kashmir is the reign of Zain-ul-abidin (1421-1472). He was a patron of the arts and industries, and as tolerant to his Hindu subjects as his father, Sikandar But-shikan, was bigoted. But though he is said to have occasionally made pilgrimages to Hindu shrines, he does not seem to have scrupled in using Hindu remains for his own purposes. The superstructure alone of his mother's tomb was erected by him. The plinth with its filleted torus cornice is entirely Hindu (Plate LXXIV); so is the trefoiled entrance and its still undisturbed massive jambs. In plan it is square, with the angles cut off and replaced by rectangular projections. The superstructure follows the same plan, and consists of a single chamber in the middle with projections recessed internally at the angles, roofed over by five domes, the largest naturally being in the centre.

"Its principal features are the glazed and moulded blue bricks, which are studded at intervals in the exterior walls, the semicircular brick projections, on the drum of the main dome, and the moulded string-courses and sunk panels on the drums of the cupolas." The wooden lintels of the ventilation apertures are remarkably well preserved.

Inside, hanging from an iron plate attached to the apex of the central dome, is an iron chain which has given rise to the misconception, common among the Hindus of Kashmir, that the structure in its present shape was originally a Panchamukha (five-faced or fiveheaded) temple, such chains being usually found in Hindu shrines, attached to the principal bell.

Immediately to the north of this building is a Hindu enclosure wall with gateway, which contains a number of tombs, one of which is said to preserve the remains of the king himself. This wall, like that of the Sankaracharya temple, has been the object of much controversy. Cunningham and Cole ascribed it to a date as early as the fourth or fifth century A.D.

This theory was contested by Fergusson, who, on the strength of the resemblance of the miniature arches which decorate this wall to similar decorative features in Muslim architecture, maintained that it was built by the Muslims themselves at the time they erected the mausoleum. But it is probable that Cunningham and Cole, who actually saw it, were nearer the truth than Fergusson, who judged only from photographs. The wall is a real Hindu one, as its materials and massiveness amply prove, though it is undoubtedly later than the fifth century A.D. A further proof of its Hindu origin is the number of carved stones still found round the site, which bear sculptured reliefs of Hindu deities.

The whole group is enclosed in a massive stone wall with a ridged coping.

This outer wall, as well as its two entrances, one on the riverside and the other opening on the road, likewise date back to Hindu times.

Since the time of Zain-ul-abidin this enclosure has been used as a cemetery, and many of the notabilities of Muslim Kashmir are interred here, among them the famous Tartar invader Mirza Haidar Gurgan, the cousin of Babar, who made his first raid into Kashmir from Turkistan and occupied it a second time in the name of Humayun, during the latter's exile from Hindustan. The following inscription on his tombstone gives the date of his death (A.H. 958=A.D. 1551).

Shah Gurgan Mirza Haidar akhir

Ba mulke shahadat zadah kus-i shahi

Qaza-e Ilahi chunin bud-o tarikh

Shuda bahr-i vaslash, Qaza-e Ilahi.

Translation: "At last the King Mirza Haidar Gurgan beat his royal drum (to announce his departure) for the realm of martyrdom. Such was the will of God and (even) the date of his union (with God) is contained in (the phrase) ' will of God.'"

The Hari Parbat Fort

The hill of Hari Parbat (Plate XI), crowned by the Pathan fort which is visible from every part of the city, has from time immemorial been a place of great sanctity in Kashmir. The name is the Kashmiri equivalent of the Sanskrit sarika-parvata, "the hill of Sarika" (har= Indian maina). Legend, corroborated by modern science, informs us that the valley was, in prehistoric times, a vast lake, which must have been one of the most beautiful in the world.

In this lake dwelt the water-demon Jalodbhava. The Sarikamahatmya tells us, circumstantially, the story of the defeat and destruction of this demon: how the monster wrought havoc among the mountains of the adjacent districts, but being invulnerable in his own element, and declining to fight at a disadvantage on land, continued his life of depredation in impudent security for a long time; how the gods fumed and stormed in impotent rage, and finally resolved to lay the matter before the Almighty Mother Sati, the controller of the titanic forces of nature; how she assumed the form of a Sarika bird (maina) and taking a pebble in her beak dropped it at the spot where she knew the demon was lying, lulled into false security; and finally how the pebble swelled into gigantic proportions and crushed the demon by its weight.

The pebble to this day survives under the name of Hari Parbat, and a depression in the ground outside the Sangin Darwaza of the fort wall is pointed out as the spot wherefrom the panting breath of the demon forced its way out, as he was struggling under the crushing weight over him. The legend adds that the gods in grateful memory of their deliverance took up their abode here, which accounts for the fact that every individual stone, large and small, on this hill is reverenced by the orthodox Brahmans as the representative of one of the thirty-three crores of gods which comprise the Hindu pantheon.

In modern times, both Hindus and Muslims have appropriated parts of the hill for their shrines; but neither the shrine of Chakresvari nor the ziarat of Makhdum Sahib possesses any architectural interest. The fort which crowns the summit is a commonplace structure (Plate XI), but this cannot be said of Akbar's rampart and its gates, Kathi Darwaza and Sangin Darwaza, and the mosque of Akhun Mulla Shah, which are well worth a visit.

The rampart, which is for the most part in ruins, is nearly 3 miles in circumference. The Kathi Darwaza seems to have been the principal entrance, judging from the fact that the inscriptions have been put up only here. It is a very simple structure, comprising a domed chamber in the middle with two side-recesses. Its only external decorations are rectangular and arched panels and two beautiful medallions, in high relief, on the spandrels of the arch.

Akbar's inscription runs as follows:

Bina-e qila'-e Nagar-Nagar bud
Ba 'ahad-e padshah-e dad-gustar
Sar-e Shahan-i 'alam Shah Akbar
T'ali Shanahu Allah-u Akbar
Shahanshah-e ki dar 'alam misalash
Na bud ast-o na khwahad bud digar
Karor-o dah lakh az makhzan firistad
Du sad ustad Hindi jumla chakar
Na kardah hechkas bigar anja
Tamami yaftand az makhzanash zar
Chil-o char az julusi padshahi
Hazar-o shash zi tarikh-e payambar.

Translation: The foundation of the fort of Nagar-Nagar was laid in the reign of the just sovereign, the king of kings, Akbar, unparalleled among the kings of the world, past or future. He sent one crore and ten lakhs (of rupees) from his treasury and two hundred Indian master-builders, all his servants. No one was forced to work without remuneration. All obtained their wages from his treasury. (In the) forty-fourth year after the accession of the Emperor (and) 1006 after the prophet. The second inscription was erected by the officer in charge of the works and runs as follows:

Bina-e qila'-e Nagar-Nagar ba-'aun Allah
Ba hukm-i Shah-i Jahan Zilallah Akbar Shah
Ba sa'ye Mir Muhammad Husain gasht tamam
Haqir banda-e az banda-ha-e Akbar Shah
Dawam-i daulat-i in Shah ta abat bata
Ba haqq-i Shahidan La-ilaha-il-allah.

Translation: The foundation of the fort of Nagar. Nagar was completed, by favour of the Almighty, under orders of the king of the world, Shadow of God, Emperor Akbar, and through the instrumentality of Mir Muhammad Hussain, the least among the servants of King Akbar. May the prosperity of this king enture for ever, through the grace of the martyrs of the Faith. There is no Got but God. The Sangin Darwaza, "the stone gate," differs from Kathi Darwaza in being more ornate. The exterior is decorated by two corbelled windows, and there are two stairs, one on each side, which give access to the roof.

According to tradition, which is still living, the construction of the Hari Parbat, or, as Akbar named it, Nagar-Nagar, rampart was started as a relief work, to alleviate the distress of the people during a famine. The historian Suka states that the emperor, on hearing of the hardship inflicted upon the citizens by the troops, who for want of accommodation had been quartered upon them, had a cantonment built on the slopes of the Hari Parbat hill, which from that time became a fiourishing settlement. Bernier, who saw it three-quarters of a century later, speaks of it as "an isolated hill, with handsome houses on its declivity, each having a garden."

Pir Haji Muhammad Sahib

Less than half a mile from the ruins described above, on the way to the Jama' Masjid by way of Safa Kadal, is another enclosure with a structure in the centre, which is now doing duty as the tomb of Pir Haji Muhammad, a Muslim saint. In plan it is similar to the tomb of Zain-ul-abidin's mother, the only difference being that this has two flights of steps facing east and west, and the latter has only one, which faces west. There is no doubt that the plinth and the corners of the superstructure, as they are at present, are in their original position, and have never been tampered with.

The spaces between the stone pilasters at the corners have been filled in with screen walls of kanjur masonry, the larger sides of which are decorated externally with three closed panels. This appears to have been a later addition. A curious fact about this structure is that the two flights of steps are also later additions, though undoubtedly they have been transplanted from some Hindu site. Proof for this conjecture is furnished by the fact that the cornice of the plinth, a cyma recta, is not bonded with the masonry of the stairs, and that carved stones evidently not originally intended for the purpose have been used in the steps.

In the eastern corner of the courtyard is a smaller enclosure partitioned off from the main area; this also contains a trefoiled niche and some fluted columns.

There is a small square Muslim brick tomb within the compound wall.

The position of these ruins suggested to Sir Aurel Stein their "possible identity with the temple of Vishnu Ranasvamin which Kalhana mentions as founded by King Ranaditya. This temple must have enjoyed considerable celebrity up to a comparatively late period."

Cemetery of Baha-ud-din

Outside the rampart at a distance of less than two furlongs from the mosque of Akhun Mulla Shah is the cemetery of Baha-ud-din Sahib. It contains numerous Hindu remains, among them the ruins of a massive gateway standing near the entrance, which is traditionally believed to be a part of the "Pravaresa "temple built by Pravaresena II. It also contains the graves of some of the most prominent personages of Muslim Kashmir. One of the tombstones bears a bilingual Sanskrit and Arabic inscription which mentions the name of Muhammad Shah, the puppet ruler who was made king and dethroned no less than four times.

Akhun Mulla Shah's Mosque

The little mosque situated a little way up the hill below the shrine of Makhdum Sahib was built by the crown prince Dara Shikoh, son of Shah Jahan, for his tutor Akhun Mulla Shah (Plate XII). It is built of a beautiful grey limestone. The stone lotus finial over the pulpit is the only example of its kind surviving in Kashmir. The only external decorations are the rectangular panels enclosing cusped arches. "Its plan is singular, the design of the prayer chamber being repeated on the east side of the courtyard and forming the gateway. On the north and the south sides of the courtyard are arcades, treated in the same way as the wings of the prayer chamber. Usually the arcades round the quadrangle in front of a mosque are treated quite differently from any part of the prayer chamber. The somewhat cramped proportions of the courtyard in this case may be due to the slope of the hill on which it stands, and the difficulty which would have been experienced in making the prayer chamber wider."

On a lower level are the ruins of the arched halls wherein pilgrims used to lodge. A little further off is the hammam, which is now closed up. On the lintel of its doorway is the following inscription:

Tarikh-i hammam-o masjid-i Sultan Dara Shikoh

Hammam-i tu o masjidat ai dida baz

Garm ast yake yake jama'at pardaz

Tarikh-i bina-i har du ra goyad Shah

Yak ja-i wazu amad-o yak ja-i namaz.

Translation: The date of the construction of the hammam and the mosque of Sultan Dara Shikoh.

Thy hammam and thy mosque: one affords warmth and the other adorns the congregation. The king tells the date of the foundation of both: the one is the place of ablution and the other the place of worship.

The last line contains the chronogram giving the date, A.H. 1059, corresponding to A.D. 1649.

Mosque and Tomb of Madin Sahib

Among the pre-Mughal Muslim buildings of Kashmir, one of the most prominent is the mosque of Madin Sahib at Zadibal. It is also interesting as it shows to perfection the way in which the early Muslims used the materials of the Hindu temples. The group of buildings at Vitsarnag and a number of others strewn about the city belong to this series.

The base is square and is built entirely of materials belonging to a plinth of a mediaeval temple. Even the arrangement of courses is identical with that of the ordinary temple base. The superstructure consists of four walls, adorned externally with trefoiled brick niches. The upper foil is pointed, but in the case of the doorway it is ogee-shaped. The corner pilasters of the walls as well as pilasters of the niches stand upon bases, and are surmounted by capitals which are purely Hindu in style. The spandrels of the arches of the niches are decorated with beautiful tracery work. Their entablature is distinctly Hindu.

The cornice over the walls is composed of half a dozen courses of wood, the most prominent feature of which is the double series of dentils and metopes, the latter bearing delicate open-work carving. Above these are the eaves, which are adorned with a row of wooden tongues projecting downwards. The chamber is covered by a pyramidal earth and birch-bark roof overgrown with a jungle of white and blue irises.

On the apex of the pyramid was the spire, the only remnants of which that exist are a single long upright pole and a few pieces of timber. The entrance to the mosque is, of course, through the east wall. The wooden doorway is elaborately carved, and is flanked by two fluted stone columns originally belonging to the adjoining Hindu ruins. The interior is plain.

The ceiling of khatamband (thin pieces of wood worked into geometrical patterns) is supported on four multi-sided wooden columns.

To the north of the mosque is the tomb of the saint. In ancient times it must have presented a brilliant spectacle, as its entire wall surface was decorated with glazed tiles, most of which have unfortunately been removed and sold out of Kashmir. A few fragments are preserved in the Pratap Singh Museum, Srinagar. When Nicholls of the Archaeological Survey of India visited Kashmir in 1905, he found considerable portions of the tile decoration in good preservation.

The left spandrel of the entrance arch was adorned with a very well executed representation of a beast with the body of a leopard, changing at the neck into the trunk of a human being, shooting apparently with a bow and arrow at its own tail, while a fox is quietly looking on among flowers and "cloud-forms." The "cloud-forms "are common in Chinese and Persian art. The principal beast in the picture is about 4 feet long, and strikes quite an heraldic attitude. The human chest, shoulders, and head are unfortunately missing.

The tail ends in a kind of dragon's head. As for the colours, the background is blue, the trunk of the man is red, the leopard's body is yellow with light green spots, the dragon's head and the fox are reddish-brown, the flowers are of various colours. Besides the spandrels there is more tile-work in the building. The jambs of the archway are lined with squares, many of which have fallen out and been put back in the wrong place. None of these is of any special interest, except that they show that tile-work was used on masonry buildings in Kashmir before Mughal days. There is, however, an interesting narrow border above the dado on the east facade representing a flowing floral pattern interwoven with the heads of donkeys and lions.

Both the tomb and the mosque were built in memory of the same person, and the inscription on the lintel of the entrance of the mosque records the date of its erection as A.H. 888 (A.D. 1483) in the reign of Zain-ul-abidin. The tomb may have been built a few years later, though it is not impossible that it was built at the same time as the mosque, for among Muslims the practice of building tombs during the lifetime of their future occupants is not uncommon.

Around these two structures, and on the way between them and the Sangin Darwaza of the fort, there are numerous Hindu remains, all of which have grievously suffered at the hands of the iconoclast. Many of them have been converted into mosques, though even these latter have now fallen into desuetude.

Mughal Gardens

The valley of Kashmir provided a magnificent field for the garden-planning genius of the Imperial Mughals. Its salubrity of climate, its inexhaustible supply of water, its grassy alluvial mountain slopes, presented opportunities which the emperor's certainly did not neglect. Some of the most charming spots in a valley which itself has deservedly obtained the title of the "Paradise of the Indies "were selected as royal pleasure haunts; and during the four successive reigns of the greatest of the Mughal emperors a series of splendid gardens was constructed, which are famous in the world for their natural charm and beauty of environment.

Among the gardens on the banks of the Dal, Chashma-i-Shahi, Nishat, and Shalimar are the best preserved and most frequented. Remains of other gardens exist, but they are far too ruinous to merit the attention of the modern visitor; among these perhaps the most notable was the Bagh-i-Nagin, the garden of Akbar. Nasim, situated opposite to the Shalimar Bagh, contains a splendid park of shady old chinars.

Chashma-i-shahi

This is the smallest, though not on that account the least attractive, of the Mughal gardens of Kashmir. It is situated at a distance of five and a half miles from Srinagar, a little less than a mile off the road to Nishat. The conformation of the ground round about shows that the garden can never have been large, but there is evidence to prove that it was not as circumscribed as it is now. The two barahdaris as well as the surrounding wall and the side entrance belong to recent times. The cascades, the plinths of the barahdaris, the watercourses, tanks, and fountains, are genuine Mughal works, save, of course, for the restorations. The lowest terrace has a tank in the centre containing five fountains arranged as a quincunx. A flight of steps on each side of the barahdari leads up to the second terrace and to the ground-floor of the barahdari itself.

This is one of the most favoured haunts of tourists in spring and early summer, for the view it commands of the Dal lake is one of the most charming that can be had anywhere, at any rate among those which are easy of access.

In spring, when the fields of the blossoming rape-seed flank the verdant hill slopes with gold; when the snowcapped mountains are being ceaselessly washed by melting snows and frequent showers; when in sunny intervals white masses of downy clouds are seen floating majestically in the translucent azure of the sky, their shadows trailing after them as if caught by the sharp mountain peaks; when the lake is free from weeds and reeds—beardless, as the Kashmiris call it—and its two small islets of Rupalank and Sonalank, the Chahar-chinar, are like two emeralds set in the sapphire shield of the Dal; when vast patches of the slopes of the Chashma-i-Shahi hill and the Hari Parbat are covered with red and white almond blossoms, the fortunate spectator stands entranced as he gazes out of the arch of the barahdari, his feelings lulled by the gentle murmur of the little fountain that plays in the centre of the hall.

The tank in the second terrace contains only one fountain and a small carved chute, down which the water of the channels in the upper terraces comes rippling joyously. All these fountains, channels, and cascades are fed by the real Chashma-i-Shahi, a truly "royal "spring, which perennially gives forth its wealth of the coolest and purest water in a lotus basin built in the centre of a Mughal platform.

The pavilion which covers it is unusually ugly and dilapidated. According to an inscription said to have been put up at the gateway, the garden was constructed in the reign of Shah Jahan, probably by the emperor himself. The exact wording of the verse which contained the date is as follows:

Guftamash bahr-i Chashma tarikhe,
Guft bar go kausar-i Shahi.

Translation: "I enquired of him regarding the date of the spring; he replied, ' say kausar-i shahi ' (the royal spring)."

The term kausar-i-shahi is synonymous with Chashma-i-Shahi, and according to the abjad system of reckoning gives the Hijra year 1042, corresponding with A.D. 1632-33.

Nishat Bagh

Returning from the Chashma-i-Shahi to the main road, the visitor proceeds 2 1/2 miles to Nishat Bagh. This is the most favoured resort of pieasure-seekers in Kashmir. "Its twelve terraces, one for each sign of the zodiac, rise dramatically high and higher up the mountain-side from the eastern shore of the lake. The stream tears foaming down the carved cascades, and fountains play in every tank and watercourse, filling the garden with their joyous life and movement. The flower beds on these sunny terraces blaze with colour—roses, lilies, geraniums, asters, gorgeous tall-growing zinnias, and feathery cosmos, pink and white. Beautiful at all times, when autumn lights up the poplars in clear gold and the big chenars burn red against the dark blue rocky background, there are few more brilliant, more breathlessly entrancing sights than this first view of Asaf Khan's Garden of Gladness" (Plate XIII).

The lowest terrace has unfortunately been cut off by the modern road, which has likewise shorn Shalimar of part of its length. The two wooden doorways as well as the gaudily painted barahdari on the third terrace are innovations which date from the time of Wazir Pannu's governorship of Kashmir in the reign of the late Maharaja Ranbir Singhji. These Mughal gardens of Kashmir owe a heavy debt of gratitude to this gentleman, if not for restoring them to their original grandeur, at any rate for arresting their further decay. He also repaired them thoroughly according to his lights; and if his barahdaris and porticoes do not bear comparison with similar structures of the Mughals, not he but the times to which he belonged are responsible.

The brightest and most fragrant spot in the garden is undoubtedly the second terrace, with its thick groves of Persian lilacs, its high, broad, and vertical cascade of sparkling water, and its beds of brilliant pansies. The twenty-three small niches in the arched recess immediately behind the cascade were originally intended to contain rows of lamps, whose flickering light, reflected and multiplied in the transparent sheet of water behind which they lay, must have presented a singularly pleasing spectacle at night.

Two flights of stone steps which survive from the date of their original construction give access to the third terrace. The barahdari is a two-storied structure. In the middle of the lower floor "is a reservoir about fourteen feet square and three feet deep, with five fountains, the one in the centre being the only old stone fountain left in the garden. On a summer day there are few more attractive rooms than the fountain hall of this Kashmir garden house. The gay colours of the carved woodwork shine through the spray in delightful contrast with the dull green running water. Through a latticed arch a glimpse is caught of the brilliant garden terraces and their waterfalls flashing white against the mountain side.

Looking over the lake which glitters below in the sunshine, the views of the valley are bounded by the distant snowcapped peaks, the far country of the Pir Panjal. Climbing roses twine about the painted wooden pillars, and nod their creamy flowers through the openings of the lattice. All the long afternoon a little breeze ruffles the surface of the lake and blows in the scent of the flowers, mingling it with the drifting fountain spray; for the terrace below the pavilion is planted after the old custom with a thicket of Persian lilac."

Here begins the long series of open terraces each rising higher than the one preceding it—which terminates in the eleventh terrace at the upper end of the garden. They are bisected by a broad watercourse, which on certain days in the week is converted into a bounteous stream with numerous fountains playing in its midst, saturating the atmosphere with their driving spray. A feature of this garden are the beautiful marble thrones which span the watercourses at intervals. These are now, as they undoubtedly were in Mughal times, the favourite seats of visitors to the garden. The tank in the eleventh terrace contains a group of twenty-five fountains. From this terrace a flight of stone steps leads to the last, and, in the eyes of its Mughal founder, Asaf Khan, the most sacred part of the garden, the zenana enclosure.

The low parapet wall which screened this terrace from the remainder of the garden is still in existence. At the upper end of the footpath near the pavilion is a remnant of the original brick pavement. An octagonal tower is built at each end of the retaining wall of the terrace, and contains a stair which leads down to the lower and more exposed parts of the garden.

Strolling down the flower-bordered walks on the right side of the channel, the visitor who makes his exit into the second terrace will notice two rather well-executed elephants, standing on either side of a vase containing lotuses, carved on the stone lintel of the doorway. The presence of these animals would show, if other evidence were wanting, which is not the case, that the Nishat Bagh was built before the time of Aurangzeb. Perhaps he did not enter the garden, as it was a private one, and did not belong to the king, which may also account for Bernier not mentioning it.

The original approach to the garden was from the lake, which was also its lower boundary. The old flight of stone steps which gave direct access to the garden is still in an excellent state of preservation.

There is a story that the emperor Shah Jahan, who visited Kashmir in 1633, "decided that the garden was altogether too splendid for a subject, even though that subject might happen to be his own prime minister and father-in-law. He told Asaf Khan on three occasions how much he admired his pleasure-ground, expecting that it would be immediately offered for the royal acceptance.

But if Shah Jahan coveted his neighbour's vineyard, the Wazir was a no less stiff-necked Naboth; he could not bring himself to surrender his cherished pleasaunce to be ' a garden of herbs 'for his royal master, and he remained silent. Then as now, the same stream supplied both the Royal Garden (Shahlimar) and Nishat Bagh, which lies on the mountain fide between Shalimar and the city of Srinagar. So Shah Jahan in his anger ordered the water-supply to be cut off from Nishat Bagh, and was avenged, for the garden he envied was shorn of all its beauty.

"Nothing is more desolate than one of these great enclosures when their stone-lined tanks and water channels are dry and empty. Asaf Khan, who was staying in his summer palace at the time, could do nothing, and all his household knew of his grief and bitter dis—appointment. One day, lost in a melancholy reverie, he at last fell fast asleep in the shade by the empty watercourse. At length a noise aroused him; rubbing his eyes, he could hardly believe what he saw, for the fountains were all playing merrily once more and the long carved water-chutes were white with foam.

A faithful servant, risking his life, had defied the Emperor's orders, and removed the obstruction from the stream. Asaf Khan rebuked him for his zeal and hastily had the stream closed again. But the news reached the Emperor in his gardens at Shalimar; whereupon he sent for the terrified servant and, much to the surprise of the Court, instead of punishing him, bestowed a robe of honour upon him to mark his admiration for this act of devoted service; at the same time granting a sanad which gave the right to his master to draw water from the garden from the Shalimar stream."

Pari Mahal

The striking group of arched terraces perched higher up on the mountain slope to the west of Chashma-i-Shahi is Pari Mahal, "the fairies' abode," a ruined garden palace, the construction of which is ascribed by tradition to the ill-starred prince Dara Shikoh, who was beheaded in 1659 by order of his brother Aurangzeb. Despite its dilapidated condition, it is easy to determine its principal features; for the garden has, probably owing to its difficulty of access, escaped the restoration to which the other Mughal gardens in Kashmir have been subjected. Pari Mahal differs from other Kashmir gardens in that it does not possess any cascades or water chutes, though it seems probable that there were fountains in the tanks. Water was mainly conducted by underground earthen pipes, though a few traces of open watercourses have also been found. The garden consists of six terraces, with a total length of about 400'. The width of the terraces varies from 179' to 205'.

In the uppermost terrace are the ruins of two structures, a barahdari facing the lake, and a water reservoir built against the mountainside. The reservoir was fed from above by a spring, which has since gone dry, and of which the only extant remains are the fragmentary stone conduit and the retaining wall against the hillside. It is a simple chamber, built of rubble stones in lime, with a facade of two small arches.

Internally it measures 11' 3" by 5', and has a recess in each of its walls. Water flowed through an arched drain pierced in the front wall which is now partially blocked up. At each corner of the terrace wall is a flight of steps leading to the lower terrace, measuring 22' 3" by 4' 3". In the middle of the second terrace exactly in front of the barahdari is a large tank with brick sides measuring 39' 6" by 26' 6". The facade of the retaining wall is ornamented with a series of twenty-one arches, including two of the side-stairs.

The arches are built in descending order of height from the centre. Each of them is surmounted by a niche, the height of which increases in proportion to decrease in the height of the arch. The central arch is covered with a coat of fine painted plaster, which seems to have always served as a favourite board for scribbling notices in pen and pencil. Various people have recorded on this the date of their visit to the garden. Among them was the cruel Azad Khan, a Pathan Governor. His amanuensis, Malik Sabir Munshi, has scribbled the following sentence in black ink:

"Batarikhi bist-o nuhum mahi Rabi-us-sani s. 1199 .... Ittifaq bahamrahi sawari kasir-ul-iqtidar Sardar Azad Khan nazim-i soba-i Kashmir mutabiq sair-o shihr warid-i in makan farhat asar gardidah "Faqir haqir Malik Sabir Munshi.

Translation: "On the 29th of Rabi-us-sani s. 1199 (A.D.1784-85) the humble mendicant Malik Sabir Munshi visited this abode of bliss in the suite of the most honourable Sardar Azad Khan, Governor of the Province of Rashmir, while (he was) on an expetition for pleasure and sport."

This terrace seems to have been screened off from the lower court by a parapet wall, which is still extant in parts.

The third terrace is, architecturally, the most interesting portion of the garden. The entrance, which is of the usual Mughal type, arched in front and behind with a central domed chamber, is in the middle of the east wall, and is covered with a coat of fine painted plaster. On either side of it are a series of spacious rooms: the one to its north seems to have been the hammam. Fragments of the water-pipe are still to be seen projecting from a corner of its domed ceiling.

Its interior is the most highly decorated of all the rooms in Pari Mahal. On the south side of the entrance are two other chambers, but it is difficult to say to what use they were put. Both of them have pipes inserted into their ceilings, the one nearest the gateway having only one, but the other, two; possibly the latter chamber was used as a kitchen. The western half of the retaining wall has recently fallen; doubtless it also contained chambers similar to those on the other side.

In the central recess of the arcade is visible the originally hidden earthen pipe which conveyed water from the terrace above. From it the water flowed through an open channel and an underground pipe, which ran side by side, and entered the barahdari at the middle of the broad end of the terrace. In all probability the channel formed a tank in the centre of the principal chamber and then emptied itself into the pipe which ran underground, of which traces are still visible on the floor of the barahdari.

It is probable that these three terraces were reserved solely for the prince's private use.

The fourth terrace has nothing remarkable in it except the ruins of the tank—perhaps it was a tank within a barahdari—whose plinth projects far beyond the line of the wall. About the middle of its north wall is the earthen pipe which conducted water to the terrace below.

In the fifth terrace a curious feature of the plinth of the barahdari, or the tank, of the upper terrace is the numerous square holes with which the upper half of its surface is perforated. They were probably intended to harbour flocks of pigeons. The retaining wall is arcaded. The arcade is a double one, the upper row of arches faced a corridor which ran on both sides of the plinth of the barahdari.

The sixth and the last terrace has a rectangular tank in the middle and octagonal bastions at the ends. The lower end is not supported by any retaining wall.

The ruined structure a few yards below seems to have been intended for a kind of a guard house.

Harwan Excavations

Harwan is the name of a small village situated about 2 miles beyond the Shalimar garden. The only distinction it at present enjoys is derived from its being the site of the head-works of the magnificent water-supply system of Srinagar. Though the name Harwan had been identified by Sir Aurel Stein with Shadarhadvana (grove of six saints), a locality mentioned in the Rajatarangini, there were no indications above ground pointing to the existence of important monuments buried under the earth. It is true that over thirty years ago a few moulded brick tiles had been exhumed in the course of construction of the conduit which carries drinking water to Srinagar; but as these were merely stray fragments no efforts were made to trace their origin. It is only recently that this much-delayed task has been undertaken.

Fortunately, at the very outset, the enquiry was facilitated by a lucky chance. It was on a brilliant afternoon that the site was first surveyed. The hillside along which the water conduit runs was waving with long-stalked Indian corn. But amid all those fields of luxuriant corn there existed a square flat patch which was covered only with thin turf, and in which there grew a solitary stunted plane tree.

This plot of land, by reason of its apparent unproductiveness, immediately attracted attention. On enquiry from the neat-herd who was watering his cattle in the brook near by, it was ascertained that this barren field owned the significant name of Kitur-i-Daj (field of potsherds), because the entire field consisted of thickly packed sherds—whence its barrenness.

The question that naturally arose was how such an abundance of potsherds could occur so high up the hillside and so far from the present inhabited areas. The only explanation (which eventually turned out to be correct) was that in ancient times there had been dwellings here—dwellings the nature of which could be ascertained only by excavation.

Within a few days of the commencement of the excavation a number of walls came to light (Plate XV). They were ordinary rubble stone structures, at first sight scarcely distinguishable from the modern mud-and-stone walls of peasants' dwellings in Kashmir. When the operations had advanced, it was discovered that there was a method in the arrangement of the stones—e.g., a number of large boulders was placed in one row with intervening spaces between each pair of them. These spaces were filled with smaller stones, so that the entire facade presented a diaper effect.

None of these stones was dressed. This style of construction was given the name "diaper rubble "style (Plate XVI). Among the buildings constructed in this style are (1) the triple base of a medium-sized stupa, and (2) a set of rooms which might have served as chapels, or for residential purposes. The stupa is built in the middle of a rectangular courtyard facing north. While digging under its foundations a copper coin of Toramana, the White Hun ruler, who flourished in about the fifth century A.D., was discovered. From this piece of evidence it was inferred that the "diaper rubble "stupa could not possibly be earlier than the fifth century A.D., though it might be considerably later in date.

Immediately around the stupa there was a narrow fringe of figured-tile pavement. A close examination of it showed that (1) nearly all the pieces were fragmentary; (2) though nearly all of them bore figures, no group of adjacent pieces completed a motif; and (3) though some were flat and might have formed part of a pavement, there were a few which bore mouldings in relief and could only have belonged to walls. The obvious inference was that these tiles were transplanted from a different structure, probably earlier, when that structure had fallen into desuetude. The question now was to find the structure to which they originally belonged.

In this area, however, the rubble stone structures—e.g., the stupa and the chapels—were not the only buildings that were exhumed. Side by side with them were other buildings in quite different styles—for example, two adjacent walls of what might have been the courtyard of some edifice of which no trace came to light. These walls had a core of rubble stones, but their facing consisted of closely packed small pebbles, transported from the bed of the neighbouring torrent. The walls are built entirely in mud, but the pebbles are so carefully packed that after the lapse of nearly two thousand years the portion of the wall that remains standing presents a very neat appearance.

But the labour involved in collecting and fixing such small pebbles in an extensive building must have been enormous. This style of construction has, for want of a better name, been termed the "pebble "style (Plate XVII). Again, another enclosure wall in a far better state of preservation was found. This is built in a peculiar style, which is evidently a cross between the older pebble style and the later rubble style, and provides a strikingly effective facade (Plate XIX). It consists of a series of large, smooth-faced, irregularly shaped boulders placed at intervals of 6" to 18" apart, the interspaces being filled with small round or oval pebbles of 1" to 2" in diameter. It appears that the builders' solicitude for the durability of their buildings in time overcame their desire to acquire religious merit by devoting extra, though unnecessary, labour in the construction of religious buildings.

Among the antiquities that this area yielded, were a large number of broken fingers and toes of terra-cotta figures, terra-cotta curls belonging to images of the Buddha, of which no other remnant was found, and a few clay votive tablets bearing in relief miniature stupas. These last are extremely interesting, inasmuch as they give an idea of the kind of stupas that were built in Kashmir in the early centuries of the Christian era. The stupa depicted on the tablets had a triple base, all the three flights of steps leading up being in line with one another, as is the case with the existing stupa at Harwan. From the uppermost basement sprang a cylindrical dome with a bulging hemispherical top, which was surmounted by a number of umbrellas, standing one over the other, and diminishing in size until they end in a pointed finial. They are supported by what appears to be a forest of poles radiating outwards. To the finial were attached several long waving streamers.

On one side of the stupa, standing in the courtyard, or it may be on the first terrace of the plinth, was a "lion" column. Below the representation of the stupa on the plaque, the Buddhist creed, Ye dharma, etc., in Brahmi characters of about the fourth century A.D., is stamped in relief (Plate XVIII).

A closer scrutiny of the hillside brought to light the fact that in the period to which the ruins belong it was arranged in level terraces, on each of which stood several buildings. There was a central flight of steps which connected them, and gave access from one to the other. It is likely that it was continued to the foot of the hill, along which runs a beautiful stream of clear water, although the shrines were not wholly dependent for their drinking water upon the stream. There exist to this day two springs, one above and the other near the ruins, and probably in the old days there was a larger number.

On the highest of these terraces, which, by the way, grew excellent corn at the time of excavation, there was a little mound whose general appearance seemed promising. Nor did the operations, carried out later, belie that promise, for they brought to light the most important of the buildings so far exhumed at this site. It is a large apsidal temple, square in front and circular at the back, built in the very picturesque diaper pebble style of masonry.

The temple accommodation consisted of a spacious rectangular antechamber with a circular sanctum behind. No relic of any kind nor any trace of an image was found, but this deficiency was made up by the wonderful pavement of the courtyard round the temple, consisting of large moulded brick tiles having various shapes and forming different patterns (Plate XIX). The favourite pattern seems to have been a large disc consisting of several concentric circles with a single central piece. Each circle is composed of a series of arc-shaped tiles, each shamped with a special motif. The principal motifs on the tiles so far discovered are (1) designs consisting of frets, wavy lines, fish-bone patterns, conventional flowers, and flower-designs consisting of different combinations of leaves; (2) leaves of an aquatic plant common in the neighbouring Dal lake; leaves of the lotus plant, some indigenous flowers in full bloom grouped in various ways; (3) geese running or flying in rows with flower petals or leaves in their bills; ducks; cocks or pheasants often placed in the centre of a floral pattern; cocks fighting; (4) rams fighting; cows suckling their young; elephants; deer looking with head turned backwards at the moon; archers on—horseback chasing deer and shooting arrows at them; (5) a lady carrying a flower vase; a dancing girl; a female musician beating a drum; a soldier in armour hunting deer with bow and arrow; men and women conversing, seated in a balcony; boys carrying a floral festoon on their shoulders.

That these tiles occupied exactly the position they were laid in by ancient workmen is borne out by the fact that each one of them bears a number in Kharoshthi script, the order of the tiles in a series being in strict accordance with their consecutive numeral order. The obvious inference is that the tile-pavement was not laid in a haphazard manner, but followed a set design, probably drawn first by the architect on paper or parchment. The potter who made the tiles and stamped them with decorative figures numbered them before baking, to prevent the comparatively unskilled layer from making mistakes and thereby spoiling the design.

Incidentally it shows that in ancient India, over fifteen centuries ago, labourers were expected to know at least the rudiments of writing and reading. The existence of Kharoshthi numerals also affords a reliable clue to the date of the tiles, and consequently to that of the monuments. Kharoshthi script ceased to be in vogue in north-western India, where it had principally flourished, about the fifth century A.D. It follows therefore that the tiles belong to a period anterior to that century, possibly a considerable period. The fact that the Kharoshthi numerals at Harwan were intended for the guidance of common labourers indicates that the script must have been at the highest pitch of popularity at the time the tiles were made. I should accordingly place the date of the tiles, and consequently that of the diaper pebble masonry with which they are associated, at about A.D. 300. This conclusion receives further support from the style of the human figures and other designs stamped on the tiles.

For example, the physiognomy and, to some extent, the dress of the men and women are wholly unlike that of any of the races at present residing in Kashmir, or for the matter of that in India. Their facial characteristics bear close resemblance to those of inhabitants of the regions round about Yarkand and Kashgar, whose heavy features prominent cheekbones, narrow, sunk, and slanting eyes, and receding foreheads, are faithfully represented on the tiles. Some of the figures are dressed in trousers and Turkoman caps.

The only period when Kashmir had any intimate connection with Central Asia was during the supremacy of the Kushans in the early centuries of the Christian era, when Kashmir formed part of the Kushan empire, which extended from Mathura in India to Yarkand in Central Asia. Indeed, then as now it appears to have occupied a pre-eminent position; inasmuch as Kanishka (circa A.D. 125), the greatest of Kushan emperors, is said to have convened here his great council of Buddhist divines.

It may be that some pious and prosperous Kushan built this shrine at Harwan, where, according to the ancient history of Kashmir, resided the great Buddhist patriarch, Nagarjuna. Further perhaps to increase his religious merit, and to show his humility, the builder had the image of his own face and that of his wife's stamped on the tiles so that the commonest people might tread on them. Among the other decorative motifs which reveal foreign influence are the figures of mailed horsemen with flying scarves tied to their heads, which are strongly reminiscent of the contemporary Sassanian art of Persia.

The tile decoration was not confined to the pavement only. Though very few moulded tiles belonging to the facade have been found, their fragments prove that up to a certain height at least, the facade also was decorated with tile-work. This is further borne out by the discovery of a long platform at the back of the courtyard, which almost throughout its length bears such decoration (Plate XXI). The peculiar interest of the Harwan monuments lies in the fact that they are the only remains of their kind in India (possibly in the world), and that they supply a life-like representation of the features of those mysterious people, the Kushans. From the above it is clear that the pebble style of buildings was the earliest in date. It was followed by the diaper pebble style, which dates about A.D. 300. This style was followed by the diaper rubble style, whose date is about A.D. 500 and later.

The dimensions of the tile pavement round the apsidal temple are 160' by 124' 6". The tiles, as stated above, are decorated with a variety of motifs, the most prominent of which are reproduced in the accompanying illustrations. It will be noticed that a striking feature of the human figures on the tiles is that the head is invariably shown in profile and the body facing front (Plates XX-XLII).

Shalimar

Shalimar is, of all the Mughal gardens in Kashmir, the one which has received the greatest attention from the later rulers of the country. The Pathan and the Sikh Governors occasionally used it as their pleasure resort, and when, from the reign of Ranjit Singh, Europeans began to visit the valley with comparative freedom, its marble pavilion was often assigned to them as a residence. But in spite of this intermittent care, the destroying hand of time and the wanton vandalism of some of the rulers themselves have robbed the summer residence of Nur Jahan and Jahangir of a great part of its ancient charm. An idea of what it was in the time of the Mughals may be gathered from the tantalisingly short description of Francois Bernier, who visited Kashmir in the suite of Aurangzeb in A.D. 1664:

"The most beautiful of all these gardens is one belonging to the king, called Chah-limar. The entrance from the lake is through a spacious canal bordered with green turf and running between two rows of poplars: The length is about five hundred paces, and it leads to a large summerhouse placed in the middle of the garden. A second canal, still finer than the first, then conducts to another summerhouse at the end of the garden.

This canal is paved with large blocks of freestone and its sloping sides are covered with the same. In the middle is a long row of fountains, fifteen paces apart; besides which there are here and there large circular basins or reservoirs, out of which arise other fountains, formed into a variety of shapes and figures.

"The summer-houses are placed in the midst of the canal, consequently surrounded by water and between the two rows of large poplars planted on either side. They are built in the form of a dome, and encircled by a gallery, into which four doors open; two looking up or down the canal and two leading to bridges that connect the buildings with both banks. The houses consist of a large room in the centre with four smaller apartments, one at each corner. The whole of the interior is painted and gilt, and on the walls of all the chambers are inscribed certain sentences written in large and beautiful Persian characters. "The four doors are extremely valuable; being composed of large stones and supported by two beautiful pillars. The doors and pillars were found in some of the idol temples demolished by Shah Jahan and it is impossible to estimate their value. I cannot describe the nature of the stone, but it is far superior to porphyry or any species of marble."

The large stone doors now no longer exist; the domes have given place to a common shingle roof; the gilding and paint and the inscription on the walls are now covered or replaced by a coat of whitewash; the view of the lake is cut off by an ugly stone wall; but in spite of these disastrous changes, the garden still preserves its singular charm. In strong contrast with the buoyant atmosphere of Nishat Bagh, with its sunlit terraces, its dashing cascades, playing fountains and sparkling streams, is the soft gloom and the gliding motion of the watercourses of the Shalimar, which is built on a comparatively flat piece of ground. The garden was a royal residence, and the court seems to have indelibly imprinted its spirit of decorum upon it. As the garden was probably designed by the Empress Nur Jahan, who in point of beauty and wit was the most pre-eminent lady in Muslim India, it would, perhaps, be more appropriate to say that the garden reflects the image of that queen of the harem, whom her fond lover designated the Light of the World. The garden originally consisted, as now, of three enclosures, the lower one of which, however, has been considerably curtailed by the intrusion of the cart-road. The outermost enclosure was used as the public garden, and its barahdari was the Diwan-i-Am (the Hall of Public Audience).

The small black marble throne still stands over the waterfall in the centre of the canal which flows through the building into the tank below. "The second garden is slightly broader, consisting of two shallow terraces with the Diwan-i-Khas (the Hall of Private Audience) in the centre. The buildings have been destroyed, but their carved stone bases are left, as well as a fine platform surrounded by fountains. On the northwest boundary of this enclosure are the royal bathrooms.

"At the next wall, the little guard-rooms that flank the entrance to the ladies' garden have been rebuilt in Kashmir style on older stone bases. Here the whole effect culminates with the beautiful black marble pavilion built by Shah Jahan, which still stands in the midst of its fountain spray; the green glitter of the water shining in the smooth, polished marble, the deep rich tone of which is repeated in the old cypress trees. Round this baradari the whole colour and perfume of the garden is concentrated, with the snows of Mahadev for a background. How well the Mughals understood the principle that the garden, like every other work of art, should have a climax (Plate XIV). "This unique pavilion is surrounded on every side by a series of cascades, and at night when the lamps are lighted in the little arched recesses behind the shining waterfalls it is even more fairy-like than by day."

Yandrahom Megaliths

From the Harwan ruins, looking northwest, may be seen, situated on the plateau of Burzahom, 2 miles away, the only prehistoric remains, save stone implements, which have so far been discovered in Kashmir. They consist of a group of eleven megaliths, five of which are more or less erect: the rest have fallen. As no excavations have yet been carried out at this site, it is impossible to state precisely what they are and to what period they belong (Plate XLIII).

5

Bumazuv Cave and Temples

The little village of Bumazuv is situated only a mile to the north of the sacred springs of Bavan (Matan). It contains the only important group of artificial caves in Kashmir. They are very unpretentious excavations and only one of them possesses architectural interest. It is carved out of a large mass of limestone cliffs overlooking a scene of great beauty, comprising the whole of the lower section of the Lidar valley. The stone in which this excavation is made is of a very friable nature. The facade of the gateway has, therefore, been built of stone masonry in lime. It consists of a single trefoil-arched doorway, surmounted by a pediment, and side walls.

On the left-side wall is a small rectangular niche measuring 2' 2" by 1' 1". Its pilasters are carved with floral scrolls of extraordinary delicacy. The lintel is ornamented with a row of rosettes and the cornice with a row of slightly projecting dentils, whose intervening spaces appear to have been filled with figures of dancing dwarfs, all of which are now defaced. In its interior is a small temple which is similar in style to other temples of Kashmir. It is 9' 5" square externally and stands on a base 4' 6" in height. A remarkable feature, which points to its being a decadent example, is the very slight projection of the porch. The corner pilasters have two rectangular niches.

In the village, at the foot of the cave, are two temples which have been converted into Muslim ziarats. Both of them are now covered with a thick coat of mud plaster, under which all the artistic and architectural features are concealed. The larger temple now goes by the name of the Ziarat of Baba Bamdin Sahib, who is said to have been a disciple of Shaikh Nur-ud-din, the famous Muslim saint of Kashmir. The pyramidal roof is buried under a mound of earth which surmounts the modern square double wooden roof. The interior measures 8' square. The ceiling consists of overlapping stones, like that of the Pandrethan temple. The uppermost stone is carved with a full-blown lotus. The entrance is in the north wall. Unless the coat of plaster is removed it is impossible to say whether the temple was open on other sides.

To the west of this temple are the ruins of a smaller temple. The exterior of the roof is destroyed, but the ceiling inside is intact and is similar to the ceiling of the larger temple. Its porches are exact replicas of those of the cave temple, a fact which leads to the surmise that all three were built at about the same time.

The larger temple has been identified with the Bhimakesaval shrine built by Bhima Shahi of Gandhara, the maternal grandfather of Queen Didda, who ruled Kashmir as the wife of Kshemagupta from A.D. 950-958, and as sole sovereign from A.D. 980-1003.

Achhabal

The spring of Achhabal is perhaps the largest spring in Kashmir. Its old Hindu name was Akshvala, but it does not seem to have been much known in mediaeval times. Abul Fazl speaks of it in the Ain-i-Akbari as "a fountain which shoots up to the height of a cubit, and is scarce equalled for its coldness, limpidity, and refreshing qualities. The sick that drink of it and persevere in a course of its waters, recover their health."

Bernier, who visited it in A.D. 1665, speaks of its beauties in the following glowing terms:

"Returning from Send-bray, I turned a little from the high road for the sake of visiting Achiavel, a country house formerly of the kings of Kachemire and now of the Great Mogol. What principally constitutes the beauty of this place is a fountain whose waters disperse themselves into a hundred canals round the house, which is by no means unseemly, and throughout the gardens. The spring gushes out of the earth with violence, as if it issued from the bottom of some well, and the water is so abundant that it ought rather be called a river than a fountain. It is excellent water and cold as ice.

The garden is very handsome, laid out in regular walks, and full of fruit trees, apple, pear, plum, apricot, and cherry; jets-d'eau in various forms and fishponds are in great number; and there is a lofty cascade which in its fall takes the form and colour of a large sheet, thirty or forty paces in length, producing the finest effect imaginable, especially at night, when innumerable lamps, fixed in parts of the wall adapted for that purpose, are lighted under this sheet of water." This description, but for the dilapidated aspect of the tanks and watercourses, the comparative absence of fruit trees, and the total absence of nocturnal illuminations, might very well apply to the Achhabal garden of today.

The cart-road and the dak bangalow have encroached upon its lowest terrace, though the original watercourse is still intact, and the foundations of its row of fountains are still visible in the water. A quaint doorway built in the time of the late Maharaja Ranbir Singhji gives admittance to the second terrace of the garden. Most of the barahdaris and pavilions belong to the repairs executed in the reign of the Maharaja Ranbir Singhji. Only the ruins of the pavilion over the fountain itself, standing solitary yet strong in defiance of the rushing waters and of the destructive vegetation, belong to Mughal times. This garden does not possess any sloping cascades. All the falls are vertical. To the west of the garden are, or rather were, the royal quarters, the present buildings being modern and contemporaneous with the pavilions. The hammam of Jahangir, however, is in excellent preservation. The objects specially noteworthy here are a piece of a timber conduit Iying in the compound and said to belong to Mughal times, and the system of earthen pipes which conveyed water to the royal bathrooms from the subterranean channel in the uppermost terrace of the garden.

Achhabal is an ideal place for laying out a garden. "Nowhere else have I seen such possibilities for a combined appeal, of a stately stone-bordered pleasance between ordered avenues of full-grown trees, and a natural rock and woodland upper garden with haunting far-reaching views, where the white wild roses foam over the firs and the boulders rivalling the sheet of water Bernier praised."

Kother

The village of Kother is situated two miles above Achhabal, a little off the Achhabal-Kashtwar road. The name is derived from Kapatesvara, which is a contraction of Papasudana-Kapategvara, an appellation of Shiva to whom the spring here is sacred. The place has for many centuries past enjoyed a great reputation for sanctity. King Bhoja of Malva, who was a contemporary of King Ananta (A.D. 1028-1063) of Kashmir, "had the round tank (kunda) constructed at Kapatesvara with heaps of gold that he sent. King Bhoja vowed that he would always wash his face in the water from the Papasudana Tretha, and this (man Padmaraja) made the fulfilment of his difficult vow (possible) by regularly despatching from this (tirtha) large numbers of glass jars filled with that water."

The tank is circular. The stone basin built by Bhoja is still partially extant. The flights of steps flanked by side-walls which are surmounted by the cornices usual in Kashmiri temples, facing north and south respectively, lead down to the water level. By the side of the spring are two small temples which seem to be contemporaneous with the stone wall of the spring. The larger temple measures 8' 4" internally and faces southwest. Its roof seems to have been destroyed by fire. The entrance is 3' 8" by 6', and it is noteworthy that the recesses on the exterior of the other three sides, which in most other temples are of about the same dimensions as the open doorway, are in this instance much smaller.

The smaller temple measures 6' 4" internally. It faces west. Its lower part is buried underground. There is a long stretch of wall 246' long and about 12' wide, on the north side of the area, which originally formed part of the enclosure wall round the temples and the tank. The fragment that is above ground on the east side shows that this surrounding wall is in reality a cellular peristyle. The top stones of the cells are visible. A curious local legend reports that a treasure lies buried somewhere in or near the spring, and that there was a stone slab embedded in the wall of the spring on which were inscribed directions for its discovery and expenditure on the repairs and upkeep of the spring and its dependent shrines. The same legend associates the name of a king Mutskund with the foundation of the temples. In support of this the people quote the adage:

Mutsakund razas manshihandi kan

Tim kati tsalanas? Kuther van.

Translaion: King Mutsukund has buffalo's ears: where will they be removed? In the wood of Kother.

He is said to have been favoured by nature with a pair of buffalo's ears, of which he was anxious to rid himself, but he could not achieve his purpose by any means at his disposal. At length, being advised to try a bath in the waters of this spring, he had his heart's desire. In gratitude he expended his treasures upon the foundation and upkeep of the temples and the spring.

Note: Since the above was written, the area round the spring has been excavated, and, as was expected, a cellular quadrangle and a number of shrines belonging to the tenth to eleventh centuries have been exhumed. Stratigraphical evidence shows that there was an older stratum of buildings also, upon which the structures of the tenth to eleventh centuries were superimposed.

Mamal

The small temple of Mamal (ancient Mamalaka) is situated on the right bank of the Lidar, exactly opposite the State Rest House at Pahalgam. For one who has seen the great temples of Martand and Avantipur, the journey to Mamal and back for the sole purpose of seeing this temple is perhaps not worth the trouble. But a visitor whom other pursuits call to Pahalgam should not miss seeing it.

The temple is 8' square internally, and has in front a porch supported on two fluted columns, one of which is missing. The superstructure has fallen down. No remnants of the ceiling are left. The walls are straight and vertical above the string course, and it is probable that originally there was no ceiling, as at Narastan.

It may well be that this temple is the same as that of Mammesvara, which the Rajatarangini mentions King Jayasimha (A.D. 1128-1155) to have adorned with a golden kalas'a, or finial. Its architecture also shows certain features which are undoubtedly decadent. One of these is the absence of projection in the corner pilasters. The temple was externally covered with a thick coat of lime plaster. It contains an old pedestal and a probably modern Shiva-linga. A spring of remarkably pure water rises under the site of the temple. Its waters are enclosed in a basin in front of the stairs. The whole was originally surrounded by a rubble-stone wall, of which the foundations are still visible on the north side.

Vernag

The spring of Vernag is the reputed source of the river Vitasta. In Hindu times it was known as the Nila-naga, and was sacred to the snake-deity of that name. The Nilamata Purana tells us that when Parvati had obtained the consent of her consort Shiva to incarnate in Kashmir as the river Vitasta in order to purify the country which had been defiled by the touch of Pisachas, who appear to have been some outlandish barbarians, he struck the earth at the site of the spring with his trident, and thus cleared the way for the issue of the waters of the Parvati-Vitasta from the nether world. Hence the tirtha also bore the alternative name of Sulaghata, "trident stroke." It seems to have retained considerable importance among Hindu places of pilgrimage even as late as Akbar's time, for Abul Fazl mentions the existence, to the east, of a number of stone temples. In his time it had already taken its present name of Vernag, borrowing it probably from the district of Ver, the name at that time of the modern Shahabad Pargana. Abul Fazl adds that "it is a pool measuring a jarib, which tosses in foam with an astonishing roar, and its depth is unfathomable, and is surrounded by a stone embankment."

The construction of the octagonal basin and the arcade (Plate LIV) which now surrounds it, was commenced by Jahangir and completed in the time of Shah Jahan. The former writes: "It is an octagonal reservoir about 20 yards by 20 yards. Near it are the remains of a place of worship for recluses: cells cut out of the rock and numerous caves. The water is exceedingly pure. Although I could not guess its depth, a grain of poppy-seed is visible until it touches the bottom.

There are many fish to be seen in it. As I had heard that it was unfathomable, I ordered them to throw in a cord with a stone attached, and when this cord was measured in gaz it became evident that the depth was not more than one and a half the height of a man. After my accession I ordered them to build the sides of the spring with stone, and they made a garden round it with a canal; and built halls and houses about it, and made a place such that travellers over the world can point out few like it."

This information from the pen of the Emperor himself probably accounts for the complete disappearance of the stone temples and caves, whose materials would afford the persons in charge of building operations too tempting a quarry to be lightly set aside. Of the buildings which Jahangir ordered to be constructed here only the range of twenty-four arches round the spring remains partially intact. The arches were originally built of stone, the walls being surmounted by a row of beautifully carved brackets which supported the eaves. A number of these are still in existence.

On two sides of the octagon are larger chambers, each containing a staircase leading to the upper storey, no trace of which is left. The brick facing of the majority of the arches, as well as ruins of the walls of the second storey over the entrance chamber, belong to the repairs done by Wazir Punnu in the reign of the late Maharaja Ranbir Singhji. Two inscribed stone tablets, one belonging to the time of Jahangir and the other to that of Shah Jahan, are built into the wall of the arcade. The inscription of Shah Jahan was originally fixed in the wall of the entrance chamber, but was for some unknown reason removed some years ago by the Public Works Department contractor who was commissioned to raise the floor of the promenade round the spring, presumably for irrigation purposes. The raising of the level of the promenade accounts for the markedly stunted appearance of the arcade. Jahangir's inscription, which is dated the fifth year of his reign, runs as follows:

Patshah-i haft-kishwar 'atalat-gugtar 'abu-al muzaffar Nurud Din Jahangir ibn

Akbar Shah Ghazi batarikh-i

Sanah 5 julus darin Sar-chashma faiz-amin nazul ajlal farmudand; tarikh:-

Az Jahangir Shah-i Akbar Shah

In bina sar kashitah bar aflak

Bani-e aqal yaft tarikhash

Qasr abad-o chashma-i Varnag.

Translation: The king of the seven dominions, the Dispenser of Justice, the Victorious Lort, Nur-ud-Din Jahangir, son of Akhr Shah Ghazij bestowed grace upon this bounteous spring (by his presence) in the fifth year of his reign: the date:

Through Jahangir Shah, the son of Akbar Shah, this foundation raiset its head to the high heavens. The source of wisdom (i.e., the author) discovered its date: May the palace ant the spring of Varnag endure (for ever).

The last line gives the date A. H. 1029 = A. D. 1619-20. Shah Jahan's inscription reads thus:-

Haitar ba hukm-i Shah-i Jahan padshahi dahr

Shukr-e khuda ki sakht chunin abshar jui

In jui tada ast zi ju-e bahisht yat

Zin abshar yafta Kashmir abrui

Tarikh-i jui guft ba gosham sarosh-i ghaib

Az chashma-i bihisht birun amatast jui.

Translation: The Lord be praised for that Haidar, by the order of Shah Jahan, the monarch of the universe, constructed such a cascade and such a watercourse. This watercourse is reminiscent of the stream that flows in heaven; and the cascade (is such) that (even) Kashmir derives honour from it. The invisible angel whispered the date (of construction) of the watercourse in my ear. "This stream has sprung from the fountain of heaven."

The last line gives the date A.H. 1036, corresponding to A.D. 1626-27. After the decline of the Mughal. Empire the Hindus reclaimed what they had lost. Some of the cells are now used as idol chambers, and priests serve as guides to visitors.

The surplus water of the spring was discharged by an underground conduit, the mouth of which is visible from above. Passing under the buildings the conduit crossed the garden and carried the water to the royal bathrooms, the ruins of which and of other buildings are still to be seen outside the rubble wall on the east side. The stream which flows from the spring is about 12' in width and runs throughout the length of the garden. It is spanned in the middle and at the northern end by two modern barahdaris. Only the upper terrace is enclosed, though the presence of the ruined water-chute, over which the stream rushes down, before leaving the garden, suggests the existence of a lower terrace.

The garden, in spite of its much curtailed dimensions, the presence of unsightly huts built by the local priests, and the general dilapidated condition of its streams and buildings, has a distinct charm, of which its royal founder seems to have been quite sensible; for the way-worn Jahangir, who expired at Chingas near Rajauri on his return journey from Kashmir, prayed with his dying breath to be conveyed to Vernag to be buried there. The garden with its shady trees, icy-cold water, and murmuring streams, overshadowed by the sombre pine-clad hills, is a place pre-eminently fitted to be the retreat of a recluse and the final resting-place of a world-weary emperor.

Monuments below Srinagar—Parihasapura

The karewas of Paraspor and Divar are situated at a distance of fourteen miles from Srinagar on the Baramula road. They were chosen by King Lalitaditya (c. A.D. 750) for the erection of a new capital city, and it is certain that, given a sufficient supply of drinking water, the high and dry Plateaus of Parihasapura have every advantage over the low, swampy Srinagar as a building site. Lalitaditya and his ministers seem to have vied with each other in embellishing the new city with magnificent edifices which were intended to be worthy alike of the king's glory and the ministers' affluence.

The Plateau is studded with heaps of ruins of which a few have been excavated. Among these the most important are three Buddhist structures, a stupaj a monastery, and a chaitya. Their common features are the enormous size of the blocks of limestone used in their construction, the smoothness of their dressing, and the fineness of their joints. The immense pile at the northeastern corner of the Plateau is the stupa (Plate LV) of Chankuna, the Turkoman (?) minister of Lalitaditya. Its superstructure has entirely disappeared, leaving behind a huge mass of scorched boulders which completely cover the top of the base. There is a large massive block in the middle of this debris, which has a circular hole in the middle, 5' deep. It is probable that this stone belonged to the hti (finial) of the stupa; and that the hole is the mortice in which was embedded the lower end of the staff of the stone umbrellas which crowned the drum.

The base is 128' 2" square in plan, with offsets and a flight of steps on each side. Its mouldings are of the usual type, a round torus in the middle and a filleted torus as the cornice. The steps were flanked by plain rails and side walls which had pilasters in front decorated with carved figures of seated and standing atlantes. Some of these are in position, while others, which were lying about loose, have been transported to the Srinagar Museum.

They are not grotesque creatures like those so commonly seen in Gandhara, but have the appearance of ordinary respectable gentlemen, whose placid features seem to indicate that the superincumbent weight sits lightly upon them. The top surface of each of the two plinths is broad and affords adequate space for circumambulation. Among the loose architectural stones lying scattered about the site are a few curious blocks in the southeastern and southwestern corners. They are round torus stones adorned with four slanting bands or fillets running round the body. As this type of torus moulding is not used in either of the bases, it is probable that it belonged to the string-course on the drum of the stupa. There are fragments of trefoiled arches also, which contained images of the Buddha and Bodhisattvas.

The large square structure to the south of the stupa is the rajavihara, or royal monastery. A flight of steps in the east wall gives access to one of its cells which served as a verandah. The monastery is a quadrangle of twenty-six cells enclosing a square courtyard which was originally paved with stone flags, some of which are extant. In front of the cells was a broad verandah, which was probably covered, the roof being supported by a colonnade which ran along the edge of the plinth. A flight of steps corresponding to the one mentioned above leads down to the courtyard. Exactly opposite to this, in the middle of the west wall, are three cells preceded by a vestibule, which is built on a plinth projected into the courtyard.

It is probable that these were the apartments occupied by the abbot of the monastery. Near a corner of it is a large stone trough, which may have served as a water reservoir for bathing purposes. A couple of stone drains passing underneath cells Nos. 18 and 21 (if we begin counting from the cell to the south of the entrance chamber) carry off the rain and other surplus water from the courtyard. Externally the plinth is about 10' high. In cell No. 25 (that is the one to the north of the entrance chamber) was found a small earthen jug which contained forty-four silver coins in excellent preservation. They belonged to the time of kings Vinayaditya, Vigraha, and Durlabha. They are now exhibited in the Numismatic Section of the Srinagar Museum. The monastery was repaired at a subsequent period. The repairs are plainly distinguishable in the exterior of the wall on the eastern and western sides.

The building next to it on the south side is the chaitya built by Lalitaditya. It stands on a double base of the usual type. A flight of steps on the east side leads to the entrance, which must originally have been covered by a large trefoil-arch, fragments of which are lying about the site. This building possesses some of the most massive blocks of stone that have ever been used in Kashmiri temples, and which compare favourably with those used in ancient Egyptian buildings. The floor of the sanctum is a single block 14' by 12' 6" by 5' 2".

The sanctum is 27' square surrounded by a circumambulatory passage. It is probable that its ceiling was supported on four columns, the bases only of which survive at the four corners. The roof, which was probably supported on the massive stone walls of the pradakshina, may have been of the pyramidal type.

The courtyard is enclosed by a rubble-stone wall which has nothing remarkable about it. In front of the temple steps is the base of a column which probably supported the dhvaja, or banner, bearing the special emblem of the deity enshrined in the sanctuary.

The flank walls of the stair were adorned with atlantes similar to those of the stupa.

Near the chaitya is the foundation of a small building of the diaper-rubble style.

While this Plateau was reserved for the erection of Buddhist buildings only, the other two were exclusively appropriated by Hindus. Perhaps the arrangement was intentional, to avoid possible friction between the two powerful religious bodies. On the karewa locally known as Gordan there are ruins of a Hindu temple which are probably all that remain of Lalitaditya's temple of Govardhanadhara. Crossing the ravine in which nestles the little village of Diwar-Yakmanpura, and ascending the Plateau opposite, are seen the immense ruins of two extraordinarily large temples—one of them has a peristyle larger than that of Martand—which may represent Lalitaditya's favourite shrines of Parihasakesava and Muktakesava.

Patan

Sugandhes'a Temple

The Rajatarangini mentions the erection of three temples at Patan, which in ancient days was called Sankarapurapattana, after the name of its founder, King Sankaravarman

(A.D. 883-902). Perhaps it would be well to remark here that vandalism of a serious kind had already begun in pre-Muslim times, as some of the materials used in the construction of these temples were removed from the older site of Parihasapura described above. The three temples named by the Kashmir chronicle are (1) Sankaragaurisvara, (2) Sugandhesa, and (3) Ratnavardhanesa.

The first, identified with the larger temple near Patan, was built by the king himself, the second, which is the one nearer Srinagar, is named after Sugandha, his queen, and the third, of which no trace has so far been found, if we exclude the architectural fragments near the spring outside the dak bangalow, was built by Ratnavardhana, his minister. All three were dedicated to Shiva.

The Sugandhesa temple does not differ materially from other temples of Kashmir. The shrine is 12' 7" square and has, as usual, a portico in front. It is open on one side only, and has trefoiled niches externally on the other sides. These niches contained images. The temple stands on a double base, but it seems probable from the flank walls of the lower stair and the frieze of the lower base, in which the panels intended for sculpture decoration have been merely blocked out, but not carved, that the temple was never completed.

The entrance to the courtyard is in the middle of the eastern wall of the peristyle, and consists, as usual, of two chambers with a partition wall and a doorway in the middle.

Among the architectural fragments lying loose on the site, the most noteworthy are (a) two fragments of fluted columns with their capitals, (b) two bracket capitals with voluted ends and carved figures of atlantes supporting the frieze above, (c) a huge stone belonging to the cornice of the temple, bearing rows of kirtimukhas (grinning lions' heads) and rosettes, and (d) a stone probably belonging to the partition wall of the entrance, having (1) two small trefoiled niches in which stand female figures wearing long garlands and (2) below them two rectangular niches, in one of which is an atlant seated between two lions facing the spectator, and in the other are two human-headed birds.

The cornice of the base of the peristyle is similar to that of the Avantisvami temple. The cells were preceded by a row of fluted columns, bases of some of which are in situ while those of others are scattered about in the courtyard.

The attention of the visitor is called to the slots in the lower stones of the jambs of the cells. These are mortices for iron clamps which held pairs of stones together. Pieces of much-corroded iron are still extant in some of the mortices.

Sankaragaurisvara Temple

Lower down is the larger temple built by the king himself (Plate LVI). It is only an enlarged copy of the queen's temple. On account of the lack of proper facilities for drainage of rain water it has not been deemed advisable to excavate its courtyard. The peristyle, the temple-plinth, and a smaller shrine in the northeast corner, are therefore still underground. The rectangular path around the temple marks the position of the peristyle, tops of some columns of which are seen peeping out of the earth in the southwest corner. The square flower-bed with a projection on one side in the northeast corner of the courtyard coincides with the small shrine below. The square space in the middle of the eastern path marks the position of the entrance.

The temple itself is an imposing pile, though a great deal of its grandeur has been taken away by the concealment of its plinth. The cella is 17' square and the central stone of the floor measures 12' 6" by 10'. It has nine circular holes arranged in three rows. It is possible that these were mortices of tenons which held in position the pedestal of the idol. The left wall of the portico has a trefoiled niche which is divided into two panels. The lower and larger one contains a number of figures, of which the principal seems to be Shiva. Above it, in the upper foil, is the squatting figure of the elephant-headed god, Ganesh, whose presence here would conclusively prove, even if there were any doubt about it, that the temple was dedicated to Shiva. The jambs of the recesses on the exterior of the temple have half-engaged columns which are decorated with well-executed geometrical and other patterns. Their capitals are surmounted by human-headed birds.

A few yards to the north of the Patan dak bangalow has recently been excavated an old baoli whose waters are confined in three rectangular reservoirs which are connected with each other. The one in the middle contains a miniature temple constructed originally of three stones (Plate LVII). The top-stone is missing. It is 2' 8" square externally and is open on all four sides. The openings seem to have been closed originally with wooden doors. These little shrines belong to the time when the prosperity of the Hindus had waned, and they were not capable of devoting so much wealth to the glorification of their religion.

Ushkar and Baramula

The village of Ushkar or Wushkur is situated at a distance of half a mile from the Baramula dak bangalow. The name is a corruption of Huvishkapura, which, according to Kalhana, was the name of a city founded by Huvishka, the great Kushan king in the second century A.D. It was a flourishing town in mediaeval times owing to its position on the principal trade-route between Kashmir and northwestern India. Lalitaditya built here a shrine of Vishnu named Muktasvamin and a large vihara with a stupa. Hsuan-tsang, the famous Chinese pilgrim who visited Kashmir in A.D. 631, entered the valley by the Baramula pass, and spent his first night at one of the monasteries here. The reigning king accorded him a very hospitable welcome, sending his own mother and younger brother with chariots and horses to escort him to the capital.

Of the monasteries and temples which Hsuan-tsang saw, and Kalhana mentions, none now remain above ground, except the ruins of a stupa and its surrounding wall, a few yards to the west of the village. On the analogy of style which is similar to that of the great stupa at Parihasapura, there can be little doubt that it is the same structure which the Kashmir chronicle states Lalitaditya built in the middle of the eighth century A.D. Only the lowest courses of its base are now in position.

An interesting fact about this stupa is that it seems to have been built over an older structure of nearly the same type, stones of which were found in situ when the silt round the base was removed some years ago. That structure may have belonged to Kushan times. This surmise is strengthened by the discovery outside the northeastern corner of the surrounding wall, of eleven terracotta heads, besides a number of fragmentary limbs of images which display the unmistakable influence of the Gandhara school of the third and fourth century. These are now preserved in the Srinagar Museum.

Fathgarh

This is the name of the small village near the mouth of the Narvav valley. It is situated at a distance of nearly three miles from Baramula. It contains the ruins of a very large temple which presents several points of interest. Internally it is 28' 9" square. The greater part of the cella was occupied by a massive platform on which was placed a colossal Shiva-linga, a large fragment of which is lying there still. The platform was decorated with a torus moulding and the space around it was no doubt used as a pradakshina.

Two fragments of the waterspout (pranali), which carried off the washings of the image, are also lying in the sanctum. The front elevation of the platform is decorated with two rows of trefoiled niches, which were probably intended to contain lamps during the evening worship. A point of special interest about this temple is the arrangement of the ceiling. In other temples, as has been remarked above, the ceiling is either composed of overlapping stones which gradually lessen the span until it is sufficiently short to be covered by a single slab, usually circular, or it is straight-lined and triangular in section as at Narastan and Naranthal. Here both these arrangements have been discarded in favour of an elaborate system of corbelling.

A late memorial stele displaying very poor artistic skill has been discovered in the excavation of the cella. The lower panel contains a pair of clumsy human figures seated on stools facing each other. The upper one contains a trident.

The dado of the portico is adorned with a row of pedimented niches.

The open doorway faces northwest and, like the closed recesses on the exterior of the other three sides, was covered by a large trefoiled arch surmounted by a pediment. Its pilasters are, as usual, adorned with half-engaged fluted columns. This temple has a particularly massive appearance and its thorough excavation is very desirable. In the southeast corner of the area is a late brick well.

Naranthal

This is the name of a village about two and a half miles below Baramula on the right bank of the river. On the old road to Muzaffarabad and situated at a short distance from the village is a small shrine which is said to have stood in a tank, though today it is on dry ground and no traces of a tank are visible. But there is a spring near by. Only the superstructure of the temple is above ground. It is built of plain blocks of slate which are now very much the worse for wear. There is only one arched entrance on the east side. Traces of a stone floor are visible inside. The second course from the top is formed of a single slab 4 1/2' square by 1 1/2' thick.

The interior is a square of 7 1/4' and is 9' 5" high. There is no ceiling.

The topmost stone of the roof has a circular mortice in the centre which was originally intended to hold the finial which crowned the apex of the pyramid. The temple is probably of the late mediaeval era, not earlier than the twelfth century A.D., and perhaps much later.

Buniar

The temple of Buniar (Plates LX and LXXV) is situated on the Jhelum Valley road, two miles above Rampur. It is by far the best preserved of all the larger Kashmir temples.

The gateway is a double-chambered structure faced on each open side by a trefoil arch surmounted by a steep pediment. The lintels of the closed arches are supported on pairs of columns which were originally fluted, though the weather has now left no trace of flutes. They have a double capital, the upper one being voluted on all four sides. The walls are externally surmounted by a cornice of kirti-mukhas, alternating with miniature trefoiled niches. Upon this rests the first course of the pyramidal roof.

The flights of steps-on the eastern and western sides respectively afford entrance to and exit from the entrance chamber. The one on the roadside is buried underground, but the inner stair has been excavated. It consists of seven steps flanked by sloping rails and upright side walls. Between this stair and the temple is a small stone platform which formed the lowermost course of the stepped base of a column (most probably a Garudadhvaja).

The priest in charge of the temple has now placed in it a small stele of very crude workmanship and late date, which he has painted with vermilion. Another similar stele, still standing in the position in which it was found, is seen in front of the temple stair.

The temple itself stands on a double base, which is in every respect similar to other structures of its kind in Kashmir. (Plate LXXIV). A lofty trefoil arch, standing upon advanced pilasters and enclosing a rectangular entrance originally surmounted by an ornamental trefoil and steep pediment, gives access to the sanctum. The jambs of the entrance are adorned with half-engaged columns. The interior is a square of 14 feet. The pedestal of the image is placed on a broad platform. The original image, which seems to have been of Vishnu, is now replaced by small Shiva-lingas originally brought from the bed of the river Narbada. The walls are covered with a coat of modern whitewash. The string course from which the ceiling springs is still visible, but the ceiling itself which Bishop Cowie saw in 1865 and described as domical, has since either fallen down or been removed. It was, no doubt, similar to the ceilings of the larger temples at Wangath.

Externally the only decorations are the trefoils of the recesses, their pediments, and the cornice of kirtimukhas and miniature trefoils from which the roof sprang.

The quadrangle measures 145' by 119 1/2', and consists of fifty-three cells and the gateway. They are rectangular, 7' long by 4' broad. Each cell has a single trefoiled entrance enclosed in a high-pitched pediment resting on half-engaged columns. These ranges of cells are preceded by a noble colonnade which stands on a base similar to that of the temple. A transverse beam connects the capitals of the columns with the roof of the cells. Over these beams rises the entablature, only one course of which, namely the frieze of miniature trefoils, is extant (Plate LXXVI).

In the centre of each range of cells, except, perhaps, the one in which the gateway stands, is an apartment of larger dimensions preceded by a pair of taller columns which are advanced about 4' from the rest of the peristyle.

The top course of the cells is also decorated in the same way as the frieze above.

On the south side, projecting from the cornice of the upper base of the temple, is the spout of the channel which carried off the washings of the image. It seems to have been shaped originally into a makara, or crocodile's head. Immediately below it is a huge water trough carved out of a single block of stone.

The rain-water in the courtyard is carried off by a drain which runs under the southeastern corner of the peristyle.

In cell No. 11 of the north range, beginning the reckoning from the corner nearest the gateway, is the side entrance, which was then, as now, closed with a wooden door. The monotony of the external face of the western wall is partially relieved by rows of small square projections. In its two corners are two cells opening outwards. Immediately outside the side-door mentioned above is a square structure built of plain blocks of stone. The middle portion of each of its four walls has fallen down, and the gaps have been filled in with small chips of stone built in mud. It is difficult to surmise what was its original purpose.

Dhathamandir (Bandi Temple)

The temple known as Dhathamandir is situated on the Jhelum Valley cart road, midway between Rampur and Uri, about two miles below Mohora. The name signifies "ruined temple."

The only material difference in style between this temple and the one at Buniar is that it does not possess any colonnade, and that the cells, which in the former are built of granite as the temple itself, are here built of kanjur, their plinth only being of limestone. The jambs of the cells were decorated with half-engaged columns, remnants of which may still be seen in the southwestern corner of the peristyle.

The central shrine faces northeast, and is built of a very beautiful green limestone, which, curiously enough, seems to have been covered with a thick coat of lime plaster, decayed fragments of which are still clinging to various parts of the walls. The pedestal of the image is extant. There are two small shrines, replicas of the main building in the north-western corner of the courtyard.

The bases of the columns which supported the trefoil arch of the gateway are still in situ. Fragments of columns as well as their beautifully carved capitals are lying about in the compound and the area outside the gateway.

On the hillside, a few yards to the southeast of the temple, are remains of two smaller shrines which, like the subsidiary temples in the courtyard, are replicas of the main temple.

Firozpor-Drang

Firozpor=drang is a small village situated at a distance of a mile and a half from Tang Marg, at the spot where the Firozpornala issues from the mountains into the open ground. The latter part of the name preserves the memory of its ancient appellation Karkota-dranga. The term "dranga "was used in pre-Muslim times to indicate a frontier watch-station, established for the purpose of collecting customs duties and of generally safeguarding the frontier. Karkota-dranga (modern Firozpor) controlled the Tosamaidan route to Punch (ancient Parnotsa; Kashmiri Prunts).

The village contains the ruins of a small temple which was probably originally surrounded by a peristyle, no part of which, except the double-chambered gateway, is now extant above ground. The chief cause of the ruin of this temple seems to have been the unchecked growth of vegetation. Several walnut trees have taken root in the masonry, and are continuing the process of destruction.

The temple faces northeast. The roof has fallen in, and has filled the whole cella with large boulders which have completely hidden the floor, and consequently made it impossible to ascertain to which particular god the shrine was dedicated. Internally it is 11' square. The ceiling seems to have been of the Narastan type. The portico was surmounted by a trefoil-arch and a pediment of the usual type.

Externally also this temple is similar to the Narastan temple, inasmuch as the corner pilasters have very slight projection and the trefoiled recesses on the sides are smaller than the arch of the portico. It stands on a base surmounted by a cyma recta moulding. Admission is gained by a flight of steps flanked by plain side-walls.

The gateway measures 15' 6" square externally.

Ascending the spur, at whose foot these ruins are situated, we come to a very beautiful piece of open ground in the midst of dense forest. Among the trees at one corner of it are the scanty remains of the base of a small temple.

The long lines of walling between the temple and the village are regarded by tradition as the ruins of the old watch-station.

Manasbal

One of the most attractive places in the valley is the Manasbal lake (Plate I). Being absolutely free from disturbance of any kind, and nestling in an oval basin surrounded on all sides by hills and uplands, the lake is an ideal abode for the happy lotus-eater, who dreams away his days reclining under the shady chinar, and passes his evenings in watching the long streaks of moonlight flitting across the mirror-like surface of the water. Naturally, such a delightful spot would not have been overlooked either by the devout Hindu or the nature adoring Mughal. The former have left a small temple, now partially submerged during the greater part of the year. It is a very small structure, and only its two pyramidal roofs are visible in the driest seasons (Plate LXI). The cornice of the lower roof, and the horizontal band which divides it from the upper storey, are decorated with series of dentils and metopes. Only the upper part of the pediment of the entrance is visible. It faces west.

A few yards from the temple, up the hill, is a natural cavern of no particular interest. Further up is the Shahkul canal brought down from the Sindh river by Zain-ul-abidin.

On the south bank of the lake are ruins of a terraced Mughal garden, the construction of which is ascribed by tradition to Empress Nur Jahan. The garden, locally known as the Jarogha, is entirely in ruins, the only parts standing being the retaining walls and the corner bastions of the terraces.

There are a number of sculptured stones, belonging to some Buddhist shrine, scattered about on top of the low ridge on the northern bank of the lake.

Andarkot

Near the entrance of the lake, on the left bank of the river, is the large village of Sumbal. At a distance of a mile from it is situated Andarkot, known originally by the name of Jayapura, the capital of King Jayapida. The site selected for the capital was in the midst of an extensive marsh, the drainage of which was so difficult a task that in Kalhana's time (twelfth century) it was believed that in the execution of his design the king had employed the services of rakshasas, "demons," whom his friend, King Vibhishana of Ceylon, had placed at his disposal. The ancient causeway which connects the island with the mainland of Sumbal is still the only means of communication in the rainy season; when the lowlands round about are covered with water.

There is not much left today of the Buddhist viharas and Hindu temples which are said to have been built here by Jayapida. Practically everything has been destroyed. The temple of Kes'ava is represented by a large heap of scorched and shapeless boulders. The only objects of interest are a couple of sculptured reliefs on two faces of the pilaster of the stair; and they too are woefully defaced. The relief on the flank depicts a four-armed Vishnu seated on a cushioned throne in what is technically known as the lalitasana (sportive attitude), while an attendant, probably a female, is standing on his left. The left foot of the god rests upon a small footstool. His upper right hand holds a mace, and the lower one is placed in abhayamudra (pose of grantirig immunity from fear). He is profusely ornamented, and wears the mandaramala (garland—of celestial flowers). Under his throne are an atlant and some other indistinct figures. The relief on the front panel contains a group of three figures: Vishnu seated between his two consorts.

The sculptures belong to about the seventh or eighth century A.D. Andarkot has a particularly sorrowful interest for the Hindus of Kashmir, for it was in the fort here that the last Hindu ruler, Queen Kotadevi, surrendered to her rebellious servant, Shah Mir, on certain stipulations which he did not fulfil afterwards.

The Wular Lake

The ancient name of the Wular lake was the Mahapadmasaras, (lake of Mahapadma), the great Serpent Deity. Its modern name is probably derived from the Sanskrit ullola, the lake with the "high-leaping "waves.

The historian Jonaraja states that King Zain-ul-abidin was anxious to build such a monument to his fame as had never been built by any king before. After much deliberation he decided to construct an island-palace in the middle of the Wular lake, but he was so greatly impressed with the magnitude of the task that he sought the wise men of his time for advice regarding the ways and means of its accomplishment. They encouraged his efforts by narrating the following legend:

In ancient times there was a city at that very place where there is the lake nowadays. The city was presided over by the great snake deity, Mahapadma. But the lapse of time, and the security given by beneficent rule, brought in its train luxury and vice among the citizens, which grew with such alarming rapidity that Mahapadma resolved upon the destruction of the entire city, including its inhabitants. But, among the residents of the doomed city was a humble and virtuous potter, whom the deity resolved to spare. He appeared to him in a dream and, warning him of the impending fate of the city, told him to save himself. Next morning the potter related the warning to the citizens, but was laughed at for his pains.

As soon, therefore, as the potter left the city, the waters began to rise until the entire countryside was overwhelmed by one tremendous deluge. To quote from Jonaraja: "The terrified children who stood, at first when the water was low, at the feet of their mothers, soon, as the water began to rise higher, got into their laps, then clung to their breasts, next jumped upon their shoulders, and finally sat upon their heads, as if they were their embodied vital breaths. The flood covered the quaking limbs of women as if it were an affectionate lover embracing his beloved whose limbs are trembling with emotion."

After the Naga had thus wreaked his vengeance upon the sinful city, he established his permanent residence in the newly formed lake.

"The Lord of the Snakes was in reality Kaliya, who, being trampled upon by the feet of Krishna, bore the mark of a lotus on his head, and from that time onwards bore the appellation of Mahapadma."

Zain-ul-abidin's wise men then wound up their story by the naive assurance that he, being an incarnation of Hari, could do as he pleased in the domain of his liege subject Mahapadma, and that his efforts would assuredly be crowned with success. He therefore set about vigorously for accomplishment of his purpose. Large cargo boats, which are still plentiful in Kashmir, were filled with boulders and sunk at the spot selected. The island was named Zainalanka after its builder, and still retains that name.

The king built a small but very beautiful mosque at one corner of it, the ruins of which are still in existence. It is built of large blocks of limestone, similar to those used in the mediaeval temples of Kashmir. Even the mouldings are those which are so common in the ancient Hindu temples. The principal decorative feature externally is a double row of trefoiled niches, which are flanked by pretty fluted columns surmounted by ribbed capitals. The lower row of niches stands on a quirked ovolo course, and is surmounted by a filleted torus. The corner pilasters have square filleted capitals. The two flank walls of the porch survive.

The interior was paved with large stone flags. The floor was on a level with the filleted torus outside.

A large assortment of architectural fragments of Hindu temples, such as fluted columns, stones from pilasters, jambs, etc., are scattered round about the site, which tends to prove that there was once a Hindu temple also on the island. This hypothesis is further strengthened by the presence of a big Shiva-linga, which is partly submerged, on the east side of the island. It is probable that the temple also was built by Zain-ul-abidin, for none of his successors on the Kashmir throne was capable of such a colossal task. There are indications to show that there were series of steps on all sides leading down to the water, though the principal landing seems to have been on the east side.

The only other structure on the island is a small domed chamber of brick masonry measuring 15' 7" square internally. This was also partly built of Hindu materials. The string-courses on top of the walls consist of projecting wooden beams. The entire surface of the chamber seems to have been coated with painted plaster. Externally the walls were adorned with shallow arched recesses which were originally covered with plaster. They were separated by glazed tiles. The square impressions of these tiles are visible on the plaster backing wherever it still adheres to the walls. Fragments of painted and glazed tiles are Iying in the debris.

The structure seems to be a tomb, and is probably contemporary with the mosque.

In 1874, Dr. Vincent-Smith discovered on this island a stone slab bearing a Persian inscription which mentioned the name of Zain-ul-abidin and contained the date A.H. 847—A.D. 1442-43.

Garur

On the northeastern shore of the lake is situated the village of Garur. It contains a small mediaeval temple 4' 2" square internally, and 7' 3" high from basement to cornice. The roof has disappeared and the base is buried underground. The temple faces northwest and stands on the bank of a spring. The steps which led down to the water are now missing. The absence of the external trefoil niches is remarkable. The roof was undoubtedly pedimented. There is a small pointed niche in each of these walls, which contains a sculptured relief. That on the back bears a three-headed Shiva. The other two figures are too defaced to be identified with anything approaching certainty.

The ceiling is built of overlapping stones.

Wangath

The Srinagar-Sonamarg high roadl branches off at Wusan to the mountain village of Wangath and the long and narrow glen known to sportsmen by the name of Wangath Nala. The dense dark green forests of pine and fir which clothe the steep and in some places almost vertical hillsides are favourite haunts of the bear in early autumn, when maize begins to ripen. The cow-track—for the Wangath road is nothing better—winds along the mountain spurs, always following the tortuous course of the Kanka-nadi torrent, whose white and foaming waters form a striking contrast to the sombre hue of the surrounding woods. On all sides the view is bounded by long ranges of hills rising higher and still higher as they recede until they terminate in the bare, jagged, towering peaks of Tilail.

An uphill trudge of eight or nine miles brings the jaded traveller to Narannag, the site of an interesting group of temples which are commonly known as the Wangath temples, though the village bearing the name "Wangath "is three miles distant. They are situated at the foot of the Butsher mountain, whose extreme steepness and slipperiness have become proverbial, arld have made it the terror and despair of Gangabal pilgrims.

Narannag is the modern name of ancient Sodaratirtha, which has been, since very early times, an important place of pilgrimage in Kashmir. The site probably owes its sanctity to the existence of a large spring, near which have been built two groups of temples belonging to the mediaeval era. All the temples are more or less in ruins, chiefly owing to the inroads of vegetation. The stone used is the greyish granite which is found in abundance at the place. The first group, that is the one nearer Wangath, comprises six temples situated within an enclosure wall. Judging by their positions, as they are by no means symmetrically disposed in relation to one another, and by the difference in their architectural details, it is probable that the various structures were built at different dates (Plate LXII).

(1) The principal temple is a square of 25', and, except in a few particulars, does not differ from other temples of Kashmir. The first point of departure from the usual style are the entrances. We have seen the temples of the vimana type, which have all the four sides open. But this one has two entrances opposite each other in the northeast and southwest sides. The second distinction is its domed ceiling, though there is no doubt that externally the roof was pyramidal. A large quantity of lime has been used in the masonry of the temple. The ceiling is built of circular courses of kanjur stone, and is crowned at the apex by a full-blown lotus. The dome springs from four large corner stones, which cut off the angles formed by the walls. On two sides of the string-course upon which the dome rests are eight rectangular slots (four on each side), which seem to have been intended to hold the rafters of a canopy over the image. The interior measures 17' square. In the centre of the floor is a square space which is unpaved. It marks the site of the pedestal of the image. The mortices of the tenons of the doors can still be seen in both entrances.

The two sides which are closed are decorated externally with square-topped recesses, each of which contains the pedestal of an image which was probably a replica of the one in the sanctum itself. The core of the roof consists of rubble-stone masonry in lime.

This temple has been identified by Sir Aurel Stein with the Jyeshthega temple of Lalitaditya.

(2) The small temple to the left possesses niches on three sides intended for images. Their pedestals with tenons are in situ. Part of the kanjur backing of the dome is intact on top of the walls.

(3) The temple immediately touching the porch of the preceding shrine is a single square structure, plain both internally and externally. One stone of the roof, which is the only one in situ, shows that the ceiling was not domical, but was built of overlapping stones.

(4) Immediately behind is the basement of another small temple. Its superstructure has fallen down.

(5-6) Of the two temples behind, one has its entrance facing northeast, and the other faces southeast. The ceiling of the former was of the overlapping type while that of the latter was probably domical.

(7) Immediately to the left of the latter is the ruined plinth of another temple, smaller than any of those described above.

The gateway of the enclosure is situated, curiously enough, at the northwest corner, and not in the middle of the wall, as is the case in other temples. It is, as usual, a two-chambered structure. In each chamber are the bases of two columns which supported the roof of the porch. Fragments of circular columns which stood on the bases-are lying strewn round about the site. The retaining wall of the plinth on which this group of temples stands is built of closely packed pieces of slate, and in places where vegetation has not played havoc with it, it is very compact and beautiful.

A broad causeway paved with huge blocks of granite leads to the second group of temples, situated about two hundred yards farther off.

Between the two groups of temples are a number of structures which in themselves deserve to be classed into a third group. All of them have fallen down, but one, the base only of which is in existence, is unique in Kashmir. It appears to have been a spacious pillared hall or barahdari about loo' long by 67' broad. The bases of the columns are in situ. They are eight in number on the longer side and four on the shorter. The staircase is built between the central pair of columns facing the first group of temples. The slots in the landing on the top of the stairs seem to have been intended for holding the posts of screens.

The lower group of temples is likewise enclosed in a massive rectangular stone wall pierced by a two-chambered gateway. Inside the wall are half a dozen structures, all in ruined condition and partly buried under the ground. The largest temple has been identified by Sir Aurel Stein with that of Shiva-Bhutesvara. Internally it is a square of 17', and was similar to the largest temple in the first group. The small temple to its right has a round-headed entrance. There are two small shrines on its south, the first of which differs from all the structures at this site in that it is built of small pieces of slate in lime mortar, placed upon a granite base. The peculiar feature of the second is an immense rectangular stone trough carved out of a single gigantic block of granite. Among the objects lying scattered about the compound, the most noteworthy are two fragments, in the southeast corner of the quadrangle, of an octagonal pedestal of a Shiva-linga, and two stones in the same corner of the quadrangle, each decorated with a pair of remarkably well-executed geese.

The long raised line of brick masonry on the enclosure wall is the debris of the cellular quadrangle which usually surrounds the Kashmiri temple.

Outside the north-western corner of the peristyle is the large spring, the real lodestone of the pilgrims, which was the occasion of all this magnificence. Its cool, delicious water, perhaps, contributed to some extent to its sanctity. The water issues out of the mountain side through the masonry walls of the tank. Slightly higher up, and more than half-buried under the ground, is a small temple whose double pyramidal roof is the only existing roof in the whole group of temples here. This has been identified by Sir Aurel Stein with the temple of Bhairava, near which the turbulent baron Dhanva was decapitated for encroaching upon the lands and revenues of these temples.

Before leaving the site, the visitor should not fail to observe the unusually massive stone retaining wall of this group of temples. The granite blocks are of so extraordinary a size and are so beautifully dressed and finely joined as to give the impression that their carvers regarded them more in the light of wooden beams than as close-grained intractable boulders to be chipped into shape with vigilant care and inexhaustible patience. It is probable that this wall served the double purpose of protecting the temple enclosure from being overwhelmed by the debris of the hill above, and also as the back wall of the range of cells on this side.

The site has from time immemorial enjoyed a very high degree of popular esteem, which remains unimpaired to this day, thanks to the pilgrims who, after consigning the ashes of their dead relatives to the Gangabal lake, make it a point to offer worship here. The temples were endowed with extensive estates, and the priests in charge seem to have been a particularly influential body. In the later mediaeval period, after the death of Avantivarman, these temples shared the misfortunes which came upon Kashmir with ever-increasing violence.

The temple treasury was plundered by Bhadresvara, the minister of Samgramaraja (A.D. 1003-1028); a conflagration in the reign of Uchchala (A. D. 1101-1111) inflicted much damage upon the buildings; during the reign of Jayasimha (A.D. 1128-1155), Hayavadana, a rebel baron, had the temples "sacked by marauding hillmen." Sumanas, a brother of Rilhana, the minister of Jayasimha, built a matha or congregation hall here. It is possible that the pillared hall is this same matha. Further excavations may throw light upon the question.

The Temple Legacy of Kashmir—An Account from Burried History: Kashmir abounds with remains of temples of antiquity characterised by a combination of massiveness and simplicity and of solidity and grandeur which symbolises power glorified with piety. They also display refinement and art. Their ponderous solidity of structure being relieved by the grace of colossal sculpture coupled with an inexhaustible variety of architectural details have called forth admiration of many that included attention of great Chinese travellers like Hieun Tsiang (631-633 AD) and Oukong (759 AD). There are few temple ruins in India comparable to those found in Kashmir. So rightly observed Dr. Ernst Neve, the famous medical missionary of Kashmir, "Ancient India has nothing more worthy of its early civilization than the grand ruins of Kashmir which are the pride of Kashmiris and admiration of travellers. The massive, the grotesque and elegant in architecture may be admirable in parts of India but nowhere is to be found counterpart of the classically graceful yet systematically massive edifices as in Kashmir temple ruins."

Ancient monuments of very great archaeological interest which disclose the existence of a lost civilization are, as stated above, numerous in Kashmir. The devotion of kings, the reserves of the kingdoms and skills of master artists in the past combined, to raise the magnificent and the beautiful temple edifices in Kashmir. They were built to endure for all times. Their solidity of construction and their gigantic size strike one with wonder that man could have built them. Many kings have come and gone and civilizations have bloomed and vanished since they were built. People go and pace around them and gaze on them with amazement and awe—amazement inspired by the stupendous might and skill of their builders and awe excited by the ruins of these edifices which look as if weeping over the departed glory of their founders.

But the disintegrating hand of time and earthquakes and the vandalistic propensities of certain bigoted rulers have laid many temples of Kashmir to waste. The climate of Kashmir too has been peculiarly destructive to them added by the frosted snow lying long over them. One must appreciate that founders of these temples were wise enough to use sculptured stones of very large dimensions as smaller ones should have under these conditions crumbled and vanished long ago.

The Kashmiris in bygone ages were called *Shastra Shilpina* or architects, an epithet applied to them on account of their well known skills in building. The people had a religious past having deep rooted connection and notions of religion based on ancient traditions and sacred mandates. Even if the present finds, ruined temples, the fact remains that their lofty arches and massive blocks of masonry were quarried and erected bit by bit by a people who expended their best on buildings which were to be set aside for nothing but the noble purpose of worship.

But alas! repeated devastations were done and havoc was wrought to them by cruel implacable zealots and vandals from time to time. It's a pity that formerly these most important and precious relics of the past glory of Kashmir were allowed to remain in a lamentary neglected condition. Unprotected from the destructive and disintegrating influences of weather the ancient temple monuments in Kashmir gradually crumbled to ruins.

In 1875, Hofrath Georg Buhler and after him several European Sanskrit scholars came and delved in the Kashmir soil. However, all honour goes to the late Lord Curzon who actuated by his great love for antiquities established an Archaeological Department in India and then the Kashmir Darbar caught the hint and instituted an Archaeological Department of their own in Srinagar. Yet the first nucleus of knowledge about Kashmir temple monuments came from the works of European Savants like Cole, Cunningham, Fergusson and foremost amongst the later source of information on these, names of Stein, Buhler, Vogel and Konow stand out.

In the course of researches, Stein succeeded in identifying a large number of interesting spots with rare account of history. Among these were the famous city of *Parihasapura*built by Lalitaditya as his favourite residence and capital of Kashmir, *Shardavanna* (modern Harwan) where the great Buddhist teacher Nagarjuna is reported to have lived and the temples of *Shiva Bhutesa* and *Shiva Jeyshthesa* situated near the hamlet of Vangath.

He also spotted *Kaptesvara*—modern Kother with its two temples and *Mamalaka* the modern Mamal near Pahalgam with its little shrine of *Mameswara Shiva* built by Jeyshthesa in 1126-1128 AD. Stein also established that a ruined temple was converted into tomb of Peer Haji Muhammad in the city of Srinagar. This probably represented the temple of

Ramasvamin attributed to Ranaditya. Buhler identified the ancient city of *Jayapura Dvaravati* founded by *Jayapida Vinayadita* grandson of Muktapida Lalitaditya, towards the end of 8th century AD with the identification of extensive remains near the village of Andrkoth.

Vogel made known the remains of temple sites near a village called Malangpura which is situated about 3 miles southwest of Avantipura. Sten Konow identified for the first time the temple in the Firozpur Nala below Gulmarg. Alongwith these discoveries also came to light two representations of *Lakulisa* or *Luktapani* on the doorways temples of *Puranadhishthana* and *Payar*. Though Cunningham recognised in the temple of *Puranadhishthana* the temple of Meruvardhan Svami-Vishnu, erected by a minister of Partha between 906-921 AD but presence of *Lakulisa* the form of Shiva proved that this temple was a Shiva fane.

The inner arrangement of Kashmir temples is essentially Indian yet the stepped roof of South and curved spire of temples in North are missing. The temples of Kashmir are either square or oblong. They are subdivided into closed (*Vimana*) or open (*Mandapa*) type. The doorway of temples in Kashmir face in all directions but care is everywhere taken to place the water spout invariably to the left of image. The former practice is also at variance with the rule that Vishnu temples should always face towards the east. The temples of Kashmir without exception are what Ram Raz designates, as *Suddha* edifices i.e. composed of one kind of material from the base to the summit. The material employed in them is lime stone of somewhat bluish colour, fine grain and susceptible of receiving a high polish. Only one temple that of Buniar is built in granite stone of whitish colour. A porous kind of stone locally called as *Kanait* and similar to *Kanjur* of Taxilla was used for ceilings and also for foundations of cells. Brick has never been found in actual use as material for the ancient temple buildings in Kashmir. This fact is established on a Sarada inscription of Ramadeva which was discovered by Konow in the village of Arigoam.

The ancient temples of Kashmir so far known to us range in date about the middle of 8th to about the 12th century AD.

The only examples of a later period being small shrines of no architectural value. Fergusson could not discover any temple site in Kashmir of a later date than 1000 AD but Stein however, established that the temples of Kother and Mamal belong to 11th and 12th centuries. With the help of many Gandharva monasteries and other Buddhist buildings unearthed at Taxilla one can reconstruct a fairly complete picture of architecture of Kashmir of that period. Unhappily no buildings of that age have survived in Kashmir above the ground.

Even in the days of Lalitaditya, earlier buildings had become scarce. However, Lalitaditya discovered by excavation deep under the ground two ancient temples with closed doors containing images of *Kesava* which on the ground of inscriptions engraved on their bases were interpreted as having been put by Rama and Laxmana, the heroes of Ramayana, a story which seems to show that the script of the inscriptions was not known to the pandits of Kashmir of Lalitaditya's time. The two images in question are stated to have been later installed in new temples at *Parihasapura*. It was Lalitaditya who imported into Kashmir for the first time, a Buddha image from Magadha.

The dedicatory inscriptions which most of the temples of Kashmir are said to have contained are lost and so has been the gradual loss of grandeur. The peristyle which was an important feature in the temples of 8th and 9th centuries disappeared in the temples of Payar, Mamal and Kother. A similar process is observed in the form of trefoil arch which gradually merges into the round arch and of the pediment which dwindles into a mere decorative ornament.

The porticoes in the side walls of the sanctum which in the earlier times were equal in dimensions to that on the entrance side denigrate in later examples into small sized niches such as we notice in some of later temples near Vangath. It is to be noticed that much of this decay in the style of architecture must have been also due to weakness and comparative resourcelessness of the later Hindu rulers in Kashmir, a few of whom were even driven to the necessity of robbing the valuable property of temples and other religious institutions.

Stupas of the Maurya time existed in Srinagar which contained each a measure of relics of *Tathagata*. A tooth of Buddha 11/2 inches in length is stated to have been enshrined in stupa attached to *Jayendravihara* in the same city. In another *stupa* which Kanishka erected in some place in Kashmir, he deposited sheets of red copper engraved with commentary on the three Pitakas. One of these, a *vihara* was erected at Arigoam in honour of Bodhistava Avalokitesvara. Parihaspura was the name of an ancient city founded by Lalitaditya in the first half of the 8th century AD. Already in the time of Kalhana, the city was in ruins and evidence shows that temples of *Pattan* were partly built with the materials carried away from this city.

From the ancient site of *Rajavihara* in one of the cells, a small earthen vessel was discovered. It contained 44 silver coins of Durlabadeva, grandfather of Lalitaditya Muktapida, Jayapida Vinayaditya, grandson of Lalitaditya and Vigrahatunga. The temples at *Parihasapura* were called *Parihasakesva, Muktakesva, Mahavarha* and *Goverdhanadhara*. Of these the temple of *Goverdhandhara* was identified by Stein at a village now known as Gurdan in Kashmir. The ruins of sacred image and fragment remains of stone lintel and a capital column is all that was located of which Vigne established that capital column had been carried away to *Puranadhisthana*. According to later Persian chronicles of Narayan Koul and Mumammed Azim, the fragments of this column were still visible upto the early part of 18th century. It is now believed that this column was converted into the road metal of the Jhelum Valley road.

At the village of Vangath are situated two groups of ruins of temples with separate enclosures named *Rajadainbal* and *Nagbal*. Stein identified the principle temple of the Eastern group with that of *Shiva Bhutesa* and the western group with that of *Shiva Jeyasthesa*. These shrines were places of pilgrimage from very early times. Ashoka obtained a son from this deity and Jaluka son of Ashoka made a vow that he would ever worship *Jeyasthesa*. A spring north to this temple site was also identified by Stein as the tank into which the minister of Avantiverman threw the bleeding body of Dhanva who had confiscated the lands endowed upon the temple of *Bhutesa*.

The temple situated two miles above Rampur, close to Jhelum Valley road and known by the name of Buniar (*Bhaniyar* or *Bhavaniyar*) due to its dedication to Goddess Bhavani is infact, a temple attributable to the worship of Vishnu. It is by far the best preserved temple of Kashmir on account of two reasons, one it is built in hard granite rock and two because it was left untouched by the *iconoclast* Sikandar due to its remote location. A temple existed between Uri and Nowshera which Cunningham relying on Baron Hugel called as *Brangutri* a corrupted derivative of *Varnakotri* meaning Golden Durga. However, the local tradition was never familiar with this name. The temple was dedicated to Vishnu as fragments of life sized statue of this deity were found in the courtyard. But fortunately, the throne of the image has escaped destruction at the hands of a road contractor who though had taken it out and left in the entrance. It has now been put back in its original position against the back wall.

The modern town of *Pattan* marks the site of ancient city of *Sankarapurapatana* founded by King Sankaravarman (883-902 AD). Here the king erected a temple and named it as *Sankaragaurisvara* while his wife erected a temple which she named as *Sughandesa* after her own name. Sankaravarman's minister Ratanavardhana built a third temple and named it *Ratanaverdhanesa*. Cunningham identified the temples built by the kings and queen. The third temple has perished and its materials today survive around the walls of baolis and near by Dak Bungalow. Cole took five pictures of these monuments. These were however, damaged only in an earthquake which took place in 1880.

The tomb of Zainul-ab-din is situated in a large enclosure on the right bank of river Jhelum below the fourth bridge of the city of Srinagar. The grave in which the remains of Zainul-ab-din lie buried is an insignificant one hardly recognizable from other graves around it but the enclosure wall surrounding it undoubtedly belonged to an ancient Hindu temple. The ancient name of this temple will perhaps never be known but there is no doubt that it was a temple of *Vaishnava* deity which was erected about the 9th or 10th century. A part of this complex encloses also in Muhammadan style structures built by Sultan Habib of Kashmir in 1573 AD.

At the village Tapar twelve miles onwards from Baramullah towards Srinagar are the ruins of a temple called *Narenderashvara* which was built by Narendraprabha queen of Pratapaditya-II who reigned Kashmir from 634 to 684 AD. It was ruined by Sikandar and his son Zainul-ab-din (1420-1478 AD) used the stones in the construction of the bund from Naidkhai to Sopur. In the Wular lake there is a small island called Suna Lank.

The island contained a Hindu temple whose traces were available till recently. It was demolished and the island was raised and shaped with same materials by king Zainul-ab-din. Thereafter, he called the island as Zaina Dab after his name and extoled it as a delightful spot for pleasure parties. But the ruins will always tell a Hindu tale.

The shrine of *Tulamula* sacred to Goddess *Kshirbhawani* or *Ragina Devi* is most popular place of pilgrimage among the Pandits of Kashmir. A curious phenomena observed here is that the water of spring changes colours occasionally like purple, green and so on. The *Ragina Kavach*—a psalm in praise of the Goddess included in Sanskrit work *Rudrya mala tantra* proves the pilgrimage is an ancient one. The *jagir* of the priests of *Tulmula* was once confiscated by King Jayapida who ruled Kashmir from 753 to 784 AD and one of the priests of *Tulmula* named Ittila cursed him for his impious deeds when a golden pole of the canopy suddenly tumbled down upon the king from which he sustained serious injury resulting in his death. The Mahatma of the shrine says the Goddess was originally in Ceylon in the house of Demon king Ravana after whose death, she was brought by Hanumana here but its account is not mentioned in Ramayana and Mahabharatha.

This place of pilgrimage was not visited by the Hindus during the Muslim rule and had been altogether forgotten by people until about 350 years ago when a Kashmiri pandit named Krishna Pandit Tapilu, whose descendents reportedly lived at Bohri Kadal in Srinagar until recent times about 50 years ago, by looking into a book called *Brihad Katha* discovered it and since then the people have again commenced visiting it. The offerings of the milk, rice and sugar that form the sediment in the spring was removed only twice within living memory. The first in 1867 by a man named Dewan Narsingh Dyal which followed a virulent epidemic of cholera.

After that, nobody dared to do it again for the displeasure of goddess until the spring nearly disappeared with sedimentation when Pandit Vidhalal Dhar, the chief *rais* of Kashmir in 1902 decided to clear the spring. The digging unearthed an ancient temple in the centre built of large sculptured white stones with marvellous images of Hindu deities. Subsequently, the whole shrine was repaired in 1907 by Maharaja Pratap Singh with the erection of marble structure and fencing on the old site in the centre of spring.

The most conspicuous temple in the heart of Srinagar the Shankaracharya temple on the hill of *Gopadari* was built by King Gopaditya who reigned Kashmir from 308-328 BC. King Lalitaditya (701-737 AD) repaired it. Sikandar the *iconoclast* (1394-1469 AD) did not for some reasons destroy it. Zainul-ab-din repaired its roof which had tumbled during an earthquake. There were steps of scultpured stones leading from *Shudashyar Ghat* of the Jhelum river right upto the top of hill. With these stones it is said *Pathar Masjid* in city was built by Noor Jehan, queen of Jahangir.

The *Shiva linga* which is now worshipped in the temple is the modern one and was erected in 1907. The original image which existed was a *linga* encircled by a snake. A small renovation was done to this temple as late as in 1925 by the Maharaja of Mysore who during his visit to Kashmir beautified the temple by getting five electric search lights, erected around it and one more on the top of it. It was atop here that Shankaracharya during the time of Abhinav Gupta (993-1015 AD) composed the well known hymn called *Soundarya Lahari* in praise of Shakti.

Turning towards the east beyond the Jama Masjid is the temple of *Pravareshvara* built by King Pravarasena II. It is now utilized as *Ziarat* of Baha-ud-din Sahib. Below the fourth bridge on the right bank of the river Jhelum, was a five domed stone temple called *Mahashri* which was built by Pravarasena II. It is now converted into a graveyard of Muslims. There is only one large tomb inside the temple which is of Sikandar *Butshikan's* wife, and one's attention is arrested farther on by a large building on the right bank between the third and fourth bridges which is called *Shah-i-Hamadan*.

There is on this spot, a spring called *Kali*. There was a Hindu temple over it which too was built by Pravarasena II (70-110 AD) and was called *Kalishri*. Today the locality is called as Kalashpora—a corruption of *Kali-Shri-Pur*. This temple was destroyed by Sultan Qutub-ud-din (1373-1394 AD) and with its material he built the *Khanaqah* which though got burnt twice was rebuilt. Today, on the wall fronting the river Pandits have put a large red ochre mark and worship the Goddess Kali there. In front of the *Kali Shri* across the river, at the *Pather Masjid* ghat stood the shrines of *Zayathesa Bhairava* and *Vishaksena Bhairava* at the Dalal mohalla. Both these shrines have been turned into graveyards.

To the west of *Jama Masjid* near *Kadi Kadal* existed a temple of *Sadbhavashri* built by Pravarasena II. It is converted into a *Ziarat* of Pir Haji Muhammad and later Sultan Qutub-ud-din was buried here. Near the 6th bridge at some distance from the right bank of the river towards the north are the ruins of the temple of *Skanda Bhavana* now called *Khandabhavana* which was built by Skand Gupta, minister of king Yudhisthira II (170-209 AD).

It stands converted into a *Ziarat* of Pir Muhammad Basur. There are also here near the river bank ruins of temple which was founded by Pravarasena II and called *Laukishri*. The *ghat* of this temple is still called *Lokhari Yar*—a corruption of *Lauki-Shri-Yar*. Passing farther below exist the ruins of stone temple called *Tribhuvanasvamin* which was built by Chandrapida who reigned Kashmir from 687 to 695 AD. A Muhammedan saint named Thag Baba Sahib was buried here and the place became to be known as Thag Baba Sahib.

Just opposite the above place, on the right bank near 7th bridge below Jhelum, Didda, Queen of Kshema Gupta built a *Matha* calling it *Didda Matha*. Today, it is called as *Didda Mar* while the *Matha* has been converted into the tomb of Malik Sahib. About two miles near Vicharnag are the ruins of the temple *Vikrameshvara* built by Vikramaditya (523-565 AD). It was destroyed by Sikander who used its stone for the construction of a mosque that exists now there. About half a mile farther east one reaches the ruins of the temple of *Amritvbhavana* built by Amritprabha, Queen of Meghavana (12-16 AD). It is now converted into a *Ziarat* and burial grounds of Vantabhavan locality.

About two miles from Vicharnag towards the south was the temple of *Ranveshvara* built by King Ranaditya (223 AD). The ruins of this temple have to be looked amidst the precincts of mosque of Madin Sahib. Farther here there is a large Chak burial ground which has remains of many unknown temple monuments and now converted into a *Ziarat*. Historian, Manakha referred to this temple as an object of his father's devotion.

The famous *Jama Masjid* was built originally by Sikander in 1407 AD from the materials of a large stone temple called temple of *Tarapida* constructed by King Tarapida (696-700 AD). Beside this, numerous ancient remains of stone temples are scattered around this mosque. The site of the mosque was considered sacred by Buddhists also in earlier times and even till recent times people from Ladakh visited it. They called it by its ancient name *Tsitsung Tsublak Kang*.

The first ancient edifice that one may encounter in the city of Srinagar is the temple of *Narendrasvamin* which was built by Lakhana Narendraditya who reigned in Kashmir from 209-222 AD. It has been turned into a *Ziarat* and even the locality is today known as Narparistan. From Srinagar at a distance of eight miles towards the Sindh valley falls a village called Amburher. Queen Suryamati (1028-1036 AD) founded two *Mathas* here. Ruins of old temple found at this place are built into the *Ziarat* of Farukhzad Sahib and are scattered here and there.

Remains of ancient temple are found in several places near Gupkar founded by King Gopaditya. Large carved slabs are built into *Ziarats* and also into basement of other Muhammadan buildings in the village itself. On the road close to the Ziarat lay a colossal *linga* 10 ft. in diameter which it is regretted was cut and taken away by somebody for building purposes in 1929. About 7 miles from Srinagar lies the village Zewan which in ancient times was a place of high rise monuments and had a pool filled with pure water sacred to *Takshanaka*—Lord of Snakes.

The pool existed even until recent times as *Takshanaka Naga* when pilgrims on way to Harshevara paid a visit to it. All this is lost now with the imposition of Muslim traditions followed on the spot.

About two miles to the east of Zewan, lies the famous village of Khonmouh where lie ruins of some old temples in the middle of tanks found here and there converted into a *Ziarat*. Some distance from Khrew lies Pampur the ancient Padmapura found by King Padma in the 9th century. He built a temple here called *Vishnupadmasvamin*. From the scanty remains of this ancient temple was built the *Ziarat* of Mir Muhammad Hamdani in which even today are visible fine columns and ornamented slabs taken from this temple. Other smaller *Ziarats* of the town also show similar materials.

A mile away from Khrew is the village of Shar known in ancient times by the name of *Shanara* as an *agrahara* founded by King Sachinara father of Ashoka. It can today be identified only as Ziarat of Khwaja Khzir amidst several small springs which is built with the remains of the temple that existed here. About two miles to the left of the road leading from Pampur to Avantipura there are two temples at Ladu, one surrounded by water and a smaller one close by a little higher-up the hill side. The small square cella and other materials of these old temples have now been annexed to a neighbouring *Ziarat*.

Twenty nine miles from Srinagar lies the town of Bijbehara the ancient *Vijayesvara*. The town contained the famous shrine of valley attributed to Shiva built by great king Ashoka who also later built two temples called *Ashokesvara*. The old temple alongwith *linga* of *Shiva Vijayesvara* was destroyed by Sikander and the remains of destruction left over and available till recent times found their way in the construction of *Bade Masjid*.

The stone receptical for temple offerings makes a part of *Ratna Haji mosque* and its pillar is found inside it.

In the Lidar valley at Mamal anciently called *Mamalaka* nestles the ruins of a small Shiva temple of sculptured stones. The temple escaped destruction at the hands of Sikandar. A remarkable account describes its best. "Sikander went up the Lidar valley with the intention of proceeding to the cave of Amarnath and breaking the ice linga there and also the temple at Mamal enroute. On reaching Ganeshbal he broke the stone image of Ganesh standing in the middle of Lambodari river. It is said that when the knee of image was struck by Sikander with a hammer, a flood of blood flowed down.

On witnessing this freightful spectacle, the *iconoclast* got terrified and thenceforth desisted, out of fear, from further destruction of Hindu temples and images. He then and there abandoned the idea of going farther to Amarnath and returned crest fallen, regretting his past sacrilegious acts and deeds. On his way back, on reaching Bijbehara, Sikander is said to have found a slab with an old inscription in Sanskrit in the ruins of *Vijayesvara* temple he had destroyed previously. In that it was stated, "*Bismillahi mantrena nashantea Vijayeswara*" meaning that with the pronouncement of *Bismillah,* (a phrase used by Muslims at the beginning of all actions), the *Vijayesvara* temple shall get destroyed.

Seeing that what he had done had already been predicted, Sikander was shaken for having been got identified and instrumental in the fulfilment of this inevitable Hindu prediction and what followed was that a few temples left were saved from destruction by him.

A small village hamlet about a mile north of the sacred springs of Mattan known as Bumzu contain three ancient temples which date to the 10th century AD. The most important among them is the temple now converted into Muhammadan tomb and known as *Ziarat* of Bamadin Sahib. The temple was erected by Bhima Sahi, maternal grandfather of Queen Didda in 950-958 AD. According to *Rishinama* this saint before his conversion to Islam bore the name of Bhuma Sadu. Another temple closeby has been turned into the tomb of Rukun-ud-din who died sometime after Baba Bamadin. These temples of great antiquity are besides the cave temples of Bumzu the vestiges of which still exist.

The temples described above were erected during the Hindu period of Kashmir history. More than these the rest must have been exceedingly numerous as is evidenced by the immense number of their ruins present in the foundations and walls of mosques and houses, besides ghats and embankments. A capital turned upside down, a broken shaft or an injured pedestal may frequently be observed embedded in a wall of ordinary office building made in stone.

But such marvellous works of art, "denote the former presence in Kashmir of a people worthy of study. And the people who built the ancient temples of Kashmir must have been religious for the remains are all of the temples or sacred emblems and not of palaces, commercial offices or hotels and they must have at least held one large idea, else they would not have built on so enduring a scale. They must have been men of strong and simple tastes averse to paltry and the florid".

In 1339 AD, Kashmir passed into the hands of Muhammadan rulers when queen Kota the widow of the last Hindu ruler was murdered by Shah Mir. No Hindu religious buildings of any consequences were erected in Kashmir in Muslim period. The Hindu remains of this period are insignificant shrines constructed by private individuals of small means which one can frequently meet within the valley of Kashmir.

Temples Along the Indus: High above the mighty Indus, on hills streaked red with salt, forts with citadels, habitation sites, and temples were built from the sixth to the eleventh centuries A.D. (Figs. 1-3). Largely ignored by scholarship in this century, and orphaned since partition, these structures form an important missing link in the history of architecture in South Asia (Mumtaz 1989). A new integrated archaeological study of these sites, undertaken by this author with colleagues in Peshawar, has begun to recover new aspects of this important period of South Asia's antiquity.

The far northwest in ancient India what now is the Panjab and Northwest Frontier provinces of Pakistan, Swat, and parts of Afghanistan is better known for the presence of eclectic cross currents over many centuries, at important archaeological sites such as the city of Taxila (Marshall 1951), and for the massive numbers of Buddhist sculptural and structural remains we associate with the region of Gandhara (Ingholt 1957). These Gandharan remains already show visually a local vocabulary that lets architectural traditions from India, Central Asia, and the classical world stand together, as in many Gandharan Buddhist narrative steles or as ornament on the famous shrine of the double-headed eagle or the Dharmarajika stupa at Taxila. The Chinese pilgrim, Hsuan Tsang, visiting Gandhara in the seventh century A.D., noted hundreds of Hindu structures as well as many declining Buddhist sites in the region (Watters 1904-5).

If there is a Gandharan legacy in Hindu temple architecture, however, it takes two paths: one, a unique tradition of pyramidal pent-roof temples built in Kashmir from before the reign of Lalit ditya in the eighth century A.D. (Kak 1933; Meister, et. al., 1988:351-93), and a separated tradition in Gandhara itself, along the upper Indus, and onto the high plateau and escarpments of the Salt Range in the Panjab (Lohuizen-De Leeuw 1959).

As an example, I might contrast the eighth-century (or earlier) temple at Loduv in Kashmir (Meister, et. al., 1988:361-3) and one of the surviving masonry sub-shrines at the Hindu pilgrimage site of Katas in the Panjab Salt Range. The square Kashmir shrine's circular interior space and hemispherical dome, for which a Gandharan prototype, a masonry structure at Guniar in Swat, is sometimes cited (Kak 1933:55-6; Meister, et. al., 1988:362), once was covered by a simple peeked pyramidal pent roof, as indicated by the pent-roofed frame decoratively surrounding its doorway.

The temple at Katas, on the other hand, while sharing the formula of a simple square plan with plain masonry walls and cantoned corner pilasters, struggled to give height to the temple by quite different means. The Katas sub-shrine's elevation can be reconstructed as a series of cornices with intermediate tiny rows of pillars and a crowning ribbed stone (amalaka), a type of "pre-Nagara" tower I have labelled "bhumi-prasada" after its use of many multiple stories. This early type of simply storied structure can best be paralleled at Sarnath, in Saurashtra, and elsewhere across northern India and the Deccan in the sixth century A.D. (Meister 1986; Meister, et. al., 1988: passim).

By contrast, the distinctive mode of monument that became the signature for Lalitaditya's powerful dynasty in Kashmir used a gabled pent roof, as is well preserved on temples at Narastan, Pandrethan, or Payar from the eighth to tenth centuries (ibid.: 351-93), a form already marked on the doorway of the earlier temple at Laduv. Antecedents for this gabled roof-type already can be seen in the architectural vocabulary of Gandhara, as can be suggested by the "classical" niche-pediments represented on the shrine of the double-headed eagle at Taxila as early as the first century B.C. (Harle 1986:74), or by the split pyramidal pediments in sculpture and on stupas from Gandhara.

At the northern Kafirkot ("foreigners' fortress") in the North West Frontier Province near the Chashma barrage north of Dera Ismail Khan, however, a true local experiment with Nagara architecture—the curved temple form of northern India—had already begun. The two earliest temples in this fort can most closely be related to early Garulaka or Maitraka dynasty temples in Saurashtra (coastal western India), at sites like Bhanasar and Dhank, from the sixth and early seventh centuries A.D., and Saindhava-dynasty temples from the same region in the eighth century (Nanavati and Dhaky 1966; Meister, et. al., 1988:167-206). Even the name of the little understood "Saindhava" dynasty seems to indicate their link with the Indus.

Scholarship in the past century including that of Aurel Stein (1937), Alexander Cunningham (1872-3:87-8), and Ananda Coomaraswamy 1927:108, 143) focused primarily on one particular temple in the Salt Range, however, that from the tenth century at Malot and on its links to the architecture of Kashmir. This whole group of temples in the northwest scholars have tended to date "post Islamic contact" because of the use of mortar, rubble-fill between masonry walls, arches, and squinched interior domes (Archaeological Survey of India Annual Report, 1920-1:6-7).

Percy Brown (1942), in his history of Indian architecture, placed these temples as a branch of Kashmir architecture, as also did James Harle (1986:197-8) in his Pelican History of Art volume. Harle, however, takes notice briefly, but only in his chapter on Kashmir temples, that "another group in Dera Ismail Khan ... forms an extension of post-Gupta Madhyadesa" (ibid.:198) rather than of Saurashtra as I suggest.

The early tenth-century temple at Malot does indeed mimic peak-roofed temples in Kashmir at a time of marital alliance between the Utpalas of Kashmir and the Hindu Shahi kings of Hund in Gandhara (Rehman 1979). It signals its difference on its walls, however, by placing curvilinear Nagara shrine models that mimic local Gandhara-Nagara temples at other contemporary Hindu Shahi sites in the tenth century, such as a pair of temples in a second important fortress, Bilot (south Kafirkot), to the west of the Indus near Dera Ismail Khan.

Sources for this Indus group of temples Malot excepted can much better be found in the Gandharan substrata and in the ferment of Nagara formation in other areas of north and western India (Meister 1981) than in Kashmir. Whether in the domed Buddhist compounds at Takht-i-bahi or the fifth-century moldings facing the Dharmarajika stupa at Taxila, antecedents are close at hand. Certainly the basic molding sequence of Gandhara-Nagara temples begins as early as Taxila, compared to those from the later temples at Bilot and Kafirkot. The typical slender pseudo-corinthian pilasters at Kafirkot as well as true arches can be seen also on the second/fourth-century Buddhist stupa at Guldhara in Afghanistan (Harle 1986:73). The characteristic sloping batter of niches and doorways (and sometimes walls) on these temples has its clear antecedents in Gandharan conventions. Even the use of interior squinches and masonry domes is not new to the region, nor is much of the architectural ornament in these temples unfamiliar in the Gandh ra region.

What is new is the Nagara modality of superstructure as it had developed in North India for the first time in the fifth and sixth centuries A.D. (Meister 1986, 1988). One might compare the shrine model on the wall of temple D at Bilot with the much better known proto-Nagara shrine model represented on the early sixth-century doorway to the "Gupta" temple at Deogarh in Central India, for example, or one on a brick stupa-base at Nalanda in Eastern India (Meister 1986:46-7).

Remarkably, this region preserves an almost continuous record of temples that define the evolution of a distinctive school of Gandhara-Nagara architecture. In this preliminary report and stylistic analysis of these monuments, let me give a brief review of these remains to frame this local and continuous craft tradition.

At northern Kafirkot, temples B and A represent the earliest experiments in this region with the developing Nagara formula. The much larger temple D at Bilot awkwardly formulates a Nagara tower on a square base, much like the pre-Nagara temple at Bile vara in Saurashtra in the seventh century (Meister, et. al., 1986:181-4), then marks its walls with a model of a proto-Nagara shrine. Temple C at north K firkot and temple A at Bilot, with damaged Nagara towers, project one central offset on each wall and modulate ornamental elements of their superstructures in a more integrated way compared to Bilot temple D, marking new confidence and knowledge of Nagara formulas late in the seventh century. Temple C at north Kafirkot for the first time tentatively introduces a version of north India's common vase-and-foliage capital for its corner pilasters, while retaining the local neo-Corinthian type for the central offset.

Two striking temples, located on hills east of the Indus opposite Kalabagh at Mari—which I would date in the eighth century—continue but refine this local N gara tradition, but still with only a single central offset on their walls. Temple A places thin pilasters on the corners of each offset, while temple B pairs pilasters for the first time on its corner buttresses. Temples in this sequence in turn seem to provide a central shrine-model on each wall to represent a slightly preceding local experiment with the formula for a Nagara temple. Each also seems to carry some architectural element forward, as in the trefoil arched niches at Bilot, trefoil doorway at Mari-Indus, and five-cusped entry to the smaller temple at Amb in the ninth century.

The first temple in this tradition that can have its date confirmed by any evidence other than style and decorative context is the elegant fired brick structure at Kallar. Its layering of five offsets making up its walls, and its developed ornamentation with vase-and-foliage pilasters and other distinctive details, place it parallel to temples in central and western India from late in the eighth and early in the ninth century A.D. (Meister, et. al., 1991), a date suggested also by a single coin found near the foundations. This comes from the reign of the first Hindu Shahi ruler, the beginning of whose dynasty can now fairly firmly be dated to ca. 821 A.D. (Rehman 1993). Only further archaeological explorations, however, and perhaps carbon-14 dating of wood beams used to support the interior domes of some of these temples, can fix the dates and historical frame suggested here more firmly.

Sub-shrines that were added above the eastern corners of the platform supporting temple D at Bilot perhaps early in the eighth century echo but re-orient two domed cells sunk into the front corners of the temple's platform. The small temple D at Kafirkot, built near the north gateway to that fort late in the ninth century, mimics some distinctive details of these sub-shrines.

In the spectacular fortress at Amb, on the southern edge of the Salt Range; at Bilot in the tenth century; and at Nandana, larger temples began to be built under the patronage apparently of the Hindu Shahi kings. These still were Latina temples, with curvilinear single spires, but they had a stairway within their walls leading to an interior ambulatory corridor surrounding an embedded upper chamber, in this respect unlike any other Nagara temples elsewhere in India.

This remarkable regional experiment with multiple levels folded within a Latina tower came to an end when the great fortress at Nandana on the eastern flank of the Salt Range fell to Mahmud of Ghazni, who sought to control the significant routes across the Panjab toward Multan and Delhi early in the eleventh century. The Hindu Shahi kings then took refuge with their cousins in Kashmir. In this sequence, only this last temple built at Nandana suggests corner turrets on its single-spired tower. These suggest, however, the multi-spired shrine-models placed on the walls of the tenth-century temple at Malot, even as they reflect a multi-spired convention common in central and western India by the tenth century (Meister, et. al., 1991).

That these forts and temples survive along the Indus must be a reminder to us of how untouched many of South Asia's traditions are; of how insular scholarship can become; and of our task as scholars to weave a comprehensive image of the past, even as we reproblematize colonial scholarship and its assumptions.

I might end this preliminary report with a footnote to demonstrate the mighty weight of finding a new monument in the field. At the site of Mari, in addition to the two eighth-century temples already discussed, there also are two mounds higher up the hill to the west, badly ravaged by treasure hunters, that past reports have labelled primarily as places of residence (Cunningham 1879:25-26; Mumtaz 1989:32). These in fact are ruins of two large temples placed on high platforms. One still preserves remains of an inner sanctum and an enclosing ambulatory wall. On the north side, this wall preserves a central niche with a distinctive "Kashmiri-style" pent roof, but the shattered remains of the temple's superstructure suggest instead a complex multi-spired tower with curvilinear Latina spirelets. This temple seems, in fact, to have been almost a reverse response to the unique local experiment with Kashmiri style found at Malot, and an answer to it. Let scholars beware!

Acknowledgments: Support for this project has come from the University Research Foundation and the Middle East Center at the University of Pennsylvania, the American Institute of Pakistan Studies, and the Lenkin Faculty Research Fund of the History of Art Department. I would like to thank Professor Farzand Durrani, Vice-Chancellor of Peshawar University, for encouragement; the Department of Archaeology, Peshawar, for early support; Dr. M. Rafique Mughal, Director General of the Department of Archaeology and Museums, Government of Pakistan; Shabaaz Khan, Director General of the Panjab Department of Archaeology; and especially my colleagues Professors Abdur Rehman and Farid Khan of the Pakistan Heritage Society, with whom carrying out this work continues to be a pleasure.

Appendix: Shrine Models as Signatures of Architectural Experimentation.

The architects of these temples in the Salt Range and along the Indus knew that they were working within a variety of options. Architecture could engage their creativity; and through their creative actions, temples could evolve in multiple ways. They seem consciously to have left a record of their architectural experiments by placing shrine models as niches on the walls of many temples.

These often seem to represent slightly earlier local experiments with the formula for a N gara temple, focusing on the nature of the temple's superstructure. Temple D at Bilot, for example, uses a proto-Nagara model. Temple at Mari, on the other hand, uses curvilinear N gara models with ornamentation placed across single cornice layers, in this respect resembling the superstructure actually built for Bilot's temple D rather than those of either of the eighth-century temples at Mari.

On the temple at Malot, the central shrine models have developed curvilinear Nagara towers flanked by extra turrets. Mari's remarkable temple, on the other hand, had central niches marked by a split pent-roof pediment framing a trefoil arch that suggests the gabled pent roof that once actually crowned the temple at Malot. The trefoil-arch pattern can be seen at Bilot, Mari, Amb, and Malot in association with either pent-roofed or curvilinear formulas.

Marking temple walls with images of past architecture provides an historical locus for architects working within a system of meaning for the temple which sees each niche as an expansion of the temple as a whole (Meister 1993). The rhetoric of architectural representation in South Asia more often relates to an a historical rather than historical reality, yet from time to time the two overlap (Dhaky 1977). In Gandhara sculpture, for example, the variety of recognizable Buddha types seems sometimes to point to specific places of pilgrimage. So also in the Salt Range architectural experimentation gave contemporary expression to the workings of the minds of architects as well as of god's creation.

Note: The Integrated Salt Range and Indus Archaeological Project The forts, temples, and archaeological sites associated with the Turk Shahi and Hindu Shahi kings will be investigated over the next three years by a team led by Professors Abdur Rehman, Farid Khan, and Michael W. Meister under the auspices of the Pakistan Heritage Society, Peshawar, with a license from the Department of Archaeology and Museums, Government of Pakistan. Preliminary excavations will begin this season in the fort at north Kafirkot.

Kaptesvara Tirtha—History and Legend: Many pilgrimages lose their importance over time. Presently pilgrimages to the holy cave of Lord Amarnath and the shrine of Tulmulla have the greatest sanctity for Kashmiri Hindus. Visits to Sarada shrine, Harmukta ganga, Bheda tirtha and Papsudana-Kaptesvara spring were highly revered in ancient Kashmir.

Papsudana (sin-removing) spring enjoyed great reputation for its sanctity for many centuries. This Tirtha is located a short distance above the village of Kother, situated two miles above Achabal. The name of the village is a contraction of Kapatesvara, an appellation of Shiva to whom the spring here is sacred.

Shiva is worshipped here under the name of Kapatesvara, having shown himself there according to the legend under the disguise (Kapata) of pieces of wood floating on the water. Large number of ancient glass fragments are strewn on the road that leads from the village Kother to the Papsudana spring. This indicates the existence of a flourishing glass industry in the bygone times.

S.No	Name of Monument / Site	Locality / Village & Tehsil	District
1	Ancient site of Chakradhar/Semthan	Semthan	Anantnag
2	Mughal Arcade & Spring at Verinag	Verinag	Anantnag
3	Martanda (Sun temple)	Ranbirpura	Anantnag
4	Bumzuva cave and temple	Bumzuva	Anantnag
5	Detha mandir	Bandi, Uri	Baramulla
6	Ancient temple	Buniyar, Uri	Baramulla
7	Ancient temple	Fatehgarh	Baramulla
8	Ancient stupa (excavated remains)	Ushkur	Baramulla
9	Partapswami temple	Tappar-waripora	Baramulla
10	Sankaragauriavare temple	Pattan	Baramulla
11	Sugandhese temple	Pattan	Baramulla
12	Ancient stupa, chaitya & monastery	Dever Yakhamanpora / parihaspora, Sonawari	Baramulla
13	Ancient site	Sumbal, Sonawari	Baramulla
14	Mosque & other ancient remains on the island	Wular lake, Bandipora	Baramulla
15	Khanpur sarai	Khanpur, Chadura	Budgam
16	Fort at Akhnoor	Akhnoor	Jammu
17	Remains of ancient site (Pambaran)	Ambaran	Jammu
18	Ancient temple (hari hara)	Bilawar	Kathua
19	Rock carving of devi riding a lion	Basohli	Kathua
20	Rock carving of Sitala, Narada, Brahma and Radha	Krishna	Basohli Kathua
21	Vishesvara & other cave temple	Basohli	Kathua
22	Trilochananath temple	Mahadera, Basohli	Kathua
23	Sculptures at drass	Drass	Kargil
24	Rock cut sculptures	Mulbeg	Kargil
25	Buddhist Monastery	Lamayuru, Khalsi	Leh

Contd..

S.No	*Name of Monument / Site*	*Locality / Village & Tehsil*	*District*
26	Buddhist Monastery	Lakir, Khalsi	Leh
27	Buddhist monestries	Alchi, Khalsi	Leh
28	Buddhist gompa	Phyang	Leh
29	Ancient palace	Leh	Leh
30	Old castle (Tsemo hill)	Leh	Leh
31	Stupa	Tisseruu	Leh
32	Ancient palace and shrine	Shey	Leh
33	Hemis gompa	Hamis	Leh
34	Ancient gompa	Thikecy	Leh
35	Shrine of four lords, Gonkhang (Tsemo hills)	Leh	Leh
36	Aliabad Sarai	Aliabad, Shopian	Pulwama
37	Avantiswami Temple	Awantipora	Pulwama
38	Awantisvara temple	Awantipora	Pulwama
39	Hirpur sarai	Hirpur, Shopian	Pulwama
40	Ancient temple	Kakapora	Pulwama
41	Monolithic shrine	Khrew	Pulwama
42	Remains of ancient temple	Khrew	Pulwama
43	Ancient temple	Loduv	Pulwama
44	Remains of ancient Stupa	Malangpora	Pulwama
45	Remains of ancient temple	Pampur	Pulwama
46	Ancient Shiva temple	Payar	Pulwama
47	Pathar masjid	Zaina Kadal	Srinagar
48	Ancient temple	Bohri Kadal	Srinagar
49	Tomb of Zain -ul-abdin's mother	Zaina Kadal	Srinagar

Contd..

S.No	Name of Monument / Site	Locality / Village & Tehsil	District
50	Khanqah of shah hamdan	Shahi Hamdan	Srinagar
51	Akhund mulla shah's mosque	Kathi Darwaza	Srinagar
52	Gates in the rampart of the forta kathi darwaza		
	b) sangeen darwaza	Kathi Darwaza Sangeen Darwaza	Srinagar
53	Ancient temple	Hari Parbat	Srinagar
54	Group of ancient temple	Naranag, Kangan	Srinagar
55	Ancient site and remains	Burzahom	Srinagar
56	Ancient monastery and stupa	Harwan	Srinagar
57	Group of structural complex	Parimahal	Srinagar
58	Shankaracharya temple	Kothhi Bagh / Durganag	Srinagar
59	Ancient site	Pandrothan	Srinagar
60	Excavated remains	Pandrothan	Srinagar
61	Pandrethan temple	Pandrothan	Srinagar
62	Ancient site, babour	Thalora, Ramnagar	Udhampur
63	Devi bhagwati temple, babour	Thalora, Ramnagar	Udhampur
64	Ancient temple dera babour	Thalora, Ramnagar	Udhampur
65	Ancient temples kala dera I&IIJ	Manwal	Jammu
66	Ancient temple nand babour	Manwal	Jammu
67	Group of temples	Krimchi	Udhampur
68	Ancient fort attributed to raja suchet singh & Samadhi of queen of raja suchet singh	Ramnagar	Udhampur
69	Ancient palace attributed to raja suchet singh	Ramnagar	Udhampur

Archeological Remains: The sacred spring now rises in a circular tank, at least sixty yards in diameter. It is enclosed by a massive stone wall, still extant partially. Steps flanked by side walls, which are surrounded by cornices lead down to the water. From the formation of the ground, it is evident that this tank has been formed by closing artificially the gully in which the spring rises on the hillside. The dam, which effected this forms the western side of the tank. Depth of the spring is quite considerable.

There are two small temples, which seem to be contemporaneous with the stonewall of the spring. Internally the larger temple measures 8' 4" and faces southwest. The smaller temple faces west and measures 6' 4" internally. Its lower part is buried underground. There is a long stretch of wall 246 ft. long and 12 ft. wide on the north side. It originally formed part of the enclosure wall round the temples and the tank.

The fragment that is above ground on the east side shows that this surrounding wall is in reality a cellular peristyle. The top stones of the cells are visible. State Archeology department carried out excavation work in this area in 1932-33. It revealed a cellular quadrangle and a number of shrines belonging to the tenth to eleventh centuries. It also showed that there was an older stratum of buildings, upon which these structures were superimposed.

Legend of King Mutuskund: Like the Sarada shrine, the construction of the Kapatesvara tank and its stone enclosure are credited to the legendary King Mutuskund. This king cursed by nature with a pair of buffalo's ears, was anxious to rid himself of this disfigurement. He had in vain sought relief by visits to numerous sacred sites. At last he learnt about the miraculous powers of Kapatesvara spring.

When near Kapatesvara he noticed that a wounded dog was healed by entering the water of the sacred spring. The King followed his example and got rid of his cursed ears. In gratitude, the King expended his treasures upon the foundation and upkeep of the temples and the spring.

The Legend of King Mutuskund is Quite Popular in this Area. It Says:

Mutsakand razas manshihandikan

Tim kati tsalanas' Kuther van

Translation: King Mutuskund has buffalo's ears; where will he get rid of these' In the forests of Kother. A curious legend reports that a treasure lies buried somewhere in or near the spring and that there was a stone slab embedded in the wall of the spring on which were inscribed directions for its discovery. This was meant as compensation for the person who would undertake the repairs and upkeep of the spring and its dependent shrines.

Sir Aurel Stein corroborates the traditional reference to treasure. He says that an inscription in various characters' had existed until Sikh times near a door in the stone enclosure on the northern side of the tank. It is believed that this inscription was thrown into the tank by a local Muslim Jagirdar during the times of King Ranjit Singh. Sultan Shahabuddin is also reported to have carried out repairs of the tank and an inscription relating to it was found by the State archeology department during one of its surveys.

The identity of King Mutuskund is shrouded is mystery. Close examination of the legend in relation to Sarada legend indicates that this King was a gauda warrior from Bengal. In the case of Kapatesvara tirtha, Raja-tarangini identifies King Mutskund with King Bhoj of Malwa. He was contemporary of King Ananta (1028-1063 A.D.) of Kashmir. King Bhoja of Dhara, who ruled over Malwa for four decades was a great patron of litterature. He was a prince of uncommon ability and laid out Bhojpur Lake near Bhopal. This lake, once covering 250 sq.

miles was formed by massive embankments and testifies to the skills of his engineers. King Bhoja, who had heard about the sanctity of Kapatesvara spring, had vowed that he would always wash his face in the water from the Papasudana tirtha. He engaged the services of merchant Padmaraja for the construction of tank and the stone basin at Kapatesvara. King sent heaps of gold for this. Padmaraja used to despatch water from this spring in big glass jars on a regular basis to King Bhoja.

Tirth Yatra: Pilgrims visited Kapatesvara tirtha every year in the month of Baisakh. Now the pilgrimage has lost much of its importance and only Kashmiri Pandits of the neighbouring villages visit it regularly.

Socio-historicity: The importance and the socio-historicity of Kaptesvara tirtha has been recorded in Nilmatpurana, Srikanthcharita of Mankha, Kitab-ul-Hind of Alberuni, Rajatarangini of Kalhan, Harcaritacintamani of Jayadratha, Ain-i-Akbari of Abul Fazal and in our own times by RC Kak, an outstanding archeologist. Alberuni mentions that pieces of wood sent by Mahadeva appear annually 'in a pond called Kudaishahr to the left of the source of the vitasta, in the middle of the month of vaisakha'.

Kudaishahr is a corrupt derivative of Kavadevsar, a prakritised form of Kapatesvara. The date mentioned for the yatra by Alberuni coincides with that given in Kapatesvara Mahatma. About Kapatesvara, Kalhana writes in the first taranga of Rajatarangini. Where, within the santuary of Papasudana, those who touch the husband of Uma in wodden form secure for reward the pleasures of life and liberation.

The great Kashmirian poet Mankha was a contemporary of Kalhana. In his celebrated Kavya Srikanthacarita, he gives description of important temples of Kashmir. About Kapatesvara tirtha, he says the temple is situated in water and in it are present the wooden images of Lord Shiva. He also mentions about its great importance. Jayadratha, the author of Haracaritacintamani (32 cantos), devotes the entire fourteenth canto to the story of Kapatesvara.

This has now become the official Mahatma of the tirtha. The author was a great poet and belonged to the Kashmir family of Rajanakas. He lived at the end of 12th or the beginning of the thirteenth century. In Ain-i-Akbari, Abul Fazl writes 'in the village of Kotiyar is a deep spring surrounded by stone temples. When its water decreases an image of Mahadeva in sandalwood appears'. RC Kak in his 'Ancient Monuments of

Kashmir', has recorded the legend of King Mutuskund and has given detailed description about the architectural aspect of Kapatesvara spring and temples.

Nilmat Story: By far the most detailed description about the origin of Kapatesva area is given in Nilmat Purana. It describes the sanctity associated with taking a bath in Kapatesvara spring. Nilmat records: One attains the world of Rudra by taking bath in Kapatesvara. In the famous dialogue on the sacred tirthas of Kashmir, which takes place between King Gonanda and Sage Brhadasva, two names Bhutesvara and Kapatesvara arouse Gonanda's curiosity. This leads Brhadasva to narrate Bhutesvara mahatma and Kapatesvara mahatma explaining the story of Shiva who appears before the sages in the guise of logs of wood. Gonanda asks the sage Brhadasva as to why the venerable Sambhu is called Kapatesvara. Brhadasva then narrates the story in detail.

Once many sages stood in great penance on the sacred bank of Drsadvati in Kuruksetra to have a sight of Rudra-the lord of the gods. Impressed by their devotion, Lord Mahadeva told them in a dream to go soon to Kasmira where there is a spacious and immaculate abode of the naga. He told them that there he would be visible in disguise. Having heard him in a dream they all reached that abode of the naga. They could not see even a little water, for the water was all over covered with pieces of wood. Moving the wooden logs with their hands, the best sages obtained Rudrahood with their bodies by merely taking bath.

However, one Vasistha Brahman, named Gauraparasar neither took the bath nor touched the wooden logs. He went on prolonged fasting and made his body decay. Hara then spoke to him in a dream and advised him to obtain Rudrahood quickly by taking bath and touching the wooden logs. Gauraparasara persisted, 'that you can be visible after the attainment of Rudrahood is a fact, 'O father of the world! But my mind is not satisfied without the sight of the lord of the gods. You have said that you would be visible in disguise in the abode (of the Naga)'.

The Brahman refuses to leave and continues fasting, sankara replies:

I have already provided to them, my manifestation in the form of wooden log. Merely by seeing me, they attained Rudrahood, O twice-born! Now, due to your penance which is greater, I give you the desired boon. Ask for what you desire and obtain Rudrahood. Gauraparasara demands that Mahesvara should manifest itself in the form of a wooden log, to all the human beings, as it did to the sages. Mahesvara agrees and remarks. O best among the twice-born, all those people who will see (the god) standing in the form of wood, (will see the gods) not always but only occasionally. With a desire to do favour to them, my gana—this Nandi in the form of wooden log shall always be visible to the human beings. And having seen (him) they would attain Rudrahood with their bodies. As I shall appear in disguise before men, so I shall obtain the name, Kapatesvara.

Sun Worship in Kashmir: The sun-god is in essence is a Vedic god and its reverential worship has been widely prevalent throughout including Kashmir. In the Rigveda we find a web of mythology woven around the sun-god known as Aditi. During the upanishadic era the sun-worship had assumed tremendous significance and the Chamdogya upanishad is replete with references to the sun-worship as it created life and also nourished it. In the Mahabharata the sun-god attained a sweeping sovereign status and in some respects was deemed more significant than most other gods in the Hindu pantheon. The sun-worship was so pervasive that massive temples were built in honour of the sun-god. The magnificent Konark temple, built in the eleventh century A.D. testifies to the importance and prevalence of the sun-god worship.

The sun-worship touched a new height during the reign of King Harsha. In his court, an eminent writer Banabhata, has made a specific reference to Harsha's father, who was an ardent devotee of sun-god and offered its worship as a matter of regular practice. Kalhana's Rajatarangini equally establishes that the sun-worship was prevalent in Kashmir too. As Kashmir had been a crucible of numerous cultural traditions and trends, the sun-god was worshipped alongwith a litany of religious gods and icons connected with Buddhism, Shaivism and

Vaishnavism. As per Kalhana, a ruler named Ranaditya as a devotee had built a sun-temple at a place known as 'Simharotsika'. The temple was said to be grand, massive and exemplary in terms of art. He has made a mention of another sun-temple, known world over as Martand. This temple is built on an elevated plateau in natural ambience in the vicinity of Mattan in Anantnag.

The temple was made to perfection by Lalitaditya, who besides being a conqueror was a great builder. Martand as a temple has been evaluated as the 'germ of Indian architecture', which set a trend in the contemporary temple architecture. The temple caused amazing wonder to medieval fanatic Zealot Sultan Sikander, who set up a government department to destroy it by the use of gun-powder. The hamlet of Mattan which has been of great religious importance to the Hindus all over India has been traditionally known as the 'Surya tirth', a place of sun-pilgrimage. After Mattan, second in importance was Kwalkhetra, not far away from Srinagar. Here Pandits would go on pilgrimage for sun-worship and for a purificatory bath to wash off wordly sins. As per Nilmatpurana, there were eight places exclusively meant for sun-worship in Kashmir. The temples built at the places were known as Aryaman Arka, Divakar, Surya, Savitra, Martand etc., all these words are synonyms of the word sun. Kashmiri Pandits still stick to a number of rituals, which are directly related to sun-workship.

Shankaracharya Temple Srinagar: Kashmir offers you an opportunity to visit one of the most revered Hindu pilgrimage destinations, the sacred temple of Shankaracharya. This temple is located on the top of the hills, southeast of Srinagar and is commonly known as the Takht-i-Sulaiman. This temple is situated at a height of 1100 feet above the Srinagar City. The temple is devoted to the worship of lord Shiva. Tours and travel to this pilgrimage involves a trek to the top of the hills in the Srinagar region.

This ancient temple dates back to 5th Century BC. It was constructed by Pandavas and completed by Maharaja Gopaditya. It is believed that the saint Shankaracharya stayed here when he visited Kashmir twelve centuries ago to preach the Sanatan

Dharma. In the ancient times this temple was known as the Gopadri. The main shrine has a circular cell inside. An inscription in Persian inside the shrine indicates that the origin of this sacred place dates back to the reign of Emperor Shah Jahan. The saint Adi Shankaracharya visited Kashmir in the first quarter of the ninth century with the basic aim of spreading the philosophy of Vedanta. The saint also popularized the worship of lord Shiva in Kashmir. It seems that before saint Shankaracharya came to this area, Buddhism was rampant in this region. Maharaja Pratap Singh did the installation of Shivalinga in the temple.

Shankarachar is a detached ridge of igneous rock to the southeast of Srinagar, separated from the Shilamar Range by the Aita Gaj Gap. The summit of the hill is crowned with a picturesque edifice. There were 300 golden and silver images in it. The Temple is built on a high octagonal plinth approached by a flight of steps. The temple is under the control of the Dharmartha Department. They have built two small buildings for the sadhus who live there. There is at the place an old stone shed which is called 'Parvatihund bana koth' (the storehouse of goddess Parvati). On the 20th April 1961 Shri Shankaracharia of Dwarika Pet installed the white marble statue of Adi Shankaria just near the temple arranged by the Dharmartha Department. The panoramic view of the valley in early April when the snow is deep on the mountains, or after rains on a summer day from the summit of the hill is one of the best that could ever be witnessed.

Location: It overlooks the Valley and can be approached by a motorable road. There are 245 steps from the end of the road before one reaches the temple.

Shankeracharya Temple has been declared to be of National importance under the ancient Monument and Archaeological Sites and Remains Act (24 of 1958) by Archaeological Survey of India.

Climate: The temperature in June-August summer is 25 deg to 35 deg C. It plummets to 7 deg C in spring (March-May) and autumn (Oct-Nov). In winter (Dec-Feb), the temperature drops to minus 10 deg C.

Khanqah-e-Moula

Location: Banks of the river Jhelum, Srinagar

Dedicated To: Mir Syed Ali Hamdani, a Muslim preacher

Constructed By: Sultan Sikander

Year of Construction: 1395

Khanqah-e-Moula is situated in Srinagar, on the banks of the river Jhelum. One of the oldest Muslim shrines in Kashmir, the khanqah was built by Sultan Sikander built in 1395. The Khanqah is a wooden structure whose chief aesthetic feature is its beautifully carved eaves and hanging bells. The interiors are richly carved and painted, and the antique chandeliers give it an air of opulence. The Khanqah-i-Mualla is dedicated to Muslim preacher Mir Syed Ali Hamdani. Also known as Shah Hamadan, the preacher came to Kashmir from the city of Hamadan in Persia in the 13th century. He is believed to be responsible for the spread of Islam in Kashmir. The Shah stayed in Kashmir for many years and then left for Central Asia via Ladakh. He also built a mosque at Shey (near Leh). The shrine gains a special significance on 6th of Zilhaj (last month of Muslim calendar), the death anniversary of Mir Syed Ali Hamadni. On this day, devotees visit the shrine in large numbers to pay a tribute to Shah Hamadan.

The Khanqah of Shah Hamadan was the first mosque to be built in Srinagar. The Shah used to meditate and offer his prayers daily on the banks of river Jhelum, at the same spot where the shrine now stands. The Khanqah of Shah Hamadan in Kashmir has undergone ruination a couple of times. The year 1480 saw the shrine being ruined in a devastating fire. Later, the shrine was reconstructed and restored by the then ruler Sultan Hassan Shah. Again, in 1493 AD, Khanqah-e-Moula was demolished and reconstructed in two-stories. A fire again struck the shrine in 1731 AD leading to first its destruction and then renovation by Abul Barkat Khan.

Shrines and Monuments

Azratbal Mosque: Hazratbal Mosque is located in a village of the same name on the banks of the Dal. Its pristine white marble elegance is reflected in the waters of the lake. Hazratbal's special significance is derived from the fact that it houses a hair of the prophet Muhammad. This is displayed to the public on religious occasions, usually accompanied by fairs. Apart from these occasions, Friday prayers are offered at Hazratbal and attended by throngs of people. Hazratbal is remarkable for being the only domed mosque in Srinagar; the others having distinct pagoda like roofs. The shrine – mosque complex is situated on the western shore of the Dal Lake opposite Nishat Bagh and commands a grand view of the lake and the mountain beyond.

Jama Masjid: The Jama Masjid at *Nowhatta,* in the heart of the old city, is the other important mosque in Srinagar at which thousands of people congregate for the Friday prayers. Of imposing proportions, the mosque is built around a courtyard and is supported by 370 wooden pillars. The hushed quiet of the mosque counterpoints the bustle of the old bazaars surrounding it. Originally built by *Sultan Sikandar* in 1400 AD, and enlarged by his son, Zain-ul-Abidin, it is a typical example of Indo-Saracenic architecture. Destroyed thrice by fire and rebuilt each time, the mosque, as it now stands, was repaired during the reign of Maharaja Pratap Singh.

Shankaracharya Temple: The sacred temple of Shankaracharya occupies the top of the hills known as *Takht-i-Sulaiman* in the southeast of Srinagar. The site dates back to 250 BC. The philosopher *Shankaracharya* stayed at this place when he visited Kashmir ten centuries ago to revive *Sanatan Dharma.*

Before this date, the temple was known as *Gopadri,* as an earlier edifice on the same site was built by king *Lalitaditya* in the 6th century AD. In fact, the road below the hill, with residences of high-ranking State Government officials, is still known as *Gupkar* road. Built on a high octagonal plinth and approached by a flight of steps with side walls that once bore inscriptions, the main surviving shrine consists of a circular cell. It overlooks the Valley and can be approached by a motorable road. A modern ceiling covers the inner sanctum and an inscription in Persian traces its origin to the reign of Emperor

Shah Jehan. The original ceiling was dome-shaped and the brick roof, it appears, is not more than a century old.

Khanqah of Shah Hamadan: Situated on the banks of the river Jhelum, between the third and fourth bridge, it is the first mosque ever built in Srinagar. The original one was built in 1395.

Shah Hamadan's full name was Mir Sayed Ali Hamadni, the surname being derived from the city of Hamadan in Persia. *Shah-i-Hamdan*, who came from Persia in the 13th century, was responsible for the spread of Islam in Kashmir. ***Khanqah-i-Mualla***, on the banks of the Jhelum, was the very spot where Shah-i-Hamdan used to offer prayers.

After staying in Kashmir for many years, he left for Central Asia via Ladakh. A mosque established by him at ***Shey*** (near Leh) attracts devotees from far and wide.

The Khanqah is a wooden structure whose chief aesthetic feature is its beautifully carved eaves and hanging bells. The interiors are richly carved and painted, and the antique chandeliers give it an air of opulence.

Hari Parbat Fort and Temple of Sharika Devi : The Mughal emperor's fort crowns the top of Hari Parbat hill. There is little left of its former glory, but the ramparts are still impressive and the old apartments within the fort, even though in a state of ruin, still convey at least a little of the grandeur of the Mughals' summer retreat in 'paradise'.

The fort was later developed in 18th century by an Afghan governor, Ata Muhammad Khan. The hill is considered sacred to the Hindus due to the presence of temple of ***Sharika,*** which is believed to be a form of goddess *Durga* or *Shakti*. The wall around the hill was built by Akbar in 1592-98 AD. The hill is surrounded by almond orchards, which make a lovely sight during April when the trees blossom, heralding the advent of spring in Kashmir.

Makhdoom Sahib: On the southern side of the Hari Parbat hill is the historic shrine of Makhdoom Sahib, which is visited by people of all faiths.

Chhatti Padshahi Gurudwara: The sixth Sikh guru travelled through Kashmir, stopping to preach occasionally. A gurudwara has been built at the exact site of each of these halts. The most important one among these is *Chhatti Padshahi gurudwara,* situated near the ***Kathi Darwaza,*** in Rainawari, Srinagar, which is held in great reverence by devotees of all faiths.

Martand: Martand, located atop a plateau, close to the township of Anantnag, has a temple dedicated to *Surya,* the *"Sun God".* Built by king Laitaditya Muktapida (7th to 8th century AD), it is a medieval temple with a colonnaded courtyard and the shrine in its centre. The temple complex has 84 columns and offers a commanding view of the valley of Kashmir.

Kheer Bhawani: The Goddess Ragnya Devi is symbolised as a sacred spring at Tula Mula village, 27 kms from Srinagar. Within the spring is a small marble temple. The devotees of the goddess fast and gather here on the eighth day of the full moon in the month of May when, according to belief, the goddess changes the colour of the spring's waters. The temple-spring complex is affectionately known as *Kheer Bhawani* because of the thousands of devotees who offer milk and *'kheer'* to the sacred spring, which magically turns black to warn of disaster.

Awantipur: Founded by *Avantivarman* who reigned Kashmir in the 9th century, this ancient township is 29 kms from Srinagar.

The site has two imposing temples, the larger one of *Shiva-Avantisvara* is marked by huge walls, some half a mile beneath the town on the outskirts of village Jaubror. The subsidiary shrines are to the rear corner of the courtyard. The complex has, over the years, lost its grandeur and been reduced to ruins, though it is still visited by the devout. Half a mile up is *Avantisvami—Vishnu,* a better preserved, though smaller temple.

The Old City: With its almost medieval charm, the old city of Srinagar has sights, smells and sounds to enchant the most jaded traveller. Its labyrinthine roads and bustling bazaars are a photographer's delight. Traditionally dressed men and women on their way to the city's many mosques and shrines, burnt brick buildings with their rich warm colour, these are some of the old city's moods which linger in the corners of a traveller's mind, long after one leaves Kashmir.

Lending the area its vitality is the presence of the river Jhelum that flows through it. Srinagar has for long been Kashmir's most important commercial town, and when one considers that boats have always been a primary means of conveyance in Kashmir, it is not difficult to see why. In time, the city has formed around the banks of the river. Today, the presence of the river Jhelum has become an integral part of the old city, despite the fact that boats are no longer so extensively used as a means of conveyance. Nine bridges span the River Jhelum, and many, many more tiny ones intersect the network of waterways that flow through the old city.

The nine bridges are Zero Bridge, Amira Kadal, Budshah Kadal, Habba Kadal, Fateh Kadal, Zaina Kadal, Aali Kadal, Nawa Kadal and Safa Kadal, *'Kadal'* being the Kashmiri word for bridge. Of these Budshah Bridge and Zero Bridge are the newest; the former having been constructed by the British in this century. Presently, the oldest bridge is Fateh Kadal, too dilapidated for actual use. However, many of the old bridges have been replaced with new concrete bridges and a few new ones have also been added in view of the increasing traffic. The most prominent among these is the Abdullah Bridge, situated near the Tourist Reception Centre.

The view from any of the old city's bridges is wholly and unmistakably Kashmiri. Old brick buildings line the banks. The distinctive pagoda-like roof of a mosque or a shrine enlivens the horizon, and in the muddy water of the River Jhelum, a straggling row of *doongas* flanks the edges. These boats, with their shingled roofs, are the forerunners of Srinagar's houseboat. A particular community lives in them. Formerly this community was associated with ferrying people, livestock and food grains along the river. The past still lingers in their lifestyles even if their occupations have changed. Occasionally one may catch sight of a *doonga* making its stately progress down the river as the owner shifts residence! *Doongas* are sparsely furnished—

virtually no furniture is seen except for the kitchen, which gleams with copper utensils of every description that line the shelves from floor to ceiling.

Roads in the old city tend to be narrow, winding and chaotic. Some are too narrow to admit vehicular traffic. Each road connects to lanes and they in turn to bye-lanes, all appearing to the uninitiated and terribly confusing. There are arterial roads, however, and major market squares where it is difficult to get lost.

In a lane off ***Nowhatta Chowk***, there are several ***copper shops***, overflowing with an amazing profusion of copper ware. As a matter of fact, such shops are situated all over the old city because every Kashmiri uses copper for tableware—even ***huqqa*** bases are made from copper. Some articles are un-patterned, others worked in bas-relief, engraving or pierced open-work. Exotic as they are, they make attractive ornaments about the house, or can be used as serving dishes.

One of the many moods of the old city is the constant reminder about its tradition of handicrafts. Well-appointed shops in the fashionable areas of Srinagar seem rather remote from the humble families of craftsmen who create tapestries and shawls; the old city changes all that. From top floor windows one catches sight of gaily embroidered fabric hanging out to dry. Occasionally a wizened old man cycles down the road, bearing a carpet, its lustrous colours glowing in the sunlight.

Kashmiri colours are not the fiery colours of the desert that sear the eyelids. They are subdued, almost purposely it would seem, to counterpoint nature's magnificence. Earthy tones of brick, the rich hue of copper, even the vermilion of Kashmiri chillies drying on window sills in autumn appear monochromatic when set off against the splendour of the Valley's backdrop. The only craft where Kashmiris revel in colour is in their carpets. Here too, the colours are never loud, never disharmonious, but always subtle and soft. At ***Habba Kadal***, shop after shop sells nothing but skeins of wool, mainly to carpet weavers. Study the muted tones and then relate them to the carpets that you see—as long as the colours remain in your mind's eye, you will never mistake a Kashmiri carpet.

The old city also boasts of Kashmir's many ancient shrines and mosques among which the shrine of ***Shah-i-Hamdan,*** situated between Habba Kadal and Fateh Kadal, is probably the most important. *Shah-i-Hamdan*, who came from Persia in the 13th century, was responsible for the spread of Islam in Kashmir. ***Khanqah-i-Mualla***, on the banks of the Jhelum, was the very spot where Shah-i-Hamdan used to offer prayers. Upon his death, a shrine, ornately decorated with papier-mache on the walls and ceiling, was built in his memory. ***Makhdoom Sahib***, ***Patthar Masjid***, ***Jama Masjid*** and ***Pir Dastagir*** are the major mosques and shrines in the old city.

Tourists are welcome to visit the mosques and shrines in the old city. There are a few points to be kept in mind in accordance with the sanctity of these places. Women are not allowed into the inner sanctum of shrines, but there is no such restriction in the case of mosques. Shoes must be taken off at the entrance. Jamia Masjid charges a fee for photography. Visitors are expected to conform to certain regulations in the matter of dress—no skimpy tops, shorts or short skirts are allowed.

One does not go to the old city to shop. The exhilaration in exploring the old city comes from peeping into a world which normally admits no outsiders and which continues at its own pace, not much affected by changing times.

Bibliography

Ahmed S.: *Making Sense of Muslim History and Society,* New York: Routledge and Kegan Paul, Ltd., 1988.

Ahmed, Ishtiaq, *State, Nation and Ethnicity in Contemporary South Asia*, Pinter, London 1996.

Ali, Mahmud: *The Fearful State*, Zed Books, London, 1993.

Allchin, F.R.: *The Archaeology of Early Historic South Asia*, Cambridge University Press, U. K., 1995.

Ammiel Alcalay: *After Jews and Arabs: Remaking Levantine Culture,* Minneapolis, University of Minnesota Press, 1990.

Anand, Mulk Raj: *Kama Kala: Some Notes on the Philosophical Basis of Hindu Erotic Sculpture*, New York: Nagel, 1962.

Anand, Raj: *The Story of India*, Bombay, Kutub, 1948.

Antoun, T.: *Understanding Fundamentalism: Christian, Islamic, and Jewish Movements,* New York, Rowman and Littlefield, 2001.

Bamzai, P. N. K.: A *History of Kashmir,* Delhi: Metropolitan, 1962.

Banta, M. : *From Site to Sight: Anthropology, Photography and the Power of Imagery*, Cambridge, Peabody Museum Press, 1986.

Burgess, J.: *On the Muhammadan Architecture of Bharoch, Cambay, Dholka, Champanir and Mahmudabad*, London, W.M. Griggs and Sons, 1896.

Cable and French: *The Gobi Desert. Mildred Cable and Francesca French*, London, Landsborough Publications, 1943.

Chandra, Pramod: *Bundi Painting*, New Delhi, Lalit Kala Akademi, 1959.

Charles, H.: *Athens and its Monuments*, New York, The MacMillan Co., 1924.

Chatterji, K. C.: *Kashmir Shaivism,* Srinagar, Research Department, 1914.

Coleridge, P.: *Res Graecae*, London, George Bell & Sons, 1898.

Cunningham. A.: *Mahabodhi, or, The Great Buddhist temple under the Bodhi tree at Buddha-Gaya*, London, W.H. Allen, 1892.

Donald, A.: *Indian Myth and Legend*, London, The Gresham Publishing Co., 1913.

Edward, P.: *Res Graecae*, London, George Bell & Sons, 1898.

Edward, W.: *Culture and Imperialism*, Vintage, London, 1994.

Ernest, A.: *Ancient Athens*, New York, The MacMillan Co., 1902.

Fanshawe, H. C.: *Delhi Past and Present*, London, J. Murray, 1902.

Fergusson, J.: *Picturesque Illustrations of Ancient Architecture in Hindostan*, London, J. Hogarth, 1848.

———: *History of Indian and Eastern Architecture*, London, J. Murray, 1910.

Fletcher, Sir Banister: *A History of Architecture*, New York, Scribner, 1921.

Forman, Werner: *Indian Sculpture; Masterpieces of Indian, Khmer, and Cham Art*, London, Spring Book, 1962.

Fraser, James: *The History of Nadir Shah (formerly called Thames Kuli Khan, The Present Emperor of Persia)*, London, A. Millar, 1742.

Frazer, Sir James G.: *Studies in Greek Scenery, Legend and History*, London The MacMillan Co., 1919.

Fred Halliday: *Nation and Religion in the Middle East,* Boulder, Lynne Rienner, 2000.

Gardner, A.: *Ancient Athens*, New York, The MacMillan Co., 1902.

Gardner, Percy : *Manual of Greek Antiquities*, London, Charles Griffen & Co., 1898.

Guha-Thakurta, T.: *Monuments, Objects, Histories: Institutions of Art in Colonial and Post Colonial India*, New York, Columbia University Press, 2004.

Harrison and Verrall: *Mythology and Monuments of Ancient Athens*, London, The MacMillan Co., 1890.

Hinsley, C.M.: *From Site to Sight: Anthropology, Photography and the Power of Imagery*, Cambridge, Peabody Museum Press, 1986.

Jevons, F.B.: *Manual of Greek Antiquities*, London, Charles Griffen & Co., 1898.

John Hubert, Sir: *Mohenjo-daro and the Indus Civilization*, London, A. Probsthain, 1931.

Khanadalavala, Karl: *Pahari Miniature Painting*, Bombay: New Book Co., 1958.

Longfellow, H. W.: *Keramos and Other Poems*, Boston, Houghton, Osgood & Co., 1878.

MacKenzie, A.: *Indian Myth and Legend*, London, The Gresham Publishing Co., 1913.

Madan, Nath: *Family and Kinship: A Study of the Pandits of Rural Kashmir,* Bombay, Asia Publishing House, 1965.

Marshall, J.H.: *Mohenjodaro and the Indus Civilisation*, London, Probsthain, 1931.

Martin, Montogomery: *The History of Antiquity, Topography and Statistics of Eastern India*, Cosmos Publishers, Delhi, 1976.

Mill, James: *The History of British India*, London, Baldwin, 1826.

Moudud, J.: *One Thousand Year Old Bengali Poetry*, The University Press Ltd., Dhaka, 1999.

Mulk, Raj: *The Story of India*, Bombay, Kutub, 1948.

Nath, Triloki: *Family and Kinship: A Study of the Pandits of Rural Kashmir,* Bombay, Asia Publishing House, 1965.

Piggott, S.: *Antiquities Depicted: Aspects of Archaeological Illustrations*, London, Thames and Hudson, 1978.

Pitt Rivers, A.H.L.: *Excavations at Cranborne Chase near Rushmore on the Borders of Dorset and Wilts*, London, Harrison and Sons, 1898.

Poole, D.: *Vision, Race and Modernity: A Visual Economy of the Andean Image World*, Princeton, Princeton University Press, 1997.

Randhawa, Mohindar Singh: *The Krishna Legend in Pahari Painting*, New Delhi, Lalit Kala Akadami, 1956.

Rennell, James: *Memoir of a Map of Hindostan*. London, W. Bulmer and Co., 1793.

Richard T.: *Understanding Fundamentalism: Christian, Islamic, and Jewish Movements*, New York, Rowman and Littlefield, 2001.

Roy, S.: *The Story of Indian Archaeology, 1784-1947*, New Delhi, Archaeological Survey of India, 1961.

Said, W.: *Culture and Imperialism*, Vintage, London, 1994.

Samuel, Wells: *The Middle Kingdom*, New York, Scribner, 1904.

Sender, Henny: *The Kashmiri Pandits: A Study of Cultural Choice in North India*, Delhi, Oxford University Press, 1988.

Tagore, Rabindranath: *Drawings and Paintings of Rabindranath Tagore*, New Delhi, Lalit Kala Akademi, 1987.

Taner Akçam: *A Shameful Act: The Armenian Genocide and the Question of Turkish Responsibility*, New York, Metropolitan, 2006.

Terry, Edward: *A Voyage to East India:Within that Rich and Most Spacious Empire of the Great Mogul*. London, J. Wilkie, 1777.

Verghese, B.G.: *Waters of Hope*, University Press Ltd., Dhaka, 1999

Weller, H.: *Athens and its Monuments*, New York, The MacMillan Co., 1924.

Williams, Wells: *The Middle Kingdom*, New York, Scribner, 1904.

Index

M

N

O

P

R

S

❑❑❑